Homosexuality as Behavior and Identity

Dialogues of the Sexual Revolution

Volume II

Haworth Series in Gay & Lesbian Studies

Series Editor: John De Cecco

Homosexuality as Behavior and Identity

Dialogues of the Sexual Revolution

Volume II

Lawrence Mass

The Haworth Press
New York • London

Homosexuality as Behavior and Identity: Dialogues of the Sexual Revolution — Volume II is Volume Number 6 in the Haworth Series in Gay & Lesbian Studies.

The Haworth Press, Inc., 10 Alice Street, Binghamton, NY 13904-1580
EUROSPAN/Haworth, 3 Henrietta Street, London WC2E 8LU England

Library of Congress Cataloging-in-Publication Data

Mass, Lawrence, 1946-
    Homosexuality as behavior and identity : dialogues of the sexual revolution / Lawrence Mass.
        p.   cm. — (Haworth series in gay & lesbian studies ; v. no. 6-<6>)
    Includes bibliographical references and index.
    ISBN 1-56024-045-8 (v. 1) — ISBN 1-56024-046-6 (v. 2)
    1. Homosexuality—United States. 2. Gays—United States—Interviews. 3. Homosexuality and art—United States. I. Title.
HQ76.3.U5M383   1990
306.7'66—dc20
                                                                90-4986
                                                                     CIP

For Arnie Kantrowitz

In memory of my father,
Dr. Max Mass

To my friends with AIDS:
In memory of those deceased
In honor of those surviving

CONTENTS

ABOUT THE AUTHOR

Lawrence D. Mass, MD, is currently medical director of Greenwich House Alcoholism Treatment Program, Greenwich House Methadone Maintenance Treatment Program, and Greenwich House Counseling Center in New York City. He was the first physician to write for the gay press on a regular basis and became the first writer to cover the AIDS epidemic in any press. He is co-founder of Gay Men's Health Crisis, a co-founder and past vice-president of New York Physicians for Human Rights, and author of *Medical Answers About AIDS*, a publication of Gay Men's Health Crisis, which has been recommended by Jane Brody in the *New York Times*.

In recognition of his medical writing, Dr. Mass received the Gay Press Association Community Service Award for Outstanding Coverage of Health Concerns. He was also a recipient of the Gay Press Association Award for Outstanding Cultural Writing for *The Housemates Who Got Nailed,* the first published installment of *Synchronicities: Memoirs of Growing Up Gay, Jewish and Self-Hating In America.* Dr. Mass is a member of the editorial board for the *Journal of Homosexuality* and of the *Colloqium of CLAGS* (The Committee for Lesbian and Gay Studies) at the City University of New York. He has written for *The Advocate, The PWA Coalition Newsline, The Sentinel,* and the *SIECUS Report.*

Foreword

Dialogues of the Sexual Revolution

"Homosexuality is behavior or acts, not people," states John De Cecco in my interview with him. De Cecco, who is Director of the Center for Research and Education in Sexuality (CERES) at San Francisco State University and a Senior Editor at The Haworth Press, Inc., believes that "the conversion of the word *homosexual* from an adjective for describing acts to a noun for lumping together individuals was the result of the social and political efforts of those who preferred their own sex to resist ecclesiastical, secular and, later, medical encroachments on their sexual activities."

At first glance, there is nothing to argue with in these statements. Everyone who is not grossly homophobic now agrees that like blacks, whites, Jews, Christians, women, men, and heterosexuals, homosexuals are individuals first and finally. We are old and young, rich and poor, liberal and conservative, shy and aggressive, intelligent and unintelligent, nimble and clumsy, altruistic and nihilistic, male and female, black and white and every gradation between these and an infinite number of other bipolar and polarized characteristics. Where the controversy arises, as it does in these dialogues, is with the corollary assumption that homosexually-identified persons are so much a product of social forces that we can safely generalize that we are entirely so and conclude, like many of today's social constructionists, repeating the history of so many psychoanalysts and sex researchers, that homosexuality is, universally, a socially learned preference arising from a biological matrix of undifferentiated bisexuality.

In 1979, when I did my first published interview — with Masters and Johnson — and first published book review — of their study, *Homosexuality in Perspective* — I believed that the question of etiology was the most important of the questions that needed to be answered about homosexuality. In those days I was a fledgling gay activist who had just completed seven years of conservative medical education and these were some of my first pieces for the gay press. I was very green, in my assumptions as in my writing, and I was wrong. The issue of etiology wasn't nearly as important as numerous other concerns, such as recognizing homosexually-identified persons as individual human beings and as fully equal to all other individual human beings and citizens in the codifications of society and the law. As these dialogues demonstrate, however, questions of etiology continue to impinge on evolving conceptualizations of sexual preference and identity. In fact, what becomes increasingly apparent in the course of these interviews and conversations is a variation on the conclusion of *Intimate Matters, A History of Sexuality in America* by John D'Emilio and Estelle Freedman: as long as sexual identity remains a source of deep personal meaning, it will also remain a source of heated political controversy and vice versa.

In *Homosexuality as Behavior and Identity*, several trends that were apparent in *Homosexuality and Sexuality*, the first volume of *Dialogues of The Sexual Revolution*, become more pronounced. The earlier collection, which contains interviews and conversations from 1979-1987, beginning with sex researchers Masters and Johnson and concluding with historian Martin Duberman, documents what I perceived to be the principal trend in thinking about issues of homosexual preference and identity in the 1980s: a gradual movement away from a naive optimism that real clarification could ever come from the sciences toward a more sober acceptance that future perceptions of homosexuality are far more likely to be determined by the outcome of the learned versus the unlearned lessons of history. In other words, pursuing a science of homosexuality that could establish our "normality," even if there were such a thing, isn't nearly as likely to help gay and lesbian people come to terms with ourselves and guide us in the personal and political decisions that will shape our future as appreciating our history and, as Michel Foucault suggests, living and exploring our potential for all kinds of relationships, for *"becoming* truly gay." Science, in fact, is no more likely to foster the understanding, integration and well-being of gay and lesbian people in the future than it has helped women, blacks, Jews and others who have suffered discrimination in the past.

Conversely, however, these dialogues, especially those in the present collection, would appear to underscore the importance of one of those lessons of history: with the experience of yesterday's science to guide us, we should be wary of entrusting any single perspective or discipline, even the currently ascendant history of homosexuality and sexuality that has exposed so many of the errors and biases of that science, to provide absolute definitions or explanations of human sexual behaviors and preferences.

As their focus changes from science to history, another important cultural and subcultural trend is discernible in the course of these dialogues: the shift in credibility of opinion about gay life from nongay experts and allies outside our community (in the exchanges with leading sex researchers, sex educators and psychiatrists Masters and Johnson, John Money, Mary Calderone, Judd Marmor, Richard Green and Thomas Szasz, all of whom were or became prominent allies in the struggle to have homosexuality declassified as a mental disorder and the subsequent struggle to maintain that declassification, and all of whom, except Green, were interviewed during the earliest years covered in the first collection, between 1979 and 1981) to the observations, experiences and research findings of gay people ourselves (beginning, in the first volume, in the interview with Richard Pillard, who was the first openly gay psychiatrist in the United States, and developing in the interviews with gay wrestler and sports observer John Handley, gay educators Charles Silverstein, Emery Hetrick and Damien Martin, gay *littérateur* George Stambolian, gay scholars and historians John McNeill, Richard Plant and Martin Duberman, and gay activist and writer Arnie Kantrowitz). This trend is especially characteristic of the second volume, wherein ten of the eleven interviewees are openly gay or lesbian.

Concentrating on the years 1985-1989, the interviews and conversations of *Homosexuality as Behavior and Identity*, the second volume of *Dialogues of The Sexual Revolution*, divide in two parts: (1) Homosexuality and Art and (2) Homosexuality and Society. The dialogues of the first part attempt to extend the work of such pioneering authorities on homosexuality, film and art as Vito Russo and James Saslow. This section opens with two discussions of homosexuality and film. The first is with Hollywood director and screenwriter Paul Schrader on the subject of his controversial film, *Mishima*. The second is with Rosa von Praunheim, the German gay activist and *avant-garde*/new wave filmmaker on the occasion of the American premiere of *A Virus Has No Morals*, his satirical film about the spread of AIDS in Germany. Then follow three dialogues on homosexuality and music, a subject that remains more closeted than any other area of gay studies in the arts (except, perhaps, dance). These discussions feature Benjamin Britten scholar Philip Brett, outspokenly gay opera authority George Heymont and Pulitzer prize-winning composer and writer Ned Rorem, who remains the best-known of openly gay figures in American music. Although there have been individual contributions to the still tiny literature on homosexuality and music, such as those explored in the interviews with Brett, Heymont, and Rorem, there has never been a book — such as Vito Russo's *Celluloid Closet* or James Saslow's *Ganymede* — on this subject, or even a feature piece in a leading mainstream publication such as *Opera News* or *The New York Times*. (I am working on what would be the first such book, tentatively entitled *Homosexuality and Music: An Introduction to Gay and Lesbian Persons, Themes and Issues in Music*.)

If the dialogues of the first part make a convincing case for identifying gay and lesbian persons, themes and issues in the arts, those of the second part, which consists of five dialogues about sexual identity in our time and over time, reevaluate such assumptions. They begin with the striking insights of James Weinrich, a leading theorist and popularizer of sexology and sociobiology. These perceptions are in juxtaposition with the scathing indictments of medicine and sex research of John De Cecco, the eminent psychologist, sex researcher and Editor-in-Chief of the *Journal of Homosexuality*, in the interview that follows. The debate then shifts from the social constructionist critique of the modern notion of transhistorical homosexual preference and identity in the exchanges with De Cecco and distinguished socialist historians John D'Emilio and Estelle Freedman to laureate historian John Boswell's Daedalian engagement of critics of his belief that there has indeed been transhistorical sexual preference if not identity based on sexual preference. Finally, there is independent scholar Will Roscoe's precocious effort to chart a future course for the odyssey of gay and lesbian studies. As they traverse this journey, these dialogues bear witness to the controversies that are reshaping our thinking about homosexuality and sexuality.

[A few words about technique and form. Except for bracketed editorial notes, each interview text was approved by the interviewee(s). In part because I am not at my best in spontaneous conversation, my preferred method is to interview others as I myself would want to be interviewed: with a greater concern for considered, fact-checked and self-edited opinion than for less but also important values of spontaneity and style. What I have found is that when interviewees are assured that they will be able to edit their responses and share editorial approval, they tend to be more open, more willing to take chances, generally if not universally, than under more restrictive conditions.

The bracketed editorial notes that often introduce and otherwise give context to these interviews contain new or additional information compiled for this volume. Any introductory or bracketed information that is not designated as an editorial note ([Ed. note: . . .]) is from the original text or is being used to clarify, but not to update, that text.]

Acknowledgements

In regard to the preparation of *Homosexuality as Behavior and Identity: Dialogues of The Sexual Revolution* Volume II, I wish to acknowledge the following persons for their assistance, information, friendship, support, insights or example: Julie Abraham, Peter Adair, Barry Adkins, Dennis Altman, Virginia Apuzzo, Bernadette Aquavella, Brett Averill, Allen Barnett, Rick Barnett, Ronald Bayer, Arthur Bell, Dixie Beckham, Mark Blasius, Chris Bram, Arthur Bressan, Michael Bronski, Len Brown, Jack Bulmash, Victor Bumbalo, Stuart Byron, Larry Bush, Joe Cady, Pat Califia, Michael Callen, Robert and Julio Caserio, John Cavendish, George Chauncey, Jr., Robert Chesley, Catherine Clèment, Bill Cohen, Ed Cohen, Ron Christopher, Douglas Crimp, Howard Cruse, Melinda Cuthbert, Peter G. Davis, Martin Delaney, Michael Denneny, James D'Eramo, Richard Dyer, George De Stefano, Nick Deutsch, Tom Duane, Lucile Duberman, Lisa Duggan, Richard Dulong, Matthew Epstein, Bruce Eves, Lillian Faderman, Nathan Fain, Anita Feldman, Robert Ferro, Ann Fettner, Frances Fitzgerald, Robin Foerster, Michel Foucault, Jim Fouratt, Dave Frechette, Sandy Friedman, Nanette Gartrell, Barry Gingell, Morris Golde, Frances Goldin, Richard Goldstein, Eric Gordon, Alex Gotfryd, Stephen Greco, David Groff, Ron Grossman, Howard Grossman, Richard Hall, Sue Kiefer Hammersmith, John Hammond, David M. Halperin, James Harrison, Michael Hirsch, William M. Hoffman, Andrew Holleran, Amber Hollibaugh, Richard Howard, Andy Humm, Joyce Hunter, Nan Hunter, Robert Isaacs, Doug Ireland, Alan Isaksen, Kris Jakobsen, Chester Jakala, Karla Jay, Mitchell Karp, Barney Karpfinger, Simon Karlinsky, Jonathan Ned Katz, David Kessler, James Kinsella, David Kirby, Don Knutson, Gregory Kolovakos, Hal Kooden, Linda Laubenstein, John Lauritsen, David Leavitt, Martin Levine, Norman J. Levy, Winston Leyland, Sal Licata, Alex Lockwood, Diego Lopez, Peter Lowy, Michael Lutin, Daniel Margalioth, Harvey Marks, Ellen Mass, Steve Mass, Jed Mattes, Andrew Mattison, Susan McClary, Boyd McDonald, Rodger McFarlane, Frank McGurk, Robert McQueen, David McWhirter, Patrick Merla, Tom Miller, Helen Mitsios, Richard Mohr, Paul Monette, Ethan Mordden, Jon-David Nalley, Esther Newton, Stuart Nichols, David Nimmons, Frank O'Dowd, Jim Oleson, Charles Ortleb, Jim Owles, Tim Page, Marcia Pally, Pam Parker, Paul Paroski, Scott Parris, Cindy Patton, George Perle, Felice Picano, Nathaniel Pier, Paul Popham, Andrew Porter, John Preston, Michael Pye, Nick Rango, Campion Read, Lou Rispoli, Darryl Yates Rist, Marty Robinson, Paul Robinson, Eric Rofes, Herb Rosenberg, Jane Rosett, Gabriel Rotello, Gayle Rubin, Frank Rundle, Ron Sable, Douglas Sadownik, Harvey Sakofsky, Terry Sandholzer, Gregory Sandow, Eve Sedgewick, Bert Schaffner, Michael Shernoff, Michael Schnur, Sara Schulman, Robert Schwartz, Jay Scott, Laura Segal, Randy Shilts, Ed Sedarbaum, Ed Sikov, Ira Siff, Michelangelo Signorile, Ira Silverberg, Ingrid Sischy, Maynard Solomon, Joseph Sonnabend, Susan Sontag, Barbara Starrett, James Steakley, David Stein, Terry Stein, Frank Sulloway, David Summers, Dee Sushi, Mark Thompson, James Tierney, Jaime Titievski, Gladys Topkis, Orlando Torres, Ron Vachon, Carole S. Vance, Judith Walkowitz, Joyce Wallace, Simon Watney, Steven Watson, Jeffrey Weeks, Edmund White, Walter Williams, Liz Wood, Ralph Wynn, Ellen Zaltzberg, Phil Zwickler, and my Greenwich House, ACT UP, GMHC, PWA Coalition and CLAGS friends and colleagues.

Very special thanks to Martin Duberman, Thomas E. Steele, John De Cecco, Jeffrey Escoffier, Norman Laurila, Arnie Kantrowitz, James Saslow, Vito Russo, Larry Kramer, Ida Walker, James Ice, Ann Schwartz, Eli Zal, Bill and Mignon Thorpe, Bruce-Michael Gelbert, Brandon Judell, David Alexander, Craig Rowland, Seymour Kleinberg and the friends from the meetings.

It is gratefully acknowledged that the interviews and conversations listed below were first published elsewhere, as indicated.

Paul Schrader, *The New York Native*, 9/16/85, pp. 21-27
Rosa von Praunheim, *The New York Native*, 1/26/87, pp. 19-22
Philip Brett, *Christopher Street*, Fall 1987, issue 115, pp. 12-27

Unmasked Confessions:
Inside the Mind
of an Artist Gone Mad

A Conversation with Paul Schrader

[Ed. note: Throughout the 1970s, during the decade in which I established a professional identity as a physician, I continued to seek personal and spiritual (group) identity by trying to understand homosexuality in a context of science. What *is* homosexuality? I kept wondering. Behind that wonder, I now see, was a belief that the phenomenon of homosexuality, like any other phenomena of sexuality, could be rendered comprehensible and categorizable in nice, neat scientific terms the way everything else in medicine was or seemed to be. As a gay liberationist in the late 1970s and early '80s, I became a lot more distrustful of medicine and science. But it's only recently that I have begun to appreciate just how much the medical model, the prejudices, excesses and other disasters of which I increasingly found myself attacking, was still dominating the way I looked at gay life and gay people, including myself, in those years.

One of the gay lives I kept looking at was that of the great Japanese writer, Yukio Mishima. In his autobiographical masterpiece, *Confessions of a Mask*, I believed I had found a kind of proof of my essentialist view of homosexuality, a view that would undergo considerable transformation over the next several years. I was convinced that Mishima's life demonstrated that in persons whose homosexual fantasies and preferences have been dominant and

1

lifelong (which applied to most of the gay men I knew of, but not to all of them or to many bisexuals), homosexuality was in fact a phenomenon of earliest childhood, probably of inheritance, and was definitely a phenomenon of cross-gender identity. In addition, I believed that Mishima's story epitomized the social context and causes—the sexism, erotophobia and homophobia—of what psychiatrists were calling "ego-dystonic homosexuality" (e.g., when a homosexual person resents and wants to be rid of her or his own acknowledged homosexuality), which I likewise believed explained this writer's flirtations with fascism. Yukio Mishima, I was convinced, was an ego-dystonic homosexual whose bravado, machismo and sadomasochism may have been sincerely and seriously patriotic, but which were probably more fundamentally the acculturated masks of a constitutionally "feminine" gay man.

I was so convinced of what seemed to me to be the straightfoward interconnections among all these factors in the life and death of Mishima that I wrote a screenplay, a kind of psychobiographical adaptation of *Confessions* that was updated to include later events in the writer's life, culminating in his public death by ritual samurai warrior suicide (*seppuku*) in 1970. This adaptation, I believed, demonstrated who Mishima *really* was and showed how and why he became an epitome of the ego-dystonicity that remains so pervasive among gay people and that seemed to be caused, simply and exclusively, by "the patriarchal values of western civilization."

I loved this adaptation, which was written in 1979-80.   I still do. Precociously and very naively (in terms of understanding how deeply Mishima touches the patriotic sensitivities of the Japanese), I sent a copy to the only person I believed, on the basis of his stunning film, *In The Realm of the Senses*, could successfully bring the life and death of Yukio Mishima to the screen—Nagisa Oshima. Unfortunately, Mr. Oshima was spending most of his time dealing with Japanese censors in court cases, as he considerately wrote me, and was in no position to consider new projects. Shortly thereafter, in 1983, he directed a film that dealt with some of the same conflicts between and around homosexuality and patriotism that seemed to me to be paramount in Mishima's life, but from a more traditionally Japanese point of view. That film was *Merry Christmas, Mr. Lawrence*.

In the early 1980s I also discussed this adaptation with Ned Rorem, who had asked me to suggest a gay subject for an opera libretto. He was intrigued by the idea of *Confessions*, which he read on my recommendation but found "too dated." I told him I wished he were right. I wish it were true that gay men, especially androgynous persons like Mishima who might easily be perceived as "feminine" or gay, I wrote Ned back, "no longer have to worry about growing up completely isolated, having to deny to everyone around them the reality of their true nature and identity . . . For me, [*Confessions*] says timeless and universal things . . . about the hatred of one's own femininity and homosexuality to the degree that one becomes a grotesque parody of the machismo that created that hatred in the first place."

Because of political sensitivities in Japan and the rigid control of Mishima's estate by the writer's wife, Paul Schrader's *Mishima*, which was released in this country in 1985 but has yet to be released in Japan, is the only feature film that has ever been made about the life and death of Yukio Mishima.

In chronological sequence, the dialogue with Paul Schrader pursues a major concern of *Homosexuality and Sexuality: Dialogues of The Sexual Revolution, Volume I*, which contains interviews and conversations conducted from 1979-1987: the reality of gay children. In doing so, it continues to probe questions of individual versus group identities and of the politics these identities engender or (as in the case of Mishima?) appear to engender. At the beginning of this collection, the conversation with Schrader also introduces a new perspective through which these questions are filtered, and which becomes the principal subject of the first five dialogues: homosexuality and art.]

The following interview took place August 23, 1985 in Paul Schrader's office. As we spoke, the handsome, tightly-muscled, soft-spoken film director seemed to eclipse the black-and-white figure of Mishima that leapt from a large, blood-red poster behind Schrader's desk. The only other adornment on the office's walls, at right angles to the poster, was a photograph of Schrader's lovely wife, actress Mary Beth Hurt, and their 19-month old daughter.

Schrader, who wrote the script for Martin Scorsese's *Taxi Driver* and *Raging Bull* and is himself the writer/director of *Hardcore*,

American Gigolo and the remake of *Cat People*, took the initiative in talking about his controversial new film based on the life of Mishima.

SCHRADER: Do you know Stuart Byron?

MASS: Yes. We had several conversations about you and your work.

SCHRADER: Not a very generous man. This prejudice that I'm homophobic started with Byron making a kind of cause out of the fact that the two antagonists in [*American Gigolo*] are gay. One is a white lesbian and one is a black gay man. That is a decision that was made on my part because of the textural world the central character [played by Richard Gere] lived in. Byron's accusation, which became a kind of *idée fixe*, seemed very ironic to me, because at the time I made *Gigolo*, my social world was 75% gay!

MASS: Vito Russo and I were among the writers who characterized *American Gigolo* as homophobic, but it wasn't just because of Stuart Byron. I think many of us felt at that time — when Hollywood images of lesbians and gay men were so relentlessly negative — that even otherwise artistically substantial or challenging films had to be criticized if they perpetuated negative gay stereotypes. The whole thing became so politicized (and appropriately so, I still think) that some of us found ourselves praising utterly mediocre but politically important films like *Making Love*, and rejecting more interesting ones, like *Gigolo*.

SCHRADER: Look, I understand and sympathize with the political needs and vulnerabilities of the gay community, but I can't be restricted as an artist by political platforms, whether from blacks, the left or the clergy. Everyone has a lot of special pleading going on, and everyone wants to make art march under some banner. I don't think art should march under banners. I think the idea of a "Marxist film" is contradictory. You can have a film that comes to certain Marxist conclusions, but if it is definitively Marxist, it's not art any more. It's a piece of propaganda.

MASS: Let's talk about *Mishima*. The introduction to Hans-Jurgen Syberberg's film, *Hitler: A Film From Germany*, asks the question, "Will we ever be free of the oppressive curse of guilt if we do not get at the center of it?" In so successfully getting inside, at the center of your protagonist, as he saw himself, were you trying to achieve in *Mishima* what Syberberg tried to achieve in *Hitler?* That is, is Mishima supposed to be *our* Mishima?

SCHRADER: Yes and no. I mean, he is *my* Mishima. Unlike *Hitler*, *Mishima* has no hypothetical or fictional scenes; but the mosaic I've created from autobiographical fragments and pieces of his works is totally informed by my own personal interest in Mishima, which is not necessarily the same as another person's. The larger truth that is created from this mosaic is really mine, yet there is nothing fictional or hypothetical in it. Syberberg's method is clearly interpretive. Mine is interpretive, but not as clearly so.

MASS: It seems implicit in your *Mishima*, as in Syberberg's *Hitler*, that we cannot fully understand such persons unless we can be made to deeply feel, to actually experience the romance that was going on between these protagonists and their audiences in real life.

SCHRADER: I think the comparison of Hitler with Mishima is spurious, even though Mishima did do a play called *My Friend Hitler*. It's spurious because one must come to terms with Hitler in a way that is not true of Mishima. Unlike Hitler, Mishima did not impose his fantasy on the rest of the world. You can treat Mishima as an interesting case for study, a cultural icon who can be seen dispassionately, but I think it's virtually impossible to be dispassionate about Hitler.

At some point, I made a statement which I didn't remember until someone asked me about it in a classroom situation in Edinburgh two days ago. I said that Mishima was going to be a combination of Syberberg and Antonioni. What did I mean by that? I explained that this sounded like the kind of thing I might have said *before* I made the film. I don't think it's true any more. Perhaps you heard that I had said this, or something like it.

MASS: No. The comparison with Syberberg was my own thought. You don't think it's valid to compare Mishima with Hitler because Mishima never succeeded in imposing a political agenda on the world. But I think the comparison is intriguing. Hitler was a failed artist who became politically successful, while Mishima was exactly the opposite: a successful artist who failed politically. Both were fascists — one in fantasy, the other in reality — whose profound seductiveness is engaged to a disturbing degree in both films [Syberberg's *Hitler* and your *Mishima*].

SCHRADER: No! Fascism is a political phenomenon. Mishima wasn't a real fascist. The politics that developed around Mishima are mostly posthumous and mostly not his.

MASS: When you began filming *Mishima*, you predicted, in an interview with film critic Jay Scott of the *Toronto Globe and Mail*, that most Japanese, including the right wing, would reject your film. Do you still believe this to be true? Why would the right wing object to a film that treats their hero with such profound respect?

SCHRADER: While we were shooting, I got a letter from one of the leading right-wing student groups. It said Mishima had died to protest the MacArthur-imposed constitution, and how dare I, a product of MacArthur's culture, make a film about him. Well, that is simply false. That's not why Mishima died. Contrary to what a lot of people think, Mishima was *not* for rearming Japan and going back to war. In fact, that was probably one of the last things he favored. On the other hand, he did favor a kind of spiritual rearmament, which was tied up with his personal aesthetics. But they weren't ever formulated into any real political thinking. That whole speech on the balcony [in the final scenes of the film] is all about *spiritual* rearmament.

Do you know the true story of the army rebellion of February 1936? This incident always fascinated Mishima, and is the subject of "Patriotism," the short story he wrote and subsequently made into a film [which he directed and starred in]. This incident is also the basis of his novel, *Runaway Horses*, which I put into the film. A group of military cadets took over the Diet and tried to overthrow the government. They were defeated after two days. Some were executed and the others committed *seppuku*. At that time, Japan was preparing for war. In fact, the army had already invaded China. (Japan periodically raped the Far East, because it had no raw materials of its own.) The military leaders and the industrialists pretty much controlled the government, and they were setting up for a widescale invasion. But this particular group of cadets said that if Japan invaded it would not only lose its traditional identity as an island culture, it would lose its soul.

Those are the kids Mishima identified with. The ones who have appropriated his legacy are the opposite. They want to rearm Japan and take certain islands back from Russia and Korea. They want to remake Japan into a military power. Because both factions — those who favor spiritual rearmament and the militarists — are considered right wing, people get them confused. This is particularly true in Japan, where, for 15 years now, the right-wing militarists have claimed Mishima. It's very hard to get back to that other kind of military thinking, the kind epitomized by the cadets, or that which has to do with "the harmony of pen and sword." That a man of action should also be a poet, that the soldier is basically a spiritual creation, and that, like the old samurai, you could go out to fight for your master and return home at night to write poems — this is what Mishima had all his fantasies about. But he didn't believe this fantasy ideal could exist in the contemporary world — because of the modernization and Westernization of Japan. So Mishima's "politics" are to a large degree symbolic and theatrical.

MASS: It's good to hear that you believe this, but what about the problem, which you just acknowledged, of the extent to which Mishima's fantasies play into the hands of the militant right wing?

SCHRADER: Well, what it is, of course, is "fascinating fascism." You know that Susan Sontag article where she talks about the fascist mentality and the sexual seduction of its accoutrements? It's those damned uniforms! As soon as you see 100 kids marching around with high-peaked caps, you think the Third Reich is coming again. Mishima was no fool; he must have known his images would have that effect. Mishima's problem was how to use a certain kind of homoerotic imagery apart from its political metaphor or simile. That's really tricky. In a way, Mishima deserves some of the misinterpretation he's gotten, by getting so involved in fascist metaphors.

MASS: I'm sure you'd agree that the current political climate is one of growing conservatism in Japan as well as in the U.S. Don't you think that the political impact of your film in Japan would be to appease conservatives and [seduce] more liberal types who had previously rejected Mishima because of the associations with fascism?

SCHRADER: I hope so, because it presents him primarily as an artist. He was not a soldier. He was a writer, and he died a writer's death. To me, the most interesting thing about Mishima is what happens when words are insufficient and one feels that one has to become a player in one's own fantasy dramas. Mishima said, it's not enough to see; one must also be seen. That's the issue that really motivates the film, and my interest in Mishima. I suppose you can't really get into that issue without getting into the political manifestations it takes at the end, but I think the film puts so little credibility in his politics. It views his politics as theater. The whole last act [Mishima's *seppuku*] is, in a way, like one of his novels. I just don't see [this appropriation by fascists] happening. The film is so intellectual. It doesn't stir those kinds of emotions.

MASS: For the intellectual, that may be true, but what about the average Japanese citizen who won't be able to understand the extremely sophisticated issues your film raises? Don't you think many people, especially right-wing militants, are more likely to respond to the film's overall tone of near-reverence?

SCHRADER: I doubt if the average Japanese citizen will ever see the film. If he does, he will never presume to make an independent judgment; he will accept the established line—whatever that turns out to be.

We've already heard from the Japanese right wing. Actually, the forces that want to stop the film from being shown in Japan find it very convenient to *blame* the right wing [implying that the right wing would be offended by the film's allegation that Mishima was homosexual, etc.]. During the Tokyo Film Festival controversy, a number of people were saying you can't show the film because the right wing will bomb the theater. But the most powerful of the right-wing kingpins got in touch with the festival and said, "Stop blaming us for this. We've seen the film and we like it." So the forces that don't want the film to be shown in Japan are many and diverse.

MASS: Do you think it will be shown in Japan?

SCHRADER: I think so, in about a year, but we have to wait until it becomes old news. Right now, it's too fresh, too controversial.

MASS: In *Mishima*, the protagonist's homosexuality is revealed for what you, like many conservative Japanese admirers of Mishima, seem to consider it to be—only one, perhaps even minor (certainly not dominant) aspect of his character. Would you characterize your attitude towards Mishima's homosexuality as more Japanese than

American? Or have you simply endeavored to convey Mishima's own sense of his homosexuality?

SCHRADER: I personally think Mishima's homosexuality was more important than the film portrays it. It's a chicken-and-egg situation. At what point does homosexuality motivate behavior? At what point is the behavior independent of the homosexuality? My feeling is that Mishima is a good case for Freud. You could probably do a pretty good Freudian reading of Mishima, because he was Western in so many ways, and he did formulate his problems in Western terms quite often. Freud doesn't really apply to the Japanese, but I think he does to Mishima.

In order to get permission for the novels from Madame Mishima, I had to agree not to show anything I couldn't document. That's her legal right. Otherwise she would hit me with a lawsuit and the film would never be released. Since my interest was never to do Fassbinder's Mishima (someone else can do that, although we'll have to wait a few more years before it will be legally possible), I agreed.

My interest was this notion of art and action. That's a rather difficult concept intellectually, whereas sexuality and politics are much more sensationalistic. In order to really keep the focus on what I wanted to do, I had to keep sex and politics in the wings. If I let them take center stage, they would never get off. It's a kind of device of the film to let the audience be aware of their presence, but to keep them in the wings so you can study more interesting, more unique aspects of Mishima. There are a lot of famous homosexuals and there are a lot of famous right wingers, but there was only one Mishima who merged art and action in his own life. *That's* the reason *I* wanted to make a film about him. It's a convenient misconception with some people that, just because someone is gay, that has to be the center of focus.

MASS: I guess I've been one of those people because I always believed that *the* mask of Mishima's autobiographical masterpiece, *Confessions of a Mask*, was the violence-obsessed machismo that covered his more natural androgyny and homosexuality.

SCHRADER: The truth is that, after *Confessions*, he went back into the closet for the rest of his life. It was as if he just briefly stuck out his head, then pulled it back in and closed the door. He was not a gay freedom fighter. In fact, he resisted any attempts to get him to come out of the closet. He was intent on maintaining that husband-and-wife persona mask. He would take his wife many places a straight Japanese man wouldn't, because he wanted to be seen in her company.

MASS: Precisely. Mishima was a self-negating, self-hating, closeted homosexual. In your film, his homosexuality is more descriptive, more intellectual than visually apparent, and his androgyny is nonexistent. Your audience has no idea that Mishima was scolded for cross-dressing as a child, no idea that the musclebound Mishima of later years had skinny, underdeveloped legs, no idea that the marriage that produced his children was one he engaged in because his dying mother made him promise on her deathbed that he would marry, no idea that many of the macho pursuits he so obsessively engaged in during those final years were ineptly performed and no idea that the *seppuku* was also botched. In your film, Mishima is comfortably masculine and believably heterosexual, like Ken Ogata [the actor who portrays Mishima in the film] and Roy Scheider [who does the English voice]; not perceivably gay, like Ryuichi Sakamoto [David Bowie's androgynous counterpart in Oshima's film, *Merry Christmas, Mr. Lawrence*]. Have you really told us objective truth about Mishima, or rather the kind of truth that would be most acceptable to his heterosexual admirers, or to Mishima himself?

SCHRADER: There is much truth to what you say. I looked around for months for someone who had a more feminine character. I just couldn't find a good enough actor. Finally, at the end of a very long and fruitless casting pursuit, I had to choose between someone who looked like Mishima and was feminine, and someone who could really act and make contact with the viewer. The choice was obvious. All through the shooting, Ogata, who is the best actor in Japan, tried to school himself in acting more feminine, but he really didn't have the physical equipment to make that crossover. That's just unfortunate. I knew the day I cast Ogata that a lot would be lost.

MASS: The sense I got was that the naturally, self-confidently masculine man we were seeing was Mishima as he idealized himself.

SCHRADER: You're right, of course, about Mishima being something of a fraud at that level. Ogata tells this wonderful story. When he was in the army, Mishima showed up one day with a bunch of photographers, to pose. He was supposed to be climbing a rope, but he couldn't climb it, so he stood on a box and posed while the other soldiers watched. A lot of the animosity Mishima had to face in his lifetime was because he was thought of as a fraud or goofball, a *poseur*. When you're going to make a film about an aberrant person, however, I think you basically have to take that person's point of view. If you look at such a person with any real outside objectivity, he looks silly and you lose interest in him. So you take characters like Travis Bickle [in *Taxi Driver*] and Jake La Motta [in *Raging Bull*], people who are basically unsympathetic and aberrant; you see the world primarily from their points of view, and at the end let the audience sort out the pieces. *Mishima* is narrated by quotes from Mishima's essays and is full of his weird thinking, which it never questions, even though this thinking is clearly not sane.

MASS: It exposes it.

SCHRADER: I think that, during the course of the movie, and certainly by the end, you're supposed to realize that this is not a very reliable narrator you're listening to. This man is not really sane. In fact, he borders on being absolutely ludicrous.

MASS: This, I think, is the film's greatest success. Just as with Mishima's writing, you are so seduced, so hypnotized by the romance of Mishima that you don't notice the extent of the contradictions that are being revealed. You see Mishima in his Western-style house, with all its Victoriana. Then you see this final scene from his novel, *Runaway Horses*, in which the villain, who is killed by a right wing terrorist, lives precisely the same sort of "decadently" Westernized life Mishima led.

SCHRADER: To some extent, these things are buried in the text of the film. You can't say right out to the audience that Mishima was a faker and a *poseur*. You have to present his case on his own terms. It gets very crazy at the end, particularly with the excerpts from the F105 [jet fighter] essay, where he's talking about being up in the heavens, where there is no oxygen so there must be death; and it's like death, and you have to wear a mask like an actor. This is batty. It's all sort of psychopathic fantasy. But it's a very intelligent fantasy — it's illogical, but it's logically worked out.

MASS: In your film, Mishima wears many masks.

SCHRADER: As Mishima began to perceive it, literature itself becomes a mask. He lost faith in writing because it appeared fraudulent to him, as did family life, the bodybuilding stuff, and all the various poses. The people who knew Mishima a relatively short time felt they knew him well. Those who knew Mishima the longest were the ones who said they knew him the least. The longer you knew him, the more mirrors you saw. Eventually, you realized that there was really nobody there, that it was just a series of masks. *That's* why he was so unhappy, and why he kept driving himself into hyperbolic fantasies that would somehow resolve his sense of being incomplete and unreal.

MASS: But so many of those masks had to do with hypermasculinity, with machismo. In a letter to *American Film*, you recently stated that you are "fully aware of the homosexuality that's at the heart of the homophobia of the central characters in *Taxi Driver* and *American Gigolo*." "I've always been interested," you wrote, "in the similarity of these two sexual impulses and have tried to exploit rather than simplify this complexity." What do you mean when you say that homosexuality and homophobia are similar sexual impulses? Is Mishima similar to the central characters in *Taxi Driver* and *Gigolo* in exhibiting a somehow characteristic mixture of homosexuality and homophobia?

SCHRADER: Not in Mishima himself so much as in one's attitudes toward him. I've always had the problem in life that, the moment an idea occurs to me, the opposite idea occurs with equal strength. Travis Bickle, for example, is racist, anti-homosexual, anti-female, a whole bunch of antisocial angers. He's just looking for another minority on which to vent his hostilities. But part of Travis's attraction is his physicality. It's the same with the Richard Gere character in *Gigolo*. You take a character who has, or who brings out, certain homophobic fears, and you present him in a homoerotic fashion. Then you just let these two impulses gnaw at each other, grind and grind, because they are so close to each other. But this isn't characteristic of homosexuality. The fact that you desire someone but fear, simultaneously and with equal force, your own desire, is something you see in *all* sexuality—and, for that matter, in all life.

MASS: But do you think, with many exceptions and very generally speaking, that gay men or a subset of gay men share with Mishima a world view that romanticizes and sexualizes violence? Would you say that Molina, in your brother Leonard's film adaptation of *Kiss of the Spider Woman*, and Mishima are somehow characteristically or stereotypically gay in their tendency to worship great displays of passion and strength, regardless of the politics those displays might be connected to?

SCHRADER: First, I have to make a sort of dreadful confession and admit that I haven't yet seen *Kiss of the Spider Woman*. But I read the script. I think that where the notion of sexuality or homosexuality and violence comes in, at least in Mishima's case, is in this notion of being the object of your own desires. There's a great quote in his novel, *Forbidden Colors*, which says that if you could combine the jealousy a woman feels when a younger woman walks into the room with the anger a man feels when he is cuckolded, you will understand how a homosexual feels every time he looks in the mirror. This idea that you are your own enemy, that what you see in the mirror is the object of your own desire and is getting older — this mixture of anger and desire at your own physicality — is what preoccupied Mishima. Ultimately, I think, he hyperbolized this metaphor into the very nature of *seppuku*, which he perceived to be both a male and a female act. In the film, he talks about *seppuku* as resolving the contradictions of being both male and female, of the sword being both sun and steel. For Mishima, *seppuku* became the sexual act. As John Nathan [a biographer of Mishima] wrote, for Mishima, death was a passionately sexual desire. So you're not talking about something that could possibly apply across the board to homosexuality. You're talking about an extreme twist on a homosexual fantasy. God knows, heterosexual fantasies have equally violent twists.

MASS: In your view, Mishima might be characterized as a sadomasochist, but not as a fascist. So you don't believe that sadomasochism and fascism are necessarily connected, whatever the proportions.

SCHRADER: Well, they cross-dress. That's for sure.

MASS: But not with a preference for one sexual orientation or another.

SCHRADER: No. There's a lot of heterosexual fantasy in fascism as well, [e.g.,] all that Hitler talk about young girls making love to Aryan soldiers and bearing many children for the Fatherland.

There's a real heterosexual fantasy going on there that transcends the political impact, particularly when you see Leni Riefenstahl's films; you see sexuality operating all across the board. We both agree, I'm sure, on this point, that the notion of hetero- or homo- is just a convenient distinction that exists only on paper; it never *really* exists in life. The whole pansexual rainbow of feelings just isn't adequately accounted for by these narrow categorizations.

MASS: You mean most people are fundamentally *sexual* — that is, bisexual and pansexual.

SCHRADER: Yes. I think everyone is originally pansexual (to use Parker Tyler's term). Sooner or later, however, most people repress one or another impulse, or legislate one or another impulse in their own minds. I don't believe anyone's sexuality is really that limited. As soon as they dream, the repressed impulses start coming back. Whatever their conscious protestations may be, at night, in their fantasies, they do the weirdest things sexually, which often include animals.

MASS: So you think that becoming self-identified as gay or straight is a cultural or temporal phenomenon.

SCHRADER: Yes. It's just a way to survive in this world, so you can find your spot, because society wants you to define yourself, for a lot of reasons. I firmly believe that Mishima was not as homosexual as he would like to have led certain homosexual friends to believe. His nickname in gay circles was Cinderella, because he always had to be home at midnight to write. Clearly, sexual activity took a secondary place in Mishima's mind to the world of fantasy. As one of his friends said to me, Mishima basically talked a good fuck and wrote a good fuck, but in his own life he wasn't that interested in it and wasn't really that sexual a person. I think if he had been more sexual, if he had been able to find a real partner in life — of either sex — he would not have been driven to excesses. He was fundamentally alone. He had no real relationship with anyone. I think that sex was an unsuccessful fantasy for Mishima, just as writing eventually became an unsuccessful fantasy.

MASS: I think a lot of us have had a simpler interpretation of Mishima: that he was a homosexual, a sexual preference or orientation that was determined in earliest childhood — that's what most experts believe, you know; that sexual orientation *does* exist, that it's multi-

ply determined and becomes permanently fixed in earliest childhood, even if there is also some pansexual flexibility—and that his
home environment, which was very erotophobic, prevented him
from being his natural self. He had to wear this mask of being
masculine and heterosexual and socially integrated, when the simple truth about him was that he was homosexual and androgynous.

SCHRADER: Let me tell you a wonderful story that Meredith
Weatherby, who did the English translation of *Confessions of a
Mask*, told me. One day Weatherby, who is gay, was going over the
text with Mishima. Mishima was going on and on about how alone
he was, how tortured, when Weatherby pointed out to him that
within a one-mile radius of them there were something like 20,000
homosexuals. "What do you mean, you're all alone?" To which
Mishima replied, "But I never knew that." He thought he was
desperately alone, but he wasn't.

MASS: How do you account for Mishima's extreme childhood re-
pression in a culture that is plenty patriarchal but was at least relatively (compared to the U.S. during the 1950s) tolerant of homosexuality?

SCHRADER: Other homosexuals who knew Mishima simply did
not share this repressive upbringing. I have a number of friends,
American expatriates, who have gone to Japan because of the relative looseness of the sexual atmosphere. They say that it's usual for
a Japanese boy to have sexual experiences with other boys, much
more so than in this country. Mishima didn't know or feel this,
because of [the isolating and engulfing influence of] his grandmother and mother. He felt totally alone and locked off, tortured
and unique. In a sense, his sexuality was formulated in a Western
context, much more than in a Japanese context.

I'll tell you the best Mishima story of all. It was told to me by a
Japanese-American friend of Mishima, who felt that people in
America were always judging him because of his homosexuality, so
he moved to Japan. He was an intellectual who knew all about
Mishima's writing and he wanted to talk ideas. Mishima would not
talk ideas with him, however, because he had categorized this person as one of his gay friends, rather than one of his literary or
"idea" friends. Conversely, as it turns out, if you were an intellectual or idea friend, you were not allowed to talk sexuality; if you

were a bodybuilding friend, you could only talk about that, and so forth. Mishima set down the rules of what could be discussed with him. He would place you in a particular box and there you would have to stay. Anyway, one day Mishima called his friend and said that he wanted to go down to the docks in Kawasaki, but was a little afraid for his safety. He wanted to be accompanied. So together they picked up a trucker and went to a small "love hotel." Inside, Mishima purposely set the door ajar, and the gay friend stood in the next room watching as the trucker turned over a coffee table, tied Mishima up, and started fucking him. It then occurred to the friend that this would not be happening if he were not there — that is, the pleasure Mishima derived from this experience was that of being watched, but not only by someone else. It was the idea of being watched by this "Western intellectual" that made it work!

I think this is the best capsule story of how Mishima's sexuality really operated. It wasn't the pleasure itself so much as a mixture of cross-cultural condemnation, prurience and voyeurism. In this idea of being raped while being seen, you have the whole febrile mix of Mishima's sexual iconography. If I were to make a film about Mishima 30 years from now (in a world where I could have complete artistic freedom), I would probably get more into the specifics, the mechanics of his sexuality; but if I would have allowed a scene like that to be in the film, I don't think I could ever have gotten out of that sexual box. That kind of sexuality is something you have to explore totally, or not at all.

MASS: I know from your interview with Jay Scott that you had an earlier script. How was it different?

SCHRADER: It was the same concept, but I had to change the center novel. I knew I had to get into the literature, because that's the only way you can get into a writer's life. Mishima's public life wasn't his real life. His real life was his fantasy life. So I felt I had to dramatize the middle-period novels. I wanted to do *Forbidden Colors*, which Mishima's widow owns (along with the other middle-period novels). We would always talk around it, yet every time I got a contract back, *Forbidden Colors* was never on it. Eventually, I realized that she would never give me this book, and the reason is that it's the only middleperiod work that has homosexual characters. So I had to find another book from that period. It turned out to be *Kyoko's House*, which I had to have translated into English. (It had never been translated.) It includes the story of a failed, narcissistic actor who is involved with two older women—his mother and a loan shark. He gets involved in a sadomasochistic relationship with the latter, which ends in a double suicide. In this episode, you see the whole rich texture of Mishima's sexual fantasy, *vis à vis* women. But the novel's protagonist, the actor, is clearly homosexual. There's no other way to read it.

MASS: Could you say something more about this business of Mishima's sadomasochism being primarily the result of Western influences?

SCHRADER: Yes. In that cloistered childhood, living in those dark rooms, his fantasies turned to literature, specifically to Western literature. I think it's very revealing that his first sexual icon was Saint Sebastian, rather than a Japanese figure. In literature, he turned to people like Gide and Radiguet. The earliest writings took Western terms, because those were the writers he was copying. Later, a number of his sexual companions were Westerners who had come to Japan because it was freer there. He ended up hanging around with Westerners, because he felt more comfortable with them and (masochistically) because he thought he was such a freak. He had a kind of self-perpetuating persecution complex. He just kept recreating the environment in which he felt most outcast.

MASS: Like the film's conceptualization, Philip Glass's gorgeous score seems to conjugate the dissonances of the two cultures that, in the film's view and more than anything else, caused Mishima such conflict. The music seems to reflect the film's viewpoint that these conflicts were resolved, however ineffably, in Mishima's *seppuku*. Certainly this was Mishima's belief. Is it yours?

SCHRADER: Yes. I have to take that point of view. Otherwise I shouldn't be making the film. It's certainly not something you can recommend to others, and it's certainly something I don't care to do myself. But Mishima really believed it, and I believe he believed it at the moment of his death. To say that Mishima at the moment of death transcended into fiction, that he became Mizoguchi in the burning temple [from the novel *The Temple of the Golden Pavilion*, which is Part 1 of *Mishima* and subtitled *Beauty* in the film], Osamu in *Kyoko's House* [Part II in the film, subtitled *Art*], and Isao on the cliff as he commits *seppuku* [from *Runaway Horses*, Part III, subtitled *Action*]; *to say that Mishima is now up in his own fantasy pantheon* [Part IV of *Mishima*, subtitled *The Harmony of Pen and Sword*, fuses Mishima's death by *seppuku* to the climaxes of the novels featured in the first three sections]—*that* is the assumption I make about Mishima. I have to believe it worked for him.

MASS: In your interview with Jay Scott, you said that you became very personally caught up in this fantasy of suicidal self-transcendence, to the point that you sometimes wondered if you would survive the making of the film. The filming is over and you have survived, but do you still entertain this fantasy at some level for yourself?

SCHRADER: The grip of that particular fantasy of suicidal glory— that I will be my own Christ, that I will save myself through death, my death—is a very powerful fantasy and one that appeals to all artists and professional makers of fantasy. Every artist entertains the notion that he can transcend real life by creating characters whose pain and death will transmogrify him. That's a common enough fantasy. What's uncommon is to see a person actually take this fantasy to its logical conclusion. Mishima is the only artist I know of who so thoroughly and successfully pursued it.

For me personally, this fantasy is not as potent as it once was, and I think it's simply because I've gotten older. I now see Mishima's fantasy of death as juvenile. It's really the kind of play-acting death that appeals so much to children and to the anger of youth. As you get a bit older, you realize how complex life is. You see that simple solutions, like a death of glory, whether it be on the battlefield or in the bedroom, are not the answer. At an age when most people outgrow such fantasies, they took over for Mishima. If Mishima had been a young man at the time of his death, his life would have been less interesting. As a middle-aged man, he died a young man's death. It's very peculiar to see someone 45 years old in the grip of a fantasy that is more logically a 25 year-old man's fantasy.

MASS: The last I heard, Madame Mishima refused to accept any monies from your film. Is this true, and if so, is she thereby expressing personal, political or other disapproval of this film?

SCHRADER: She has gone on record officially disapproving of the film. That happened even before the filming started. I honestly believe that the only reason I got this film made is that nobody thought I could do it. The people who wanted to stop me didn't mobilize until it was too late. About a month before we were going to start shooting, when it became clear to her that I was going to make the film, she started asking for changes beyond what we had agreed upon. She wanted *all* references to homosexuality deleted. She wanted the stuff in the general's office taken out.

I reminded her that this was not our agreement and that, in any event, it was too late; the sets were built and we were going ahead. I think she believed she could control the film, even though that was never negotiated. Maybe that was part of the subtext of her being Japanese, that we would do whatever she said, regardless of the contracts, because the Japanese don't operate by contract so much as by consensus. Because she has such ironclad control over Mishima's legacy in Japan, and because she can keep books from being published about him, I think she assumed that she would have that same degree of control over me. When it became clear to her that she didn't, she had no choice but to go on record opposing the film — even though she had signed the contract and a check had been delivered to her. The check is now in escrow, where it will probably remain in a sort of zen state forever.

MASS: What, exactly, is she saying to the press?

SCHRADER: She says that the film is an exploitation of Mishima's alleged homosexuality and violence (violence being a kind of code word for *seppuku*). She feels that the movie centers on these issues when, in fact, the opposite is true. As you of all people know, most of the criticism I've received is from people who say the opposite — that the film cops out because it doesn't get into the sexuality more.

MASS: What I'm really trying to get at is whether or not she is allied with any political faction, like the right wing?

SCHRADER: Her power base? I don't think she has much communication with the right any more. She used to, but not now. Her power base is primarily the old boy network, which is the social circle of publishers and politicians.

MASS: Is the Shield Society [the private army Mishima founded] still active?

SCHRADER: No. The Shield Society was really Mishima's social group. It wasn't a genuine political or military organization. As they say in the film, "We are a spiritual army." The group could not exist without Mishima. It was an extension of his thinking. Without Mishima, it was a body without a head.

MASS: Mishima was not named Best Film nor you Best Director at Cannes. Could it be for the same reasons that Mishima couldn't win the Nobel Prize, despite three nominations? That is, do you think the judges were afraid they might be endorsing something politically incorrect?

SCHRADER: Yes. I know this for a fact. For about a week, all the papers were saying we were going to win the Golden Palm. Then, after an interview we did, a Spanish journalist pulled me aside and said, "You're not going to win, because there is this faction, *Liberation* in Paris and some people in West Germany and the Iron Curtain, that says Mishima was a fascist, and that the film, because it doesn't explicitly condemn Mishima, tacitly approves of fascism. "With its rich left-wing tradition," he said, "Cannes cannot give a Golden Palm to a film that implicitly approves of fascism. This debate reached the jury." I immediately realized that the Golden Palm was out of the question and some consolation prize would be agreed upon. [Production designer Eiko Ishioka and soundtrack composer Philip Glass received awards.]

MASS: I know that you deeply believe that your film reveals objective truth about Mishima, the kind of truth that transcends today's politics, but that could perhaps help us to better understand and shape those of tomorrow. Why is it then, that no leftist intellectuals have yet come forward to praise your film?

SCHRADER: Honestly, like I said before, I think it's the uniforms. If the uniforms weren't in the movie or his life, the response would be different. The movie triggers a knee-jerk reaction many people simply can't get past. Mishima must have known this. If I had a picture of Hitler on my wall, I could talk for hours about my leftist beliefs, but as long as that picture was on the wall, everything else would be negated. The fact that Mishima chose that sartorial metaphor for his Shield Society removes the subject from the arena of argument for many people.

MASS: So, even if the film were more narratively critical and judgmental, it would still be unacceptable to leftist ideologues, simply because of its subject matter?

SCHRADER: It's like films about drug abuse where they have handsome junkies shooting up. People complain that the end result is that it makes drug abuse look glamorous. The fact that Mishima is handsome and charismatic makes the uniforms he's associated with seem glamorous. That's a political reaction, and I understand it.

MASS: My last question plays the devil's advocate with a lot of what you've said. Like Francis Ford Coppola (to some extent) and Syberberg (to a more disturbing degree), you seem to get awfully close to the subjects you are ostensibly trying to expose. After all is said and done, aren't Coppola, Syberberg and Schrader just a little bit like Molina in *Kiss of the Spider Woman*, interested in the truth, perhaps, but intoxicated and seduced, finally, by the glamor, romance and great passions of larger-than-life human beings who just happen to be politically incorrect?

SCHRADER: If Mishima were actually a fascist, I think I would have had great qualms about making the film. But the last thing Mishima wanted was to set up an organization that would inhibit freedom. This would have been illogical, since Mishima was regarded as a total freak in Japan. A person like this is dependent on the tolerance of others. I just can't see him agreeing to any system that limited the freedom of others, unless it was an act of self-hatred. But Mishima never got that far in his political thinking. He wasn't *really* political until the last couple of years of his life, until he knew he was moving toward death. What triggered that knowledge was his awareness of how deeply involved he had become in acting out—as a photographic model, as an actor, as a public speaker. And then this confrontation with the radical left happened. They took over Tokyo University and had all these clashes. It was all over the front pages. I think that's when it became clear to Mishima that the arena of art was not a big enough theater for what he had in mind for himself. Politics was the bigger stage he needed. If he was going to make his death into an ultimate, extra-artistic statement, it had to be in an arena where he was taken more seriously than as an artist.

He once said jokingly to someone that he got involved with the right because the left was full. But I'm sure that if the right had been full and the left empty, he would have chosen a leftist death. That's why he said, when he confronted the students, "We're really the same." He could never really articulate what he believed, because what he believed was really a personal expression, not a political one.

If Mishima had actually been a functioning fascist, I don't think I would have made this film. I don't think I would make such a film about Hitler. It's one thing to get inside the head of Mishima and to attempt to interpret his way of thinking, as an artist gone mad. But Mishima didn't kill anyone. All of his anger was really directed inward. You can study Mishima's life as the life of an artist, but not as a political figure.

Ein Mann Wie Rosa
(A Man Like Rosa)

A Conversation with Rosa von Praunheim

[Ed. note: When *Native* editor Patrick Merla asked Rosa von Praunheim who he wanted to interview him at the time of the American premiere of *A Virus Has No Morals*, Rosa said, "Larry Mass." I was not sure why I had been chosen, but being a friend of Rosa's and an admirer of his films, I was very motivated to do this project. Coincidentally, this assignment turned out to have a subtext as well as a context—falling, as it did chronologically, between the interview with Paul Schrader I had recently completed, the interview with Richard Plant I was preparing, and in the midst of *Synchronicities: Memoirs of Growing Up Gay, Jewish and Self-Hating in America*, an autobiographical project I've been working on since 1983 (four chapters have appeared in *Christopher Street*) that explores my naive, inevitably masochistic infatuations with such icons of Germanic culture as Richard Wagner and Carl Jung. Most important—in fact, urgent—at the time of the interview, was the opportunity to discuss the impact of AIDS on the gay community and on the gay rights movement in Germany. Of course, Rosa's achievements transcend boundaries of topicality, nationality and sexual orientation, just as they transcend rigid political definitions of "left" or "right." As an artist and as a cultural and political figure, in fact, Rosa has been singular, independent, and an international sentinel of the sexual revolutions of our time. Best of all, he has always been wittily (if not always wittingly) so.]

The following interview took place November 23, 1986 in New York City, on the occasion of the first major retrospective in the U.S. of the films of Rosa von Praunheim. Von Praunheim is regarded as one of the leading independent filmmakers of the New

German Cinema and is well-known throughout the U.S. and Europe
as an early and consistently outspoken gay activist. The retrospective, which was held at the Collective for Living Cinema, Goethe
House and the Museum of Modern Art, included *Tally Brown, New
York*, (1978), *Army of Lovers* (1979), *Death Magazine* (1979), *Red
Love* (1981), *Our Corpses are Still Alive* (1981), *City of Lost Souls*
(1983), *Horror Vacui* (1985), and featured the American premiere
of von Praunheim's latest film, *A Virus Has No Morals* (1986).
[Ed. note: Since this interview, Rosa von Praunheim has completed
several films, including *Anita — Dances of Vice*, and *Dolly, Lotte
and Maria*. He is currently at work on six films, including a documentary about the AIDS epidemic in New York.]

MASS: My interviews are usually very structured, but in your case,
I haven't been able to preconceive a logical sequence of questions.
So this conversation is going to have a little of the improvisational
quality you seem to prize so highly in your films.

Last spring you were in New York and we had lunch. I had heard
some negative reactions to your film, *A Virus Has No Morals*, from
people who had seen it in Germany. When I questioned you about
this criticism you smiled philosophically and sighed, "Have you
seen *Buddies*?" When I nodded that I had, you deadpanned,
"Well, it's not *Buddies*." What did you mean?

VON PRAUNHEIM: I meant that it's not a commercial film. I
didn't want to see *Buddies* as something that was just created to be
the first AIDS movie, and I know Arthur [Bressan] and I know how
much he genuinely cares about our community and about AIDS.
But I did resent the sentimental aspect of the film. I mean, it was the
kind of thing you see on American television, like the ending of *The
AIDS Show*, which I found totally sentimental and self-pitying. Or
like the episode of *L.A. Law* that had a gay character with AIDS. It
was *so* sentimental. All they wanted to do was make you cry. Then
there are the documentaries just showing sick people and dying people and how terrible it all is. And the talk shows! On one program,
Phil Donahue asked a man with AIDS if he regretted being gay. I'm
sorry, but . . .

MASS: But don't you think the kind of sweetness and compassion —
the "sentimentality" — you so resent in *Buddies* and *The AIDS*

Show infuses some of your own best work, like *Tally Brown, New York*?

VON PRAUNHEIM: There is sentimentality in *Tally Brown* and in some of my other films, but I use it very consciously, with a distance and often with a sense of parody. I try to make people aware of *their* sentimentality. You know, Brecht also did this.

Look, I'm glad that there are other films dealing with AIDS. I think it's good that there are lots of different views expressed and that filmmakers are zooming in on personal experiences. And I admired the small format and tightness of *Buddies*. But I want something more to come out. I want people to become more conscious, and especially more *politically* conscious, about AIDS and what it means to be gay. In Germany, one of the big commercial producers was considering a film about AIDS, but he wanted it to be the standard illness, death and tears film. Instead of cancer, he wanted AIDS. For me, that's not acceptable.

MASS: In *A Virus Knows No Morals* you've got plenty of political consciousness, and there isn't even a hint of sentimentality, but to the point that I began to wonder, where's the compassion? You know, I had lunch with Felice Picano recently, and I mentioned to him that I had just seen the film, which I characterized as a kind of black comedy about AIDS. Not having seen it himself and in view of the staggering pain and losses and raw nerves we all share here in New York, where the epidemic is so much worse than most Berliners—even now—can imagine, he could only observe that maybe comedies about AIDS need to wait a few years. But I should add that his tone of understatement made us both giggle.

VON PRAUNHEIM: I think humor, especially black humor in a time of crisis, is vital to survival. As a doctor, you, especially, must know this. In medicine, I think, having a sense of humor often helps you develop the coolness, the distance you need to approach things logically and realistically. As a gay man, you also feel this, I'm sure. Humor is often a means of survival for minorities in times of crisis. I have Jewish friends who survived the concentration camps. They've told me how, in the most extreme and cruel situations, they would burst out laughing. It was the only way they knew to endure and survive.

MASS: That's fascinating. Jews are well known for their sense of humor, but I had never heard much about Jewish humor under the Nazis or in the camps. [That would be a good subject for research, for a book, if one doesn't already exist.]

But there's another problem with the black comedy of *A Virus Knows No Morals*. When you made the movie more than a year ago, many of the future projections that seemed so ripe for parody really were preposterous. I mean, the idea of shipping persons with AIDS off to an island *was* the stuff of genuine satire. I say "was" because on the very eve of the showing of the film in New York, an Edinburgh politician was interviewed on the national, prime time news programs, and that was precisely his response to an abrupt outbreak of AIDS among drug users in Edinburgh — that they should all be shipped off to an island! So what was conceptualized to be such outrageous satire in your film turned out to be almost totally unexaggerated, contemporary reality.

VON PRAUNHEIM: The film only goes to Spring '88 and not just this one, but many of the satirical situations are already real. And it *is* scary and happening now. In January, there will be elections in Germany. If a right-wing government comes into power, we don't know what's going to happen. (The right wing is already in power in Bavaria.) In Germany, we have this pervasive semi-liberal situation, which I think is much more frightening than if you have Anita Bryant types to galvanize resistance. This more "liberal" intolerance aggravates the internalized self-hatred of gay people, the sense of difference from the mainstream. So instead of rebelling, many gay people are trying to adapt more to conventional society. They are actually helping to elect these conservative governments! The number of radical or left-wing gays, the ones who are politically conscious and active, is getting smaller and smaller.

MASS: Can you say more about what you think is happening to the gay movement politically?

VON PRAUNHEIM: I think most self-identified gay men have gotten political notions of gay emancipation mixed up with the freedom to fuck. For a lot of gay men, that's all there ever was to being gay — having the freedom to fuck. They didn't see any political side, such as solidarity with other minority and political groups. I've admired the gay movement in America, especially the early [post-Stonewall] movement I depicted in *Army of Lovers*. But that kind of political radicalism is increasingly unrepresentative.

MASS: So generally speaking, you're pretty disappointed in what you see happening to the movement politically.

VON PRAUNHEIM: I can't judge too much about America because I haven't lived here in recent years. But I can say a lot about Germany. It has been incredibly frustrating that we haven't been able to learn more from the AIDS experience in America. But the attitude has been that we can't let sexual liberation be threatened or even modified by something as unimportant as AIDS.

MASS: You're on record as one of our movement's most outspoken defenders of fundamental principles of sexual freedom. So the knowledge is implicit, automatic and absolute that, unlike some spokespersons in our community, you're not arguing in an either-or way against ideals of sexual liberation so much as in favor of modifying risk behaviors and adapting to the AIDS crisis, instead of trying to ignore it.

VON PRAUNHEIM: Yes. Frank Ripploh [*Taxi Zum Klo*] did a big article on me in Germany and accused me of not acknowledging that people have a subconscious death wish. He thinks a lot of gay people want to die anyway, and who am I to be trying to tell them otherwise. This kind of unbelievable irrationality makes you think you're living in a madhouse.

MASS: What's happened to Frank Ripploh?

VON PRAUNHEIM: He did another film recently, which was a failure. Now, he's talking about doing "Taxi Zum Klo II." The same thing happened to Craig Russel with his second film, and he's now talking about doing "Outrageous II" or, as he says, "Two Outrageous"!

MASS: Can you say more about what's been happening in Germany?

VON PRAUNHEIM: Well, the first thing that happened is that lots of West Berlin gays tried to go over to East Berlin, to fuck there, with the idea that fewer persons were likely to be infected, the same way — for the same reasons — gay men looked for sex in third world countries. Then, when the first cases began showing up in East Berlin, the authorities suddenly decided to make it very easy for gay men who are infected to leave East Germany. That's what I've *heard.* I don't know that this is what will happen in Russia, though, because there are a lot of Russian workers in Africa who may be a source of this disease.

MASS: So eventually, they're going to have to deal with it.

VON PRAUNHEIM: Yes. And the laws there, of course, are very strict. Everything has to be reported. If you have syphilis or gonorrhea, there is some sort of forced confinement. In East Germany now, they seem to be unusually free and liberal about homosexuality. But they may be doing this as a means of finding out who is gay.

MASS: And then they would sort of zoom in at some point and take everybody by surprise. That's frightening.

VON PRAUNHEIM: That's what I meant when I said that the current, semi- or pseudoliberal atmosphere in Germany is ominous.

MASS: I want to get back to this issue of gay political consciousness and involvement in films. At the screening of *Virus*, someone asked you about Fassbinder and that seemed to open a whole can of worms. You said, "Well, you know, I hate Fassbinder. . . ."

VON PRAUNHEIM: Wait. With Fassbinder, of course, there was a competitive feeling. But my dislike of him was personal rather than professional or political. He was a tyrant who didn't treat his actors as equals. Also, I found that his films are really very self-pitying. They always had this depressive message, that everything is shitty, everything is terrible, people can't be helped and it's all so tragic.

MASS: What intrigues me is that although you were/are both gay filmmakers [Fassbinder is deceased], the degree to which you were/are involved in being gay seems drastically different. In your case, you have this very explicit, politically articulate and committed gay identity that constantly informs your personal identity as well as many of the characters and situations in your films. With Fassbinder, it's sort of the opposite. Gay is one of many things he is, but not necessarily as worthy of comment as being male or being German or being West German, etc. I mean, it disappointed me more than I can say that one of the greatest filmmakers who ever lived and who was gay couldn't find a way to be more explicit about the political and social oppression of gay people. He always abstracted specific issues into essentials of human relations: you know, that the problems gay people have are often of their own making, that we act out our oppression on each other, or that our dilemmas are, in essence, simply the timeless and universal problems of human beings. There was always this implicit attitude of why emphasize that so and so or such and such was "gay"? In fact, why even mention it, except in passing or incidentally? This is especially characteristic of his early attempt to expose what he saw to be the viciousness and pettiness of gay subcultural life in *Fox and His Friends*. And it's even more true of the otherwise brilliant *Petra von Kant* and the execrable, homophobic embarrassment, *Querelle*. Despite his extraordinary talent and deep humanity, Fassbinder was, I can't help but conclude, seriously homophobic.

VON PRAUNHEIM: In TV appearances, he was quite open about his homosexuality and would often appear in public wearing his leathers. He loved to shock people. But I know what you mean. He said *Fox and His Friends* was just a crime movie, and he was much more concerned about its narrative and setup than about its political content. When he saw my film, *It's not the homosexual who is perverse*, he didn't react to the film as a political statement, only to its technical methods. But he *was* politically aware. He had a lot of solidarity with . . . independent filmmakers.

MASS: In *Tally Brown*, there are shots of Andy Warhol, who you've acknowledged to have had a substantial influence on your work.

VON PRAUNHEIM: Yes. Actually, I was quite influenced by the whole American underground. Maybe not so much by Warhol as by George and Mike Kuchar and Gregory Markopolis and Jack Smith and so on. I saw their films for the first time in Belgium, at the Knokke festival in '67-'68. Their work definitely shaped my approach to documenting the gay movement in America.

MASS: In *Tally Brown*, I watched Warhol and Divine and I thought to myself about the different directions you've all taken over the years. Like the way Divine has teamed up with John Waters on so many projects and Warhol. . . .

VON PRAUNHEIM: I think the main difference between them and me is that most of these people are no longer political. Or rather, they just prefer to ignore politics, for which they have contempt and which they think isn't good for anything except making fun of. I questioned Warhol a lot about gay issues, but despite the political consciousness in some of his early films, I don't think he ever took the concept of gay liberation seriously.

MASS: I know exactly what you mean. Warhol's attitude, LIKE THE OVERWHELMING MAJORITY OF WELL-KNOWN LES-BIAN AND GAY PERSONS, seems to be something like this: "Gay people are privileged enough just to have such a great, famous and important artist among their ranks. I'm not married and I don't always pretend to be straight, not too much, and I still hang out with gay people, at least sometimes (especially if there will be photographers), and even if the Reagans are also my good friends. I went to an AIDS fashion show and donated a print. In fact, I've indirectly helped raise a lot of money for AIDS. You're damned lucky to have all that, so don't bug me with the piddling, boring, no publicity, no glamour, unimportant people stuff, (unless it's a sure bet they'll become famous or important soon)."

VON PRAUNHEIM: I'm afraid that is true, and certainly true of many gay filmmakers. They resent me for always "parading" the political thing. They think I'm this monster who wants only to get them to be publicly gay and who doesn't give a shit about artistic vision.

I mean, look at the gay film festivals, at how conservative they've all become. They just want to show nice, erotic things that aren't too political. The biggest hits at the San Francisco and New York gay film festivals were also the most conventional films. And it's the filmmakers' faults because it's the artists, the people you expect to be more radical and lead the way, who have become conservative.

MASS: I couldn't agree more. I think this is also evident in the excitement about films like *My Beautiful Laundrette*, in which being gay is treated the same way it is in Fassbinder's films; that is, subordinated to being human and neither more nor less important or worthy of explicit identification or political context than anything else. At a very superficial level, this is quite appealing. I myself fell for it. That's what we *want* to believe and what we want straights to believe. This is not to say that the film is *endorsing* being in the closet, but what kind of lie is it, who's kidding who, when we join the protagonists and the straights in the audience (and the director?) in pretending that the street kids, ghetto Pakistanis and working classes of London won't think too negatively about homosexuality — as long as it's kept quiet — and that, consequently, there really is no pressing need to make an issue out of it? I think we still need the kind of explicit political consciousness you bring to your films.

VON PRAUNHEIM: I think it says something that as gay men are dying by the thousands, the principal commercial successes are things like *La Cage Aux Folles* and *Kiss of the Spider Woman*.

MASS: Well, *Spider Woman* was a blessing compared to the frank homophobia that's back in Hollywood films now. There must be twenty recent films that freely use the word "faggot." In one or two examples, you might argue the legitimacy of the usage, even though the word "nigger" wouldn't be tolerated in comparable circumstances. But in most instances it's so bad that it's being cited in the headlines of mainstream film critics who are otherwise (sometimes) being accused of homophobia themselves, like David Denby in *New York* Magazine.

Going back to the subject of independent filmmakers, how do you feel about Syberberg?

VON PRAUNHEIM: I think people in the same profession tend to be hypercritical of one another. That's true of me too. There are very few other contemporary independent German filmmakers whose work I like. I think Syberberg has a lot in common with Werner Schroeter, though I think his work is more superficial than Schroeter's. What I like about Syberberg is that he's an extreme example of — in German we have a word, "groessenwahn," to describe it — [megalomania]. He thinks he's the greatest. He thinks he's a cultural god and that everybody should kneel down before him and honor him for his mastery. I mean, the man is totally convinced his work is *so* wonderful. He really fights for that kind of recognition and I think it's fascinating how often and how thoroughly he can convince others.

MASS: He sounds a lot like the romantic fantasy of Richard Wagner with which he seems to be so utterly obsessed (perhaps possessed is a better word), quite the way Hitler was. Unlike Susan Sontag, I found his Hitler film rather disturbing and do not trust his said purpose of exposing the romanticism he would actually infect us all with again.

VON PRAUNHEIM: I thought the Hitler film was interesting, but I can't say much else because I'm not very interested in Wagner and in a lot of what Syberberg is doing.

MASS: My lover, Arnie Kantrowitz, was among many persons — excluding, strangely, Vincent Canby in the *New York Times* — who were very distressed by the recent German television series, *Heimat.* Did you see it?

VON PRAUNHEIM: Yes. The director is a friend of mine. I think it's wonderful that very costly series like *Berlin Alexanderplatz* and *Heimat* could get produced. It's so rare to get something on television, in Germany or in America either, for that matter, that's so sensitively and artistically made, that gives independent filmmakers a chance at that level.

MASS: I think *Berlin Alexanderplatz* was an unqualified masterpiece and I haven't seen *Heimat,* which I'm sure is artistically impressive. But what has Arnie and others, including Judith Miller in the *New York Times,* so upset about *Heimat,* among other products of German culture in recent years, is the apparent obfuscation of the awareness and participation of the German masses in what was happening to the Jews. Let me read you a passage from the Judith Miller piece, which is called "Erasing the Past" [from the *New York Times* Magazine, 11/16/86]:

> *Heimat* — an almost untranslatable word that refers to home, native place, homeland — is the saga of the inhabitants of the fictional, tranquil village of Schabbach before and after the war. Its citizens are basically decent folk, who live through the brutal Nazi era without in most cases changing significantly. There are hardly any Nazis in Schabbach. The subtle, unmistakable message of "Heimat," observes Hans Mommsen, is that "this terrible thing, National Socialism, was done to us by a few brutes called the Nazis, a tiny minority who seized power and distorted the peaceful life of ordinary German people. Evil occurs in the script but it is almost incidental.

VON PRAUNHEIM: No. I think that's wrong. I don't think that's the filmmaker's attitude at all. I think what he's doing is not narratively and directorially excusing the people. On the contrary, I think he's trying to show how they excused themselves.

[Ed. note: The following quote by Edgar Reitz, the creator of *Heimat*, is from *Film Quarterly*, Summer 1986:

> For 40 years we Germans have been asked the question, "How was the Third Reich possible?" That it was something politically disastrous and morally evil, that this Nazi rule brought endless misfortune to millions of people — no one denies that except for a few stubborn idiots. There were 80 million Germans of whom at least 90 percent cooperated with Hitler in one way or another. If one asks this question morally, then one would have to say it is completely impossible. That would mean that these many millions of people wanted in one way or another what happened there, that is, that there was a real shaping of opinion or at least that a mood had developed which makes an entire nation into criminals. I can't believe that. . . .]

MASS: You acknowledge that your parents were, as you put it, "nice Nazis," and this can't always be an easy subject for you to deal with, but have you ever thought of doing a comedy about Bitburg?

VON PRAUNHEIM: [no response]

MASS: OK. Next question. In *A Virus*, are you a mummer?

VON PRAUNHEIM: A mummy?

MASS: No, a mummer. M-u-m-m-e-r.

VON PRAUNHEIM: I don't know. I've never heard the word before.

MASS: Somebody uses the word in *A Virus*, during the scene that has the skeleton and costumes. The dictionary says it's a person, often an actor or pantomimist, who wears a mask or fantastic disguise on festive occasions. In gay pride parades in past years, a group of people from Philadelphia have marched with us. They never had any clear gay or political affiliation or purpose but always had these extremely elaborate costumes. They call themselves mummers.

VON PRAUNHEIM: Perhaps I'd recognize the German word.

MASS: Another question about words. Where did you get the name "Horror Vacui"?

VON PRAUNHEIM: It's an expression from the baroque era and refers to the baroque dread of leaving any space empty. You know, everything had to be ornamented decoration. Now, there's a book about me in which a critic says this expression applies to me. I can't leave things empty. I have to always fill everything up with people and decoration and ideas. I rather liked the expression and thought it would make a good title.

MASS: I've heard similar criticism, but it was more negative. One person said, "Rosa's still making these ragged, improvisational, hippie films that have a kind of sixties mentality."

VON PRAUNHEIM: What these people are saying is that my films never became slick and commercial.

MASS: Maybe, but I know one critic who really admires your work and your unwillingness to sell out to commercialism. He really respects that, as do I, but he also points out that there's room for you to become somewhat more, shall we say, disciplined or professional, without necessarily compromising your artistic integrity.

VON PRAUNHEIM: I suppose that's true. I can be undisciplined and superficial. I get too many ideas in my head. I don't consider myself a genius or somebody special. But I do think of myself as belonging to . . . a way of living, a way of looking at the world, which is quite outside the traditional, clean cut mainstream. I love being able to create, to make my dirty little political films with very little money. I love the freedom of expression, without the corruptions of commercialism.

MASS: I think you can be legitimately criticized for not being more technically proficient, more professional, but then if you had been this other person, you may have made different films, and I can't say I'd want that. I think that despite their roughness and limited appeal and technical problems, many of them have turned out to be important historical documents and period pieces. Even Fassbinder couldn't claim that. What I'm saying is that films like *Army of Lovers* and, especially *Red Love*, to cite only two examples, will have as much or perhaps even more durability as historical documents and glimpses of their time than Fassbinder's films will as works of art. I really believe that.

When *Horror Vacui* was shown at the gay film festival last winter, there was controversy in the community about faith healers and holistic people. In this sense, your film seemed very timely and specific for our community.

VON PRAUNHEIM: Horror Vacui was inspired by the Bhagwan Shree Rajneesh cult and by Jonestown, but also by Moon and Scientology and cults and cult leaders.

MASS: To be honest, we thought you had a specific cult leader in mind, someone who was active not only with gays, but with gays who have AIDS.

VON PRAUNHEIM: Actually, I haven't been all that in touch with what's been going on here in the last few years. When AIDS started, I wanted to go back to Berlin. I was really scared and somehow I felt safer there. Then, when AIDS came to Berlin, I realized I couldn't keep ignoring it and that's when I really began to get politically active [with regards to AIDS]. I got involved with fundraising and benefits, and attempting to explore AIDS issues on film. Now, I feel safer here in New York, because in Berlin people are still living with the illusion that nothing has changed. For example, the baths are all still open and very, very crowded. They don't monitor for safer sex practices, but they do sometimes give out condoms.

MASS: But there are AIDS groups in Germany and a lot of politically conscious people there, people such as yourself.

VON PRAUNHEIM: Well, yes, but the AIDS groups in Germany are modeled after the ones here. They have a very conventional approach. They want to shake hands with mayors, raise money, be like the mainstream. You know, the suit-and-tie mentality. As more and more homeless gay men with AIDS accumulate, as more and more are denied access to basic medical care, the timid, let's cooperate approach just isn't going to work. [In *A Virus Knows No Morals*, a radical group of persons with AIDS presses its demands at gunpoint.] There have to be radical actions because just saying how bad things are isn't enough. Even conservative and establishment institutions agree with radical gays that not enough money is being spent on AIDS research and care. That's become very official. You can read such things every day in the *New York Times*.

Homosexuality and Music

A Conversation with Philip Brett

[Ed. note: Of all the interviews I have conducted, "Homosexuality and Music" is the dearest, not because the piece is somehow qualitatively superior to the others (though I do think Brett's personal charm and exceptional gifts for polemical discourse establish him as the undisputed star of the series), but because it was the hardest earned. As I had related in an autobiographical essay called "Confessions of an Opera Queen" (*Christopher Street*, issue 69, 1982), the world of opera was "the first and only gay world I had ever known." I then went on in the piece to lament the extreme closetedness and homophobia I had encountered in that world, even as gay liberation proceeded apace: "During the Seventies, the decade of gay liberation, most of what was written about [Benjamin] Britten emphasized the 'universality' of the composer's themes while conveniently ignoring the importance of homosexuality in the expression of those themes." A little like Anna Bolena's denunciatory cabaletta, "Coppia inqua," "Confessions of an Opera Queen" concluded on a high note of indignation and accusation: "What's keeping the gay contribution to opera in the closet is not straight society. It's the gay fans and gay music critics themselves. Gay opera lovers should no longer have to imagine themselves in the soprano's gown as the *only* way of feeling connected to the world of opera. Today we can also draw pride and strength from the mature, diverse gay creativity which has helped to make opera into such a genuinely universal aesthetic experience."

As it turns out, there *was* somebody outside the gay press, somebody with impressive scholarly credentials, who was finally doing this work and presenting it to the public at large. (In the gay press, Bruce-Michael Gelbert and George Heymont began writing about gay aspects of opera in the late 1970s and became the first columnists to regularly review opera from gay perspectives. During this period, important pieces on homosexuality and music and/or opera were also written by James Saslow, Stephen Greco and others.) And the case he was presenting turned out to be greater and more persuasive than even devout believers like myself had imagined possible. That person was Philip Brett. With the publication of "Homosexuality and Music," I felt as if this most personal, lonely and longlasting of my struggles for gay identity and liberation (preceding, as it did, my confrontations with psychiatry and medicine), had finally been won.]

Philip Brett is Professor of Music at the University of California at Berkeley. He is the author of numerous scholarly articles on the life and works of Benjamin Britten, and editor of The Cambridge Opera Handbook on *Peter Grimes*.

[Ed. note: This interview was conducted by mail in the summer of 1987.]

MASS: In the mid to late 1970s, you were writing pieces that spoke with unprecedented depth and scholarly authority about a subject most music critics (many of them gay) were still loathe to even mention: the dominant, pervasive and altogether profound significance of homosexuality in the life and works of Benjamin Britten. During this time it had finally become "officially" acknowledged that Britten and his lifelong collaborator and "companion," Peter Pears, were homosexual, but nobody, including Britten and Pears themselves, seemed to want to deal with that fact beyond perfunctory acknowledgement.

Or so it seemed. Following Britten's death in 1976, Peter Pears gave a truncated but astonishing interview for *The Advocate* in which he frankly and generously talked to Stephen Greco about the significance of homosexuality in several of the composer's works. I remember how excited I got. I immediately brought the interview to the attention of two gay music critics who were close friends. Although the younger critic, his curiosity getting the better of him, finally condescended to skim-read it, neither was receptive to my urging them to try to get more such interview material before Pears died.

I pleaded with them to pursue the project, but to no avail. The reasons for their reluctance eventually became clear. Politically unconscious and very closeted, both realized at some level that such an endeavor might imply guilt by association or, much worse, inadvertently coming out to their editors, colleagues and readers, the vast majority of whom had long since figured out that they were gay and had wondered why they were so closeted. Like Peter Grimes and Britten himself, they had internalized society's prejudice and intolerance and with a strikingly parallel lack of conscious awareness. Like the homophobic establishment whose spokespersons they had become, they actually believed that homosexuality wasn't a real, legitimate subject and that, in any event, Britten's operas were about "timeless" and "universal" human truths. They weren't about the composer's private sexual peccadillos!

First, to your knowledge, is there any more of this kind of interview material with Pears? And what about Britten himself? That is, did Britten ever *really* (verifiably) discuss his homosexuality and how he believed it may or may not have influenced his works?

BRETT: Britten did not to my knowledge ever publicly say anything about homosexuality. It would have been highly uncharacteristic of him to have done so. Ronald Duncan, a sub-Eliot poet who was one of his librettists, is not the most reliable witness in all matters, but the statement in his book, *Working with Britten*, that the composer "remained a reluctant homosexual," together with the evidence he gives in support are probably as near the truth as those of us who didn't know Britten are likely to come. The closest Britten ever came to discussing any personal influence of this kind on his music was in an interview Murray Schafer printed in 1963 (in *British Composers in Interview*), where he related the plot of *Peter Grimes* to his and Pears's situation as conscientious objectors. I am not the only one to have read "and homosexuals" into that text; in an essay on the Church Parables in *The Britten Companion*, Robin Holloway interprets "peace" as the "pass- or code-word" for homosexuality in Britten's work. I don't think one has to doubt the composer's sincerity as a pacifist to see how that might be true.

With Pears, it was ultimately a different story. His courage in making all things plain after Britten's death was nothing short of heroic, given his background. I wrote to him after that interview in

The Advocate — largely to say why such statements were important, and to defend the use of the word "gay," which he said Britten hated. He must have received a lot of such encouragement because in Tony Palmer's film, *A Time There Was*, one of the most interesting and moving of all composer documentaries, he talked about their relationship quite openly. Imagine turning on BBC-TV at prime time on Easter Sunday, 1980, and hearing Pears say in that extraordinarily dignified and cultured manner of his, "He died in my arms."

I am sorry that I did not myself follow up your suggestion. I think Pears might have talked to me as someone who wrote sympathetically about their experience of homosexuality. But by the time I got to see him I was deeply involved in the documents surrounding *Grimes*, and I remember feeling the need for a certain distance. Peter, like most living witnesses, had a selective memory, and I gradually realized that what he told me was often a rather garbled version of something I later pieced together more accurately from documentary evidence. The fact that I wasn't able to separate dispassionate scholarly inquiry from the issue of sexuality and to work on the latter with him is a sign of my own conditioning. Nevertheless, it was he who made me realize that the absence of psychological elements in the plot of *Grimes* was a deliberate strategy to emphasize the social argument. When I asked him one day why Grimes's father, the ghosts of the dead apprentices, and various other features of the early drafts of the libretto had been excised, he replied "Once we had decided that it was a matter of the individual against the crowd, all those things had to go, of course."

MASS: Your essays make very clear the principal reason why there are no explicit indications of homoeroticism or homosexuality in *Peter Grimes*: The reason, "perhaps ultimately of greatest importance, was that whereas universal meaning could have been extrapolated from the predicament of many other kinds of 'minority' hero or antihero, an obvious homosexual — even an obviously repressed homosexual — in the title role would have either spelt outright failure for the opera or caused it to be dismissed as a matter of 'special interest.'"

Unfortunately, critics still don't seem able to get your point. For example, in the Autumn 1986 issue of *Opera Quarterly*, which is devoted entirely to Britten, composer Carlisle Floyd reviews your book, *Peter Grimes*, and concludes as follows:

> In the final two articles Philip Brett confronts the question of Britten's homosexuality in relation to *Peter Grimes* by stating categorically at one point that "it is to the homosexual condition that *Peter Grimes* is addressed." Having made this statement, however, he wisely qualifies it in the "Postscript" by saying that "we should avoid making the simplistic claim that here [in Britten's sexuality] lies the single key to Britten's creative personality: no inner mystery in the music is revealed by the simple acknowledgment of his homosexuality and its consequences, but the way is at least cleared for us to approach the works a little closer and with more understanding." Brett goes on to say on the last page of the book that "in order to make Peter so powerfully symbolic and to render the action of the opera so successfully allegorical, Britten could not allow the story to have homoerotic implications. . . . In doing this he made it abundantly clear that the opera's concern . . . is purely the social issue of "the individual against the crowd."

Isn't Floyd conspiring with the viewpoint that universal meaning would not have been extrapolatable from the predicament of an overt homosexual?

BRETT: Yes. And by means of the ellipsis he manages to make me say what he wants to hear. I don't mean to complain. He was kind about the book, grasped its nettle firmly, and told the editors he'd like to meet me one day. Dale Harris, reviewing the recordings of *Grimes* in the same issue, showed his hostility by adopting the Grimes-is-really-a-criminal view that I thought I had successfully exploded, and by studiously avoiding all mention of my arguments. But of course, that is only a sign that he had been unable to come to terms with what I wrote. The opposite reaction came from the Organist of the Chelmsford Cathedral, whose curious essay on the religious in Britten appears in that *Opera Quarterly*, and who keeps reiterating that Britten's operas aren't homosexual, as if to reassure himself. As you have noticed, mention of homosexuality among musicians sends nearly everyone, gay or straight, into a "for" or "against" corner, or simply into incoherence. What hope is there, then, of being able to get across a critical argument of any complexity?

I was trying in that "Postscript" to refine the statement of the earlier piece, "Britten and Grimes," and to elaborate on the subject of the mechanics of oppression, an aspect of the earlier essay which I thought had been little understood. (I also aimed to give young gay musicians a basic reading list.) I wanted in those closing pages to show that although Britten very probably thought of himself as "sick," and that although the opera was written long before the American Psychiatric Association took homosexuality off its official list of disorders, the work contains a clear vision that the difficulties arising from homosexuality are at bottom purely social, and that most of the psychological problems suffered by gay people grow from the social condition, not from "the homosexual condition," which of course is only a social construction. Like much good art, *Grimes* is prophetic. More important than its reflection of the composer is its prophetic vision, in dramatic terms, of truths that were articulated twenty to thirty years later by the thinkers of the liberation movements, first the feminists, then by such writers as Dennis Altman, Michel Foucault, and Jeffrey Weeks.

MASS: In your essay *"Peter Grimes* On Stage," you ask,

> We might wonder why so few [serious critics, especially British critics] looked beneath the surface of the plot. Can it have been fear (conscious or unconscious) of what they might find there?

Why do you use the word "fear"? Do you think these critics were "afraid" of discovering allusions to homosexuality because many of these critics were themselves gay?

BRETT: Yes. The absence of any allegorical reading (other than Edmund Wilson's) is truly remarkable. Yet Colin MacInnes's notebooks show that at least one "reluctant homosexual" of the period made a connection: "The theme and tragedy of *Peter Grimes* is homosexuality and, as such, the treatment is quite moving, if a bit watery," he wrote, adding "Grimes is the homosexual hero. The melancholy of the opera is the melancholy of homosexuality." (See

Tony Gould's biography, *Insider Outsider*, p. 82; I owe this reference to Donald Mitchell.)

What really scared and annoyed the critics was that Britten was homosexual *and* puritanical. They didn't approve of Forster either, for similar reasons. (He lived with his mother; horror upon horror.) They couldn't understand why these two didn't conform — there was no problem about being "queer" so long as you belonged to a cozy London coterie. As I've suggested, *Grimes* provided catharsis for Britten himself by projecting a worst-case scenario in which the "hero" is twice pursued by crazed mobs and ends up committing suicide. What the opera suggested, what no homosexual could avoid noticing at some level, and what is still so relevant about the work today, is that any accommodation with society might suddenly count for nothing when things turn ugly. That made critics, especially homosexual critics, both nervous and resentful. One can only say in these critics' defense that in the '40s and '50s, with CIA pressure on the British government (revealed by Peter Wildeblood in *Against the Law* after the notorious Montagu case, and more recently by Andrew Hodges in his marvelous biography of Alan Turing), there was cause for fear and reason to band together in little circles.

There was also something of the spurned lover about the inconstancy of the British critics towards Britten during his life. In the '60s they were rude about his staying away from London and becoming "out of touch" with the "latest developments." The last laugh on that kind of London provinciality is that meanwhile Britten was out in Asia studying its musical traditions, several of which he assimilated into his own personal musical language more successfully, perhaps, than any other composer of his time.

One further thing about Britten and his critics. I had always taken at face value the line about his "morbid sensitivity to criticism," but I couldn't believe my eyes when I started reading the early reviews of *Grimes*: they are so patronizing and superior and intellectually empty. A whole vocabulary of words, such as "clever," "facile," "devilish smart," "immature," was invented as a sort of code to signal the "inevitable failings" of a "queer" composer who hadn't learned to conform. What fear there was there!

It is a fear that lasted right through the time of gay liberation and is still strong today. When I was on the Board of Directors of the American Musicological Society two years ago, I was encouraged by then President Margaret Bent of Princeton to set up a forum at the national meeting in Vancouver which I ended up calling "Lesbian and Gay Perspectives in Musicology." Sadly, a lesbian could not be found to co-chair. The many senior members of the Society who are gay were conspicuous by their absence at the event, which was a tense affair. I failed to get a scholarly session going the following year—we had a party instead—largely because few can see that there might be serious intellectual issues, new approaches to musicology, etc., involved. One excellent scholar working on the biography of a gay composer wouldn't deliver a paper on that aspect of his subject at a national meeting because it would be "too sensational," and of course that was an accurate diagnosis by him of the state of the profession on the issue.

I have naturally thought a good deal about this "fear" and can offer a preliminary explanation. Given the mechanism by which internalization of societal and parental disapproval leads young gay persons to doubt the validity of all their feelings, and to suppress them (with the resulting onset of depression and worse), music appears to many of us at a critical time as a lifeline. It is a brotherhood of "lovers"—music lovers—who communicate in a language of feeling that has no exact connotations. No labels. Just pure emotion. And one can show emotion in music, especially while performing it, without being labeled in any way.

But since the attachment to music, which is always very powerful, was undertaken in an unconscious and diabolical bargain by which the rights to a sentient life were signed away, there is a special need for gay musicians to deny their gayness. It's a case of internalization of society's values by grateful adoption of one of society's own safety valves. Music is an escape from issues surrounding sexuality in the first place, but it comes to dominate one's life to such an extent and one invests so much in it that the last thing one wants to discover is that one went into it for the "wrong" reasons. It is clear to anyone in the profession that it houses many people who are "using" music in a special way. I look on this spectacle in sorrow rather than in anger, and I acknowledge with gratitude the guarded support of many of my more reticent gay colleagues—given in spite of a lack of sympathy for what I am doing, and an inclination not to upset their own accommodation to society through music. I hope that answer about "fear" and self-oppression rings true. It could easily be developed by someone more adept than me in these matters.

MASS: As you point out in your essays, a number of critics and other writers, Andrew Porter most prominently among them, have made fitful, intermittent attempts to be explicit about the significance of homosexuality in Britten's works. But your analyses are of unprecedented authority and scope. Can you tell us something about how you came to write these essays and how they were received (i.e., did you encounter much homophobia from editors, publishers, musicological colleagues, music critics, Britten people, opera people, etc.)?

BRETT: I can pinpoint the precise moment when it all started. It was 1973. I was just 36, and coming out of a failed six-year relationship. Dennis Altman's *Homosexual: Oppression and Liberation* was working away at my consciousness. It was at the back of the stalls in the San Francsico Opera House (the standing room crowd there is often more interesting than the opera) during their production of *Grimes*. As we reached that marvelous moment in Grimes's soliloquy before the storm interlude when he sings three lyrical phrases of long, even notes over a glittering Brittenesque pedal chord—they ostensibly portray a vision of the safety and comfort of Ellen's embrace—I tried to give myself over to that special chord, which had always thrilled me. It didn't work. Instead, my attention was drawn to the fussy phrases of quick, staccato notes that occur between the lyrical sweeps: "Away from tidal waves, away from storms"; "Terrors and tragedies." What an odd musical strategy, I thought. And then it suddenly struck me that the notes were a musical inversion of the theme associated with the hostile Borough crowd in the Prologue, in the inquest scene. In that moment, with Altman's diagnoses of oppression fresh in my mind, I "understood" the opera. It was a moment that ultimately gave me new ways of dealing with my own life.

One of the results of my subsequent "coming out" process was a revulsion against musicology, which I felt I had used in my twenties in order to escape the real issues of life. I was so resentful I could hardly sit in a music library without shaking. (I had begun to de-velop as a conductor since going from Cambridge to Berkeley in the mid-'60s), and wrote snide, anti-musicological program notes of great length. My colleagues in the Berkeley music department were extraordinarily patient, and encouraged my subsequent work on Britten; I owe them a lot.

A few years later, in 1976, when the American Musicological Society asked for papers about American music or about European composers in America for their conference in the Bicentennial year, I saw the chance of putting my newfound gay identity in touch with my old musicological self. I had another issue besides sexuality to deal with, the question of roots. Where did I belong, in Britain or America? Writing about Britten in America—*Grimes* was con-ceived in Lawrence Welk's town, Escondido, of all places—was one way I managed to decide not to go back.

So I delivered my first Britten paper in front of a representative assembly of the profession. I had fantasies that the chairman would say "This is not scholarship, this is pornography." Instead he bur-bled about alternative lifestyles and grasped me warmly by the hand. (I noticed he didn't touch the other paper-givers in the ses-sion.) Though there were some mildly homophobic responses, I think there was a general sense of relief that someone had men-tioned the word "gay" in such circumstances, but it was of course women (and one straight man) who came up to thank me for doing it. I don't remember a single gay male, outside my immediate cir-cle, saying a word of encouragement afterwards.

Afterwards I sent the paper to the *Musical Quarterly*. Joan Peyser had recently become its editor. Those who know her books, an earlier one on Boulez and a recent one on Leonard Bernstein, will be amused to hear that she dismissed the piece as a "personality study." So I sent it to Stanley Sadie, editor of London's *Musical Times* (and since then editor of *The New Grove*). I was impressed by his obituary of Britten, who died that same year (1976). It was difficult for him to contemplate publishing the article in England so soon after the composer's death, but he did so without editing any further than insisting on putting "gay" in inverted commas on the grounds that not all the readers would know the use of the word. (This was the year of the notorious trial of Britain's *Gay News* on the medieval statute against blasphemy, which even the *Daily Telegraph* had to report, but never mind).

You must not imagine that I found Britten an easy subject. To a newly politicized gay person, the composer's reticence about his sexuality was a cause for anger and dismay. I found myself bitter about my upbringing in England, a society that combines a smug "tolerance" for eccentricity with an equally smug and superior refusal to accept difference of any kind. It was particularly bad that no one acknowledged what everyone "knew" about Britten and Pears—because nothing confirmed the attitude of society toward homosexuality more succinctly than the keeping of the true nature of a partnership unparalleled in musical history as a dirty semi-secret. Looking back now, I see that the scholarly training I then despised stood me in good stead. It taught me to work through things and not to accept immediate face values. And if my analyses do have any authority, as you kindly suggest, it must be because I have to work through an initial flush of anger (toward Britten, Britain and myself) before I weed out the rhetoric, come to some understanding of what the more important issues are, and try to encapsulate those in words. It is a slow process.

As to reactions to that first article. . . . Well, Donald Mitchell, Britten's musical executor and biographer, made it clear he didn't agree with the emphasis I was placing on Britten's sexuality. However, he willingly opened up the archives, and became absolutely encouraging, as did all the "Britten people," none of whom has ever tried to influence what I write. This support is one of the things that made the *Grimes* handbook such a pleasure to work on, and I am very happy to acknowledge it.

The only really awkward encounters I have had, as a matter of fact, have been with the Royal Opera House, Covent Garden. Andrew Porter (who wrote a long, interesting and generous response to the *Musical Times* article) recommended a piece on *Billy Budd* I had written for the San Francisco Opera to the editor of Covent Garden's magazine, *About the House*. I sent it, he liked it, but wouldn't print it because its mention of Britten's homosexuality might upset Sir Peter, who eighteen months later, as I've explained, came out on prime time television. That was 1978.

We move now to the Olympic Year, when the Royal Opera

House brought *Grimes* and other operas to Los Angeles. I got a call from a young man at the Garden asking me to write the note. At the end of our amicable conversation, I asked in jest, "Now you aren't going to get upset again if I mention the word 'homosexuality,' are you?" Of course they weren't, this *was* 1984, after all. A week later I was disinvited on the grounds this time that Jon Vickers, who sang the role of Peter, might get upset. You can imagine the punch line: an article in the *Los Angeles Times* (July 8, 1984) in which Vickers was quoted as saying, "Let's be honest . . . the opera is about homosexuality!" Well, that's an opera house on the way down, and it's stuffier than the Met. I think all the people I dealt with there were homosexual. On the other hand I was given a free hand by the English National Opera in writing about *Lucretia*, and of course the San Francisco Opera always welcomed anything directed at its predominantly gay clientele.

MASS: At approximately the same time as the *Advocate* interview with Sir Peter Pears by Stephen Greco, according to your "Postscript" in *Peter Grimes*, Jon Vickers was still claiming "on the one hand that Grimes is 'totally symbolic' and that he could 'play him as a Jew' or 'paint his face black and put him in a white society,' and on the other hand declare that 'I will not play Peter Grimes as a homosexual' because this 'reduces him to a man in a situation with a problem and I'm not interested in that kind of operatic portrayal.'"

Do you know if Pears or anyone else ever attempted to confront Mr. Vickers with his illogic and homophobia? Jon Vickers as Peter Grimes was among my most cherished operatic portrayals.

In view of Mr. Vickers's pivotal involvement in the majority of our generation's new productions and revivals of *Peter Grimes*, I'm now beginning to wonder just how great a factor, just how negative an influence, this man has been, behind the scenes, in our generation's failure to come to grips with the reality, as you put it so simply in the *Peter Grimes* Handbook, that "it is to the homosexual condition that *Peter Grimes* is addressed." Any comments?

BRETT: I've partly answered your question. Vickers, like everyone else, changes. I rather dislike the modern cult of personality which demands that performers explain themselves. He could probably see the inconsistency of those remarks, or maybe someone helped him. Pears was articulate in his condemnation of Vickers's interpretation, but too much of a gentleman to confront anyone with anything. On the whole, I think all of us should be grateful to Vickers for what he did for *Grimes*, which was to make the title role much larger than life—large enough to spill off the stage into the overlarge opera houses of the U.S.—and to endow it with an elemental tragic force that left few untouched.

And, after all, *Peter Grimes* is an allegory. And allegories by definition are symbolic, not prescriptive. The failure to come to grips with the reality of *Grimes*, as you put it, has surely nothing to do with Vickers. (I rather enjoy thinking of all that burly intensity being put to service in the interests of a gay issue.) It has to do with people seeing something of themselves in *Grimes*, hearing other possible meanings in the allegory (Edmund Wilson, for instance, related it to the brutalization of postwar Europe), not wanting to understand the mechanics of oppression, not wanting to give up their scapegoats, and ultimately not wishing to believe that the inspiration for such a modern, universal character could have anything to do with homosexuality. My favorite review of the *Peter Grimes* handbook was from a British writer named Clifford Bartlet, who said, "I hope that Brett's interpretation will not make the work into a homosexual's opera." (This was in *Brio*, vol. 20, 1983, p. 30.)

MASS: Christopher Isherwood was originally approached to do the libretto for *Peter Grimes*, which he declined. Did he ever discuss his sense of the importance of homosexuality in *Peter Grimes*, or, more generally, in the life and works of the composer? Was homosexuality any kind of background issue in his declining this opportunity?

BRETT: The Isherwood letters Donald Mitchell printed in the handbook as part of his remarkable interview with the widow of the librettist, Montagu Slater, are purposely misleading. Isherwood didn't think the story would do, but couldn't actively discourage Britten. When I saw Isherwood and gently raised the issue, he explained that he had thought the story too homophobic to work; at least, that's how I interpreted what he said. So clearly he saw the homosexual component, and probably thought the plot too much of

"another-fag-bites-the-dust" yarn for him to be able to deal with it. Slater, a Hampstead communist, was the perfect choice. Marxism offered the only model of oppression current at the time after all.
MASS: Do you know if anyone has ever done a production of *Peter Grimes*, *Billy Budd*, or *Albert Herring* in which the title characters were clearly intended to be perceived as gay? (A great project for the otherwise oh-so-daring Peter Sellars, don't you think?)
BRETT: I don't know of such productions. And somehow I think I'd dislike the *Grimes*. If Peter Grimes himself is gay, then, because of the silent boy, the opera is in danger of becoming a sadomasochistic fantasy and losing its social meaning. He's got to be, as I've said, *de*-sexualized, for the point about society's guilt to come over strongly. Vere and Claggart, could be — are — physically and emotionally excited by Billy Budd, and, though it would be difficult to make him reciprocally interested in them (to put it mildly), it should be possible to suggest that he is a creature of natural affection who will "share" with his mates (as Forster, surely knowingly, puts it in the libretto). Albert is sexually unrealized, so there's not much to go on, but I must say I'd find it refreshing for him to look wistfully at Sid rather than Nancy once in a while. Surely that could be accepted in the spirit of comedy? In Aschenbach we do have a bona fide homosexual character, of course. But having taken some gay friends unfamiliar with Britten to *Death in Venice*, I realize only too well what a downer that can be. Britten was a sorry case, an artist who was showered with honors (including a peerage, which he would have done well to have refused), and who lived a full, accepted, and, above all, *shared* life, and yet who perceived chiefly his own shame and loneliness. This he expressed so powerfully that in a way he encapsulates the social experience of gay people since "homosexuality" was defined in 1869. He sums up a century of oppression. So in fact his characters are not "gay," and his message is not, except in *Herring*, consoling or uplifting for gay people.
MASS: Where do we go from here with regard to integrating our knowledge and understanding of homosexuality with our knowledge and understanding of homosexuality in the life and works of

other composers, as well as Britten? Are you currently working on anything in this area? Are others?

BRETT: As I've said, I've been trying to get something going in the American Musicological Society, but it's not got very far yet (in sharp contrast of course to the state of affairs in the Modern Language Association). There isn't much interesting feminist work in music yet, either. The trouble is that our field is so dominated by certain concepts of what musical scholarship consists of—concepts powerfully attacked by Joseph Kerman in *Contemplating Music*, but equally powerfully maintained by the Eastern Establishment. Interestingly, many young gay musical scholars seem to lean towards ethnomusicology, a less structured atmosphere, perhaps, where they can quite respectably take on studies of the growth of gay men's choruses or the work of self-identified gay composers.

But what a world there is waiting there for adventurous scholars. A student of mine did an essay for the Britten issue of *Opera Quarterly* on women in Britten's operas. It's a start. But why don't we have a study of "homosocial desire," as Eve Sedgewick calls it, in Verdi's operas, for instance? Then there's the obvious spadework to be done on who is and who isn't. I have an idea that all the early romantics are going to be, so to speak, food for thought. Peter Ostwald's biography of Schumann reveals his "Greek love" episodes, which need exploring. Maynard Solomon, the Beethoven scholar, published an article in 1981 in *American Imago* (a psychoanalytic, not musical journal) on Schubert's homosexuality, which will become plain in his forthcoming biography. Beethoven and his nephew obsession could be reconsidered. And going back, there's the case of Handel, whom the most recent biographer found it necessary to defend from the charge of homosexuality. So you can see how close it all is.

The common objection of course is that links between composers' lives and their works are hard to establish. It is difficult enough in this century, when many of the most important composers (after Schoenberg, Stravinsky, Berg, Webern, and Bartok) have been gay. One scholar I know believes he can make a case for the nature and juxtaposition of the musical gestures in some of Poulenc's instrumental compositions being understood best as a manifestation of the aesthetics of camp. Perhaps comparable but different critical perceptions can and will be made about aspects of the works of Ravel, Copland, Boulez, Henze, Tippett, Maxwell Davies, and the rest. But how can we know that it's impossible to say something interesting and important until someone at least *tries* to do it? No one thought English literature was susceptible to feminist analysis until women critics got busy. Now they've changed the face of literary criticism in some areas. We haven't even got the words sexuality, homosexuality, and gay in our bibliographies and dictionaries yet.

MASS: Ned Rorem is among the few leading musicians who has attempted to engage the issue of what we can legitimately call "gay," versus what we can't or shouldn't, with regard to music and musicians. The following are some excerpts from his 1974 interview with Winston Leyland in *Gay Sunshine Interviews* (Vol. II).

To be homosexual is too generalizing; I can't say "we," not even "we composers," or "we writers," or "we fifty-year olds." I say "they." Therefore I can only refer to my *sexuality*. Now a black person is demonstrably black, there's nothing he can do about it. He's black if he's a scientist, he's black as he looks into a microscope, he's black as he reads Plato. We can see that he is. Meanwhile, a homosexual is only homosexual when he's being homosexual. He's not demonstrably so when he's writing music, or when he's thinking about a recipe for carrot cake. Homosexuality is a condition, whereas to be black is not a frame of mind, it's a physical identity.

I don't claim I'm not gay, but my sexuality is only one section of what I am. . . . I feel more discriminated against as an artist in our America than as a queer.

Could one say there is such a thing as homosexual music?

The thing is, I am first of all a composer, and anything I can do for any group of people, I want to do as a composer, as Benjamin Britten does with his concerts to raise money for peace in the world. I would willingly give a concert for Gay

Liberation. Not as a gay musician necessarily, just as a musician.

I'm not sure what you mean by homosexual art, but it's a beguiling question and there could be many definitions.

Please comment on these statements.

BRETT: The key to Mr. Rorem's feelings and views seem on the face of it — I haven't read the rest of the interview — to lie in that second quotation: "I feel more discriminated against as an artist in America than as a queer." I don't fully understand the sentiment, because it seems to me artists have it no worse (and often a good deal better) in modern America than anywhere at any time in Europe, except perhaps for the hundred years between 1850 and 1950, when they tended to be put on a pedestal. But of course it's the feeling that matters, not the historical fact.

The rest of his statements seem wooly to me, because like nearly all gay musicians he seems to deny the possibility of oppression in himself. Such points of view as his are first of all dangerous because they play into the hands of conservative moralists who cannot see any justification for a movement based on sexual activity. Second, they are not to be trusted because, as Altman puts it, "the oppression faced by homosexuals takes on a number of forms, and at its most pernicious may be internalized to a point that an individual no longer recognizes it as oppression."

Moreover, as I observe my black colleague, the composer Olly Wilson, teaching courses in Afro-American music and counselling minority students, I realize that being black is much more than a "physical identity" in America today. There are two things I would see as important in differentiating the gay from the black experience: when you are young, you cannot go home and cry on your mother's shoulder over those things that pertain to your being gay; and later on you can, if you choose, hide your true nature. Black people have neither of those disadvantages.

I'm not whining, for these things are ultimately a source of strength. If we can overcome them, we can build for ourselves a person with whom we can live — our own person, at last, not the one who we thought someone else wanted us to be. If we choose to identify ourselves as gay as a result of this process then our gay identity is as important to us as a physical identity or a racial one. I can't see that this is merely a "frame of mind": "homosexuality" itself is a social construction, but the labeling and its consequences have been as important for homosexuals as for blacks or Jews. Even if we don't believe it is important to identify as "gay," then I believe the experience of oppression, conscious or unconscious, acknowledged or simply internalized, still informs our lives, all parts of them. Clearly it informed Britten's music, which can very justifiably be claimed as "homosexual art."

I certainly know it informs all parts of my own work. I've just been writing an essay on editing early music (part of my scholarly work is a new edition of the music of Elizabethan composer, William Byrd). In it, I portrayed the early music movement as subversive of the authoritarian "classical music" tradition. I emphasized its achievement in cultivating earlier music as a different kind of music and showing us how we can delight in that difference (rather than simply assimilating the music thoughtlessly to our tradition, as people did earlier this century). That perspective wouldn't have occurred to me in the '60s, before I came out.

MASS: "Gay art," wrote James Saslow (author of *Ganymede: Homosexuality in Renaissance Art and Society*), "really includes several different aspects. First, gay artists and gay subject matter are separate, though related, issues. Second, within gay subject matter it is necessary to consider separately the twin categories of male eroticism and female eroticism."

We routinely speak about German, Italian, and French music and musical traditions, but we wince at such categorizations as "black music" or "Jewish music" or "women's music." We may never be able to talk about "gay music" *per se*, but why shouldn't we be able to claim a gay musical heritage? Do you have any suggestions as to how we can begin to establish a vocabulary and method for categorizing gay and lesbian persons, issues, themes and traditions in the worlds of music and opera?

BRETT: At the forum at Vancouver in 1985, I began by rather playing down the gay composer issue. We didn't need, I felt, an A. L. Rowse book on Great Gay Composers of the Past. I was quite properly reprimanded by a graduate student who said we needed our heritage, we needed the straight world to know whose music they are using. And he was right. It's time for poor old Tchaikovsky to retire. For so long he and his "homosexual tragedy" symphony were all there was to our music; and that is worth a book in itself. But just imagine. Schubert is a gay composer. Perhaps one should print that in capitals. It might sink in better. No one has yet drawn any conclusions from what must be the most startling assertion in classical music biography of the decade.

So what? one might respond. Well, it is up to us to say what. We haven't begun to imagine what we could say in answer to that question. There may not only be the possibility of, but good reason for, a gay studies program in music history, but I am very far from being the one to suggest its theory or methodology — at least, not yet. I was lucky enough at a crucial time of my life to find a subject for criticism which badly needed its terms redefined. I worked along traditional Anglo-American pragmatic lines, thanking my lucky stars that I had found a way of integrating the respectable scholar in me with the rank outsider. The more musicologists and music critics that overcome the reluctance to be honest with themselves, the more varied and more interesting perspectives we shall have on all aspects of the relation of gay experience to music.

Homosexuality and Music II

A Conversation with George Heymont

George Heymont writes prolifically about opera and gay life for a broad range of publications. Since 1977, he has covered the San Francisco and national opera scenes in his column, "Tales of Tessi Tura," for the *Bay Area Reporter* and has conducted master classes on "The Young Artist and the Media" with aspiring singers in most of the nation's leading opera apprentice programs. George Heymont is also a regular contributor to *Opera News*, *The Advocate*, *Outweek*, *Opera Monthly*, and is national editor of *Opera Monthly*.

The following interview took place on October 27, 1987, in New York City.

MASS: Most gay opera people I've known, and all the other gay music critics I've known (with the exception of Bruce-Michael Gelbert [who writes about music and opera for the *New York Native*]) remain in the closet. Before Bruce-Michael, in your "Tessi Tura" columns for *B.A.R.*, you were the sole exception, a real maverick as the first and only gay activist music critic writing for a newspaper. Generally speaking, how have these two roles — gay activist and music critic — meshed with one another in your experience?

HEYMONT: I have been in the gay movement since Stonewall, and part of what that means is that I'm used to articulating my thoughts about being gay the same way I'm used to articulating my thoughts about music — with great passion!

There are very few opera queens who could or would hide their passion for music, yet so many of these people want to hide their passion for the very soul of who they are. I don't think the "safety" of the closet is worth it. Because I'm willing to say in public what I really feel, as a gay man with gay insights and perspectives, my writing about music and opera is more relaxed and honest. There's less dichotomy between George the passionate opera queen and George the dispassionate music critic!

MASS: When did you first start writing these gay opera pieces?

HEYMONT: In March 1977, and I should add that Bruce-Michael was one of the people who encouraged me then. My column became the first openly gay coverage of opera to be regularly featured in any press. In earlier days of the [post-Stonewall] gay movement (in the early '70s), I had already begun lecturing on gay rights in New England. Then I thought, why not use my gay lib vocabulary since so many people in the movement will understand the references. Why not sneak in the vernacular this readership is used to hearing? That will help to make the points clearer and also more accessible to those people who may not know very much about opera but understand gay vernacular.

MASS: It sounds as if it all happened very naturally.

HEYMONT: Let's put it another way. As I said before, I'm not an academic or scholar. I did not want to write Harold Schoenberg-style, mainstream reviews, which I found pretty deadly. I've always wanted to write to entertain an audience, and if you want to do that, you have to talk to them in their language. It's like safe-sex brochures. You can't really talk about safe-sex unless you talk clearly about rimming and fucking and sucking. If you don't use those everyday words, the words we really use, you're going to lose a lot of the people you most want to reach. With music and opera, it's the same thing. If you're going to reach a gay readership, and hopefully try to educate some people who don't know that much about music or opera, you have to talk to them in a language they can understand.

MASS: You were also a pioneer in urging some of the operatic powers that be to look to the gay community for support. But as Beverly Sills pointed out when you interviewed her for your piece on this subject in *Christopher Street* (issue 69, 10/82), that outreach wasn't happening primarily because gay media reps had never tried to solicit advertising from opera companies. Now, who isn't reaching who? Is the problem more the gay community or the opera establishment?

HEYMONT: It's a two-way street. Gay people buy tickets and buy tickets *en masse*. You can go to the Met or City Opera on any night and see a large block of gay people in the audience. However, those people have never bought tickets as a [gay] group. Some of them may have gone to cruise and to make new friends, but they never tried to coordinate this kind of social networking because gay people, as a rule, tend to be single consumers. At the same time, most opera companies do not have the kind of budget that allows them to advertise everywhere they might want to, even if they weren't squeamish about any connections with the gay community. So you have this two-edged sword.

On one side we have gay people who, partially because of their own independence but also because of a feeling, in many cases, of self-loathing, do not want to be identified with gay groups. For instance, Beverly has approached people who are gay and asked them to donate, and they have, but they did not want their money identified as gay money. These are older people, more closeted, who have made their fortunes and have a completely different mindset about who they are. At the same time, gay people are now becoming *more* visible in the arts, partially because of the AIDS crisis, but also because some opera management people are finally getting wise to the fact that they have to sell tickets and that it's no longer a question of "Can we afford the societal risks of seeing our ads in a gay newspaper?"

There's also the fact that the ad rates are much cheaper than for a mainstream daily. You'll get ten times the space for the same amount of money and you'll be impacting on your target audience. The bottom line is that you will definitely sell tickets. The proof of all this is an experiment that was conducted by the San Francisco Opera. They coded an ad for a specific event, setting aside 250 seats. The ad was in the *Bay Area Reporter*. It came out on Thursday and all 250 seats were sold by Saturday. The marketing director, who is gay, said, "Well, I no longer have to prove this market. You get the business because you're bringing us the business."

MASS: So the problem has really been on both sides of the stage.
HEYMONT: Yes. Speight Jenkins, who is now head of the Seattle Opera, has begun to do preview talks with a gay group in Seattle. His feeling is that a gay group is just like any other neighborhood group. I also just met with the head of Opera Guilds International

and pointed out the fundraising potential of the gay audience. I emphasized that this audience is never reached out to, never specifically invited to participate. Her response was very interesting. In Chicago, they have a black chapter of the Opera Guild. They tried to get this chapter to mingle more with the other chapters, but it just wasn't happening. She said she realized that they would just have to leave it that way and that that was OK. These people preferred to mingle with other persons, not only with similar interests in opera but with others who were actually like themselves. She proposed that we begin to look at gay people similarly, to think of them almost as an ethnic group. If you do that, she felt, you will get them, because they'll be happy to have an excuse to get together and talk about opera.

MASS: For years, you weren't getting press tickets to the San Francisco Opera (SFO) because you and the paper you were writing for, the *Bay Area Reporter*, weren't considered to be "legitimate." Is that correct?

HEYMONT: Yes.

MASS: And the press people who were causing you the most trouble turned out to be—surprise—closeted gays.

HEYMONT: Yes, but there was another major factor. Apart from being homophobic, Kurt Herbert Adler, who was manager of the SFO at that time, seemed to hate the press altogether. His feeling was that if he had to allow any press into the opera house, it would only be major dailies and nobody else. And that was the policy and overall attitude taken by the SFO press department. If a paper had a print run of a million, it instantly got access, whereas a local paper with a print run of twenty thousand, even if it hit many more people who bought tickets, was not considered to be of any value. So it became crucial to explain to Adler that he didn't understand his market.

What finally happened is that there was an incident. I had requested tickets to the opening night of a Spring Opera Theater production and was told I could not get any press seats. But friends of mine who were working at the SFO Symphony said the opera company was papering the house and that they were told they could have as many seats as they liked. So I wrote the whole thing up in the paper and claimed that I had been discriminated against. I wrote that it seemed strange that they would refuse to give press seats to a gay paper when they were all but dragging in winos off the streets of the Tenderloin for the musical equivalent of a charity fuck. Well, they took tremendous resentment to my use of the phrase "charity fuck." Tom O'Connor, the SFO marketing director, sent me a letter on SFO stationary saying that I was a boor and that I didn't belong in the Opera House. They would, however, consider giving press seats to a different critic from our paper. At that point, it was a question of drawing sides. Does the opera house have the right to dictate which critic a paper should send? No newspaper is going to stand for that. Now, the technicality was that the SFO is a tenant in the War Memorial Opera House, which is a municipal building, and San Francisco has a city code which states that you cannot do business with people who are discriminating against minorities. And *B.A.R.* had helped elect three members of the Board of Supervisors, including Carol Ruth Silver and Harry Britt. So the Board of Supervisors began to apply pressure on the opera company. Eventually, we got a written apology from Adler, who had never been known to apologize to anyone, ever. When I met Adler later at a press conference, he came right up to me and said: "I want you to know that between you and me there was never any problem. It's this middle-level crap shit that caused all the trouble." From then on, I got press seats.

MASS: I don't suppose any of the other music critics or reporters — neither in the mainstream dailies in the San Francisco Bay area and Los Angeles, nor even in the gay press (except for *B.A.R.*) — picked up on this confrontation. Has there ever been a case of discrimination, based on sexual orientation, that has gone to litigation in the music business?

HEYMONT: Yes, the Michael Raines case, which has gone to trial three times. Let me also mention the related case of [soprano] Lucine Amara, who took the Met to court, alleging discrimination based on age, and she won.

[Ed. Note: Michael Raines was the managing director of the San Francisco War Memorial, the commission that manages the Opera House, Herbst Theater and Davies Symphony Hall. When Raines was fired by the Board of Trustees of the War Memorial commission, he sued, claiming that he was being discriminated against on the basis of his sexual orientation. The case went to trial in 1/80, 6/83 and 7/87. Each time, the jury ruled in favor of the city. Matthew Coles, the ACLU attorney in San Francisco who represented Raines in all three trials says he knows of no other case of discrimination, based on sexual orientation, that has ever gone to litigation in the music business.]

MASS: B.A.R. had a piece on you entitled *"B.A.R.'s* own critic, George Heymont" (12/3/81), in which you talked about your evolution as an opera critic and writer. It says, "One matter George was sure of was his desire to review within a gay context. There were enough straight and closeted critics already."

During the period when you began doing your "Tessi Tura" column for *B.A.R.*, there was a smattering of other writers in the gay press who were beginning to address this subject. In 1977, Stephen Greco did an interview with Peter Pears in *The Advocate* that frankly addressed Benjamin Britten's homosexuality. In the late '70s and early '80s, James Saslow wrote gay-conscious pieces about the arts, including music and opera, in *The Advocate*, as did Bruce-Michael Gelbert in *Gaysweek* and *G.C.N.* and Michael Bronski in *G.C.N.* And I wrote my first piece on this subject, "Confessions of an Opera Queen," in 1980, which was published in that same opera issue [69] of *Christopher Street* that featured your piece on "Opera Companies and Opera Queens."

But there were other music and opera reviewers in the gay press — for example, Scottie Ferguson in *The Advocate* and Ivan Martinson in *The Native*.

HEYMONT: First, let me say that I have occasionally used pen names, but not because I'm in the closet. In most cases, it has been because the editor was using more than one piece by me and didn't want my name to keep appearing on the masthead. But there was another circumstance. I used to write for the airlines a lot and when the government of Mexico nationalized Mexicana Airlines, I emerged as "Jorge Jimenez" because they felt there were too many "gringo" writers on the masthead!

Now, neither Ferguson nor Martinson were writing under their own names. But there was another, more important (though perhaps not unrelated) difference between what they were doing and what I was trying to do. I wasn't just writing "straight" reviews. I was writing a column. Nor was I merely writing straight reviews in which I was openly gay and used gay vernacular, although being openly gay and using gay vernacular did sharply distinguish me from Ferguson and Martinson. Except for Andrew Porter in his *New Yorker* pieces, which have always tended to be scholarly and academic, there weren't any critics, gay or not gay, who were regularly covering opera on a nationwide basis. They might hit an occasional special production or premiere in another city, but they weren't following the operatic pulse of the nation. In that sense, what I was doing was very different.

MASS: If closeted critics were asked to defend themselves, I think they'd say such things (as they've said to me over the years) as, "we are writing for large readerships, most of which are straight. What purpose would it serve for me to be openly gay? And in any case, what does my being gay have to do with whether a singer or a staging was good or not? Art is timeless and universal. It doesn't depend on political fashions that have nothing to do with the artist or the work or the production." What are the answers to these questions, George?

HEYMONT: The reason being openly gay is so important for a critic is that reviewing is subjective as well as objective, and being subjective, it is a reflection of who you are as a person. And if you're gay, however much you may wish to deny it, a very important part of who you are as a person is the fact that you are gay. As we both know, there are many leading music critics who are closeted, and I do think it's a problem. I believe that being out of the closet affects the very language you choose as well as your opinions. Much of my writing includes the street language of gay people – e.g., "so and so screamed her tits off." Many times, other critics as well as readers have come up to me and said, "you know, what you wrote is exactly how I felt about such and such, but I would never say those things in public." Beyond any issues of propriety, that's a reflection of their own closetedness.

Look at the whole phenomeon of gay choruses. It took a long time for the mainstream press to review these concerts. During their first few seasons, I went to the *New York Times* and urged the music critic I spoke with, Allen Hughes, to look at this thing. His response was, "Well, certainly if anything of musical interest is happening in New York, we at the *Times* should know about it." So I said, "But obviously, you don't because it is being marketed differently—in bars and on street posts. I'm sure a lot of people who read the *Times* are going to these concerts, and it's a phenomenon that's happening around the country." It took years for the *Times* to acknowledge gay choruses.

MASS: I think our generic critic-in-the-closet would say, "Well, the gay chorus is arguably a musical event of some general interest, and it should receive some coverage commensurate with the degree of its general musical interest. But I still don't see what purpose it serves for me to come out in an article and say that *I* am gay. I'm also not saying anywhere that I'm white or English or a Texan or that I'm a Disciple of Christ. . . ."

HEYMONT: If there were a festival of music by black composers, I think there would be a certain amount of editorial pressure or desire to use someone who knows black musical history; or who knows something about how music is composed out of a heritage. Whether the heritage is one of slavery or jazz isn't the issue. The point is that it helps if you have someone who is sympathetic and familiar with the history, the heritage, of the musicians as well as with their idiom. As we've already said, for the sake of honesty, it *is* appropriate, if not always extremely important, for the reader to know if a critic is black or Polish or American or English or gay or Jewish, though I think it's less important that the critic be openly identified as black or gay or Jewish or Polish or American or English than that he or she be tuned in to what it means, in terms of the music and its appreciation, that the composer is a representative of a certain musical or artistic heritage. In San Francisco, there's now a Society of Lesbian and Gay composers. So this is clearly a heritage that a growing number of gay and lesbian musicians themselves, in addition to the larger gay and lesbian community and the public, are taking seriously and want to explore.

When the gay marching band and gay chorus went on their national tour, I went with them to Washington. One of the most moving experiences I ever had, as a gay person *and as a music critic*, is when the gay chorus stood inside the Jefferson Memorial singing

Randall Thompson's "Testament to Freedom." In this instance, everything came together. Here you had a chorus of gay people, singing a piece of music that has tremendous political meaning to them. Whether or not the composer is gay, his music was being sung in a gay context in view of the White House. So this is a good example of an event coming together that wasn't just music for music's sake. You don't just write about whether or not they hit the notes on pitch or on time. It was music in its relevance to society. *That's* what was appropriate to write about.

MASS: Of course, no one outside the gay press, and certainly not any of the closet cases we're discussing—who knew very well what this concert meant—acknowledged that meaning.

HEYMONT: Look, you can find books about why Maria Callas farted during a performance. OK, but if there's that degree of curiosity about every other aspect of music history, the question is not why should critics and musicologists explore gay aspects of a performance or artwork. The question is, why are they so inconsistent? Why are they running in the opposite direction with their tails between their legs?

MASS: But there's also this basic issue of honesty. Just as Don Henahan occasionally mentions his wife and John Rockwell his dates, so gay critics should occasionally be able to mention something about *their* lives. When Frank Rich became senior theater critic of the *New York Times*, the *Times* announcement concluded with a statement that Rich was married and was the father of a son. Why shouldn't a gay critic be able to make an occasional reference to his life partner, especially if it's in the context of discussing a work that speaks to gay people? In their insistence on "neutrality" and "objectivity" to the point of excluding any and all references to the personal, their writing, without their realizing it, neutralizes and objectifies reality.

HEYMONT: A good example of how this works is the critical response to *Cry To Heaven*, Anne Rice's book about the castrati. According to Anne, the reason the market picked up the book very quickly was because the *gay* market picked up the book very quickly, and that was because the book is about a person's sexual odyssey, going through all these phases of sexual identity and sexual adventures, including sex with a gay cardinal. But the reviews—many of which were written by gay men—of course stressed what a wonderful picture it gave of Italy and its music in whatever century it was. Predictably, there was no discussion of the sexuality. The critics wrote about the history and the music, but almost nothing about the sexual identity crisis that, to Anne, was what the whole thing was all about.

To get a perspective on what's going on here, you really have to go back to our elementary school days in the 1950s. Remember those Dick-Jane-and-Spot readers? Remember how there were no black people? Why do you think magazines like *Essence* and *Ebony* got started? And look at what they've done in terms of advertising. Now *Essence* has a TV news magazine, which is all about black achievement and is sponsored by black sponsors. It took years of doing, but it happened because the black community made it happen.

MASS: You've done a huge number of interviews with stars. With some, like Barbara Cook and Beverly Sills, you talk comfortably about gay fans and gay audiences and other gay issues. With others, like Renata Scotto, you don't raise the issue at all. Is that just a coincidence or does it reflect a policy?

HEYMONT: A number of these interviews were done specifically for gay publications like *Stallion* and *The Advocate*. For these readerships, an *emphasis* on gay subject matter was appropriate. But the interview with Scotto was for a Canadian music magazine which couldn't have cared less about gay issues. My overall purpose in interviewing Scotto for that magazine was not to see what her thoughts were on gay issues. That is not a standard interview question. Interviewing someone for, say, *Musical America* is very different from interviewing someone for *The Advocate*. On the other hand, I certainly don't make it a policy to avoid gay subject matter, such as AIDS, that's relevant and should be of interest to a broader readership.

Sometimes, if I am interviewing someone and know that I can spread this material over several magazines, I will ask those questions. Beverly Sills and I have known each other for years. We just had another meeting yesterday, and we've talked about this issue a lot, because I keep trying to get her to do fundraising in gay circles.

She's been very conscious about this because so many of the City Opera people are gay and so many have died of AIDS.

MASS: Why is it that Beverly Sills, who is straight, is frequently speaking out about AIDS and gay issues in her conversations with you and elsewhere in print, but James Levine, her counterpart at the Met, hasn't yet uttered one public word on these subjects? On the other hand, Levine has participated in several AIDS benefits. What has the New York City Opera done?

HEYMONT: I don't know if the City Opera has done anything specific, yet, to raise money for AIDS. I don't think either City Opera or the Met, *as companies* [a benefit at the Metropolitan Opera House was not sponsored by the Metropolitan Opera], have done anything yet. But I do know that Beverly cares very deeply. Plenty of her friends have died. Yesterday she said she has given so many eulogies she's starting to feel like a ghoul. Beverly has spent a lifetime raising money for the disabled and has a number of family members and relatives with disabilities. She is very sensitive to these things. But she ran into a tremendous amount of hostility when she had to raise money for *X: The Life and Times of Malcolm X*. A number of the City Opera's Jewish supporters said, you want us to raise money for an anti-Semitic opera about a black person? But she persisted because she believed it to be an important work.

MASS: Well, if she believes AIDS is important, shouldn't she then proceed with at least one fundraising project, even if there might be opposition, as you imply, from some of her supporters?

HEYMONT: It's important to understand that most AIDS organizations have their own executive directors who are supposed to be handling each organization's fundraising needs. The job of General Director of an opera company [In 1988, Sills resigned as General Direcor of the NYCO] is to run the opera company and raise funds for the opera company rather than for peripheral organizations and causes, however worthy. It's a question of professional priorities.

On a more personal level, because of the fact that their son, Bucky, is autistic, and their daughter, Muffy, is deaf, Beverly and her husband, Peter Greenough, made a family decision many years ago that if Beverly personally did fundraising for organizations and causes other than opera, the first priority would be the March of

Dimes. That is their family's charity of choice and I don't think anyone would begrudge them that decision.

MASS: As we've noted, Levine has not spoken publicly about AIDS, or about anything else that touches the political, for that matter, and certainly not about his sexual orientation. He seems to be yet another shining example of that common and predominant figure in the arts, today and throughout history—the artist who is above politics or whose politics or absence of politics is excused by art. During the Waldheim fracas, Anthony Lewis wrote an Op Ed piece for the *New York Times* suggesting that Levine should cancel his Salzburg concerts, the way Toscanini cancelled his performances in Nazi-occupied Europe. There were two or three of these editorials and letters in subsequent issues of the *Times*, but, to my knowledge, Levine never responded. Nor did he cancel his appearances in Salzburg, which are overseen by Herbert von Karajan, who has never publicly stated any regret for being a Nazi party member and who has consistently lied about the details of that membership. It's distressing to see how naturally being in the closet fits in with a *weltanschauung* of artistic exclusivity, noninvolvement and unaccountability; although it's always the exception—in this case, the politically sensitive and activist conductor, Leonard Bernstein—who proves the rule. Primarily for political reasons, as I understand it, Bernstein has never conducted at Bayreuth and I don't think he conducts at Salzburg, but he has chosen to maintain his close associations with Vienna despite Waldheim. In her astoundingly homophobic and slovenly biography of Bernstein, Joan Peyser suggests that these associations have continued because the Vienna Opera agreed to stage Bernstein's opera, *A Quiet Place*, the only opera currently in the international repertoire that features an explicitly homosexual character who doesn't die at the end.

HEYMONT: Of course, it's all part of a package. I don't expect the conductor of a major orchestra or opera house to be "professionally gay." Nor do you. In fact, even I am not professionally gay. But I am a gay professional. In reality, I lead a frequent flyer lifestyle more than anything that could be called a gay lifestyle. But I am openly gay.

MASS: Did you see the Patrice Chéreau production of the *Ring* cycle that marked the centennial celebration of the Bayreuth Festival and was broadcast internationally? It was very striking and clever and intelligent. Chéreau may well be the most original and interesting director in opera today. But it was also grossly anti-Semitic, albeit in the guise of exposing Wagner's anti-Semitism and therefore, perhaps, unwittingly anti-Semitic, at least on Chéreau's part. In this production, the Nibelungs, the unequivocally bottom-line villains of the saga, are portrayed as Jews (which is the way Wagner perceived them). The production created a furor but ostensibly for other reasons, such as having the Rhinemaidens portrayed as common prostitutes. The fact that the Nibelungs were being portrayed as Jews was noted, but not one of our leading critics, in New York or anywhere else that I know of—and certainly not John Ardoin, who wrote the intermission text for Wagner's granddaughter, Friedelind, that concluded: "Who knows when another Alberich [the chief Nibelung and *Ring* cycle villain] will come along to set the entire cycle in motion again?"—expressed one word of concern that this production might be, intentionally or unintentionally, anti-Semitic and therefore political and offensive. (The festival production was supported with large West German goverment subsidies and was a major German and European cultural event.) Now, the way this ties in with our discussion is that I began to realize, when I saw this production on television, just how serious this problem of being in the closet really is from a political standpoint. The same critics, many of whom were and are gay closet cases, who couldn't see what their homosexuality had to do with reviewing an opera performance, who couldn't see or acknowledge that Benjamin Britten's homosexuality had anything to do with his operas, and who said next to nothing about AIDS as it was decimating the music community, despite desperate appeals (until much later in the epidemic, when it became fashionable to make one- or two-sentence comments and add one's name to huge rosters of mostly straight celebrities), were the same critics who couldn't see what an artistic staging of Wagner's operas had to do with politics. These are the same people, incidentally, who, today, still don't acknowledge that Wagner's operas *per se* ever had anything to do with Nazism. To my absolute horror, I've come to realize that the music establishment that we are dealing with today was and remains substantively indistinguishable from the music establishment that said little or nothing as the Nazi evil unfolded.

HEYMONT: What you're talking about is a conspiracy of silence that is identical to what we're seeing with the gay situation. It's nothing new. It gets repeated in cycles. In medieval times, nobody wanted to criticize the church because that was a quick way to get your ass chopped in half. In various times in our history, nobody wanted to criticize slavery. There were some rich plantation owners who happened to like it and benefit from it. You can see this going from period to period. There will always be such situations. What we have to understand is that if you go out on a limb and take the risk of saying what you believe, you not only risk alienating people, but you also risk going so far that you'll never be able to come back. That's my situation. Yours too. But after a while, it doesn't matter. If you have enough confidence in what you're doing, you just go ahead and do it and don't worry about the consequences.

People have to understand that, yes, music can be very political. You can't look at operas like *Malcolm X* or *Paul Bunyan* or *Willie Stark* or *The Crucible* or even *Un Ballo in Maschera* and say that they aren't political. . . .

MASS: The Marriage of Figaro is one of the best examples of an opera that was so political in its time that it can be said to have influenced the politics of its time. And that's what I think is special and different about the *Ring* cycle. I feel that it not only did for its time what the *Marriage of Figaro* did in its time for the politics of its time, I fear that it is continuing to do so. That is, I fear that its ugly message of anti-Semitism, usually so hushed up in a conspiracy of silence, continues to influence the politics of our time in a manner that is regrettable and dangerous. I don't think modern productions of *Un Ballo in Maschera* are linked with a growing trend toward political assassination (though there was so much concern about this in Verdi's day that he had to rewrite the opera; and there was the interesting coincidence of a scheduled production of *Un Ballo in Maschera* in Dallas when John F. Kennedy was assassinated), but I do worry that ongoing presentations of the *Ring* cycle, as exemplified by the Chéreau production, play into new waves of anti-Semitism, especially in Europe. If you know of one other critic in Europe or America who has expressed this concern, please let me know.

HEYMONT: When you have a conspiracy of silence, it's also a conspiracy of cowardice. When the AIDS crisis was first starting and I was trying to sell some stories on it, I met an editor at United Airlines who said, "Well, I know it should be done and my husband is doing research on it, but this is a very conservative magazine and we don't want to give our readers any bad news while they're in flight." This is a standard ploy of the in-flight magazines.

MASS: We've discussed how shocked and insulted every gay reader of *Opera News* we know was by the magazine's failure to acknowledge, in a memorial tribute, that its editor, Robert Jacobson, was gay, that he died of AIDS and that he was survived by his life partner.

HEYMONT: So far as I know, *Opera News* has never published a feature piece of any kind about gay people and opera or about homosexuality and music.

MASS: I don't think *any* mainstream publication, such as *The New York Times*, ever has. I don't think they've ever even done a feature such as "The Phenomenon of Gay Men's Choruses" or "Homosexuality and Music." Has *The San Francisco Chronicle*?

HEYMONT: You might want to check with Randy Shilts as to whether or not the San Francisco Chronicle or Examiner has done these kinds of features, but I really doubt it. While there are now occasional reviews of some gay concerts in the dailies, there is another problem that we have not discussed.

Often, the people doing the PR for gay concerts are not very media-wise. Sometimes they don't alert the mainstream press or invite them to cover an event because they think that (a) those people already know about their concert and have automatically assigned a reviewer; (b) a straight reviewer wouldn't come, anyway, so why bother trying? (Are we talking internalized homophobia here?); and/or (c) they feel that since this event is a "community concert" and they only want media stroking for doing good deeds, their music-making should not be reviewed objectively on the basis of its artistic merits. (This translates into "We want you to buy tickets because we need your money, but we don't want any bad publicity or negative criticism which might make us think that we're anything less than wonderful, or that, God forbid, the public should find out that we sometimes sound like re-heated shit." Note: If you don't understand this peculiar phenomenon, ask some pushy Jewish stage mother to explain it to you.)

MASS: Of course, *Opera News* has published Ned Rorem's pieces (during Jacobson's term as editor and at his invitation), which contain these tiny little tidbits of things gay or maybe gay, and, of course, Ned is widely known, as he has put it, as the country's "official queer," but that's the extent of the magazine's tokenism, so far as I know. I suppose the bottom line of this featuring of Ned's pieces in *Opera News* is that it marked the first rattlings of the locked closet doors of that magazine, and for that, both Jacobson and Rorem do deserve credit.

HEYMONT: I was pretty offended when Bob [Jacobson] died that there was no mention that he was gay, but I wasn't really surprised. *Opera News* is published by the Metropolitan Opera Guild, which is run mostly by rich, white-gloved old ladies who like things kept white and nice.

MASS: How many Guild members do you think are gay?

HEYMONT: Oh, lots, but not board members. Let me go back to Robert Jacobson for a minute because I think you're missing something very important. Jane Poole, the managing editor, was very prissy about anything sexual and had a lot of trouble dealing with Bob's illness, but Bob himself wasn't exactly a screaming liberal, you know. In fact, he was a closet case. Wearing a mink coat to the opera and being known as gay among your gay friends is not the same as publicly identifying yourself as gay.

MASS: In the interview you did with him in *The Advocate* (8/6/85), Jacobson talks about how important it is for gay artists and other professionals in the music business to come out of the closet. At one point, he actually says something like "James Levine and Leonard Bernstein are now more open about themselves." Nowhere, however, in this interview or elsewhere did Bob himself actually come out and say "I'm gay" or "I'm homosexual."

HEYMONT: The closest we got was when Bob said something to the effect that he used to throw up a lot of smokescreens about his identity, but when he saw a transcript of the interview, he sent it back to me with that line edited out.

MASS: In your interview with Jacobson, you refer to some homophobic remarks made by Regine Crespin [in the mid-1970s] in *Musical America*. As I recall, her good friend (and mine at the time), [*New York* Magazine] music critic Peter G. Davis, was well aware of this offense, but never discussed it with her or in his writing. If anything, this incident seemed to perversely complement his growing adulation of her and, in any case, it certainly didn't hurt her career at the Met. To your knowledge, did any critic complain about Crespin's remarks in print?

HEYMONT: I don't know. You'd have to ask [openly gay impressario] Matthew [Epstein].

MASS: In an interview you did with Rorem, he restates his belief that he has felt and continues to feel far more discriminated against as a composer than he has ever felt in his sex life. . . .

HEYMONT: As a free-lance writer, I can understand and sympathize with him on that point. For him, this may well be true. Ned was always very handsome and probably had little trouble finding sexual gratification and love, despite the prejudices of society. My situation has not been the same. I've always been overweight and it hasn't been so easy for me. Now, if you're a free-lance writer or an artist or a musician in society, most people assume that you'd be happy to take less money for what you do because you love it. And people will ask you time and time again to do things for free because they know you love doing it. They seem to have no concept that there is a cost to doing business. Or they don't care.

What Ned is talking about here is that he has been more discriminated against *economically* as a composer than as a homosexual in our society, and he gave a very specific example of this in the interview he did with me. Some major foundation asked him to fly to Washington to present an award. When Ned asked them to pay his expenses and they declined, saying they didn't give money for such things, he pointed out that they (the people who were asking him to make the presentation) were getting paid for their work, so why shouldn't he at least get reimbursed for his traveling expenses. I agree with Ned on this point wholeheartedly. This nation does not pay its artists commensurate with their skills in the professional marketplace the way it does for dentists or lawyers or doctors.

MASS: Yes, that's definitely true. But Ned's point isn't simply economic. I think he still maintains what he said back in the mid-Seventies, in his interview for *Gay Sunshine*, that being gay is not a legitimate identity:

> To be homosexual is too generalizing. I can't say "we," not even "we composers," or "we writers," or "we fifty-year-olds." I say "they." Therefore I can only refer to my *sexuality*. Now a black person is demonstrably black, there's nothing he can do about that. He's black if he's a scientist, he's black as he looks into a microscope, he's black as he reads Plato. We can see that he is. Meanwhile, a homosexual is only a homosexual when he is being a homosexual. He's not demonstrably so when he's writing music or when he is thinking about a recipe for carrot cake. Homosexuality is a condition whereas to be black is not a frame of mind. It's a physical identity.

HEYMONT: I don't agree with him on that point, not at all, but I remain sympathetic with his situation. Ned resents the fact that as a living composer, he doesn't get the kind of coverage he would if he were a dead composer. The fact is that Ned does not make a lot of money because he is not writing commercial trash. If he were writing jingles for Raisin Bran, he'd be a millionaire. On the other hand, Ned has been let into the club, so to speak. Despite all his kvetching about how tough it is to be a composer, he's done pretty well. It's really a question of which side of the issue you're looking at it from. If you're looking at it from the side of the person who has privilege, as Ned does to a very real degree, it's really a pain in the ass to hear all these other queers who haven't been let into the club beefing all the time. If you're a gay activist who hasn't been let in, and the vast majority are still aggressively excluded if they make any claim to a gay identity, I think you're very justified in making noise. Go back one step further, to the Sheridan Square [Stonewall 1969] riots. The people who threw garbage pails, who led the demonstrations, were not the respectable queers. They were the most disenfranchised — the drag queens.

MASS: At its most tolerant, the club mentality will allow an occasional homosexual to be openly queer. At the same time, it insists that being gay doesn't mean anything more than sexual orientation, which in turn doesn't mean anything more than eye color. Look, says the official queer, I make tarts and I pay my electric bill. I'm like you in everything except what I do in bed. Yes, I'm homosexual, but . . . I think this was the attitude of most homosexuals of Ned's generation, before Stonewall, and it is the attitude of most gay yuppies today, who look back nostalgically with the rest of the country to the 1950s.

What a contrast with Lou Harrison, the unofficial queer of American arts, who is so openly and proudly gay, who acknowledges that being gay has colored every aspect of his existence as a man and as an artist, and who is nonetheless a clubmember, if not a very visible one, in that he is widely acknowledged to be among the most distinguished of contemporary American composers.

HEYMONT: The people who came out in Ned's generation, and even the people who come out today, have been educated that their sexuality has nothing to do with their careers. What's the old line? "I don't care what you do in bed . . ." Well, some of us don't do it in bed. Some of us do it hanging from the rafters.

Let's go back to your earlier question about whether or not City Opera has done anything to recruit gays? How many people do you know who go to the opera?

MASS: These days, less and less.

HEYMONT: Well, say you have fifteen friends who go. Why not get together and go to the marketing director and say, we want to change our subscriptions and go as a theater club. If you did that, you'd be demonstrating to the company that there is a reason why you are banding together, and there is a reason why you want a discount, as a group. That would make them pay more attention to you, as a gay person, than they would had you remained individual subscribers. This hasn't yet happened in the opera world because gay opera people are so closeted, but it has really taken off in the travel industry. There are gay tours and packages all over the place.

Typically, you're seeing groups of twenty going and that allows them the group discount that is standard throughout the industry.

MASS: You are entirely persuasive, but how does this connect with our discussion about Ned?

HEYMONT: It connects at this level. Ned's generation believes that there is no such thing as gay culture, that gays don't represent a legitimate designation of people, but the truth is that gays are no different from any other block of people. Like Jews and blacks and women, we were always disenfranchised. Then Jews and blacks and women discovered that they could add their dollars and votes together and turn their powerlessness around. By organizing themselves as a group with something in common, they could empower themselves. The bottom line is always the same: involvement. How many people are willing to take the risk of (a) being identified, (b) letting themselves be part of a group and (c) saying yes, I'm gay.

I know the historical significance of people like Ned. There is no question that their contributions have been very important. But I also think that we, and that includes gay liberationist historians, should stop beating dead horses. They should move on and give the attention and the space to the people of today, the ones who are openly gay and making a contribution to the gay movement. It's the same problem I run into with opera queens. One of the book proposals I'm working on now is about singers who will be prominent in the 1990s. I'm talking about the generation of Erie Mills and Carol Vaness. But today's queens still want to hear about Eleanor Steber. We have to reset our sights.

MASS: What other projects are you working on?

HEYMONT: The working title of the first book is *The New Golden Age of Opera*, about the period of 1965-1990, when opera really became a popular art form in America. It covers regional performing arts centers, videotapes, supertitles, performance opportunities for American artists, new works by American composers, opera into the eighties and beyond, etc. Another book I'm trying to get published is a collection of some of my interviews, the working title of which is *Stouthearted Men* and the theme of which is the search for gay male role models. It's also about the maturation of our movement which in 1990 will be twenty-one years old and legal! There are several other projects, a collection of anecdotes, a collection of "Tessi Tura" columns, and a murder mystery about opera and gay people.

MASS: In your interview with him for *Musical America*, Simon Estes states flatly that he has been denied work because of his refusal to sleep with gay opera administrators and conductors. In the interview, you don't really challenge him on this. Is that because you believed him?

HEYMONT: Yes, I believed him. Simon has this reputation for being a crybaby because he was discriminated against for being black. But Simon Estes is not a crybaby. He's a very articulate man, and he told me quite openly how in Germany, in the early part of his career, one of the opera house directors tried to put the make on him. When he said, sorry, no thanks, he found that he was not getting jobs. Someone else was always getting cast for various reasons. I believe him. The casting couch exists on both sides of the fence. There are exploitative and unscrupulous gay people just as there are exploitative and unscrupulous every-other-category of people.

MASS: It's accusations like that that our closeted music critics and artists—and I think this is likewise very true of Ned—are most afraid of, that they'll be perceived to be some sort of special interest group conniving and machinating and doing favors for each other and wielding power behind the scenes and unjustly. And let's face it, a lot of that kind of networking and power playing, which is the way of all flesh and of the world, does indeed go on among gay artists and musicians, just as it does among straights. So I would think such an accusation would be disturbing to them and would drive them further into the closet.

HEYMONT: I don't agree. I think you are missing a very important point. The closet cases have spent so much of their lives believing they can pass—meanwhile, of course, everyone knows they're gay and thinks it's more peculiar and suspicious that they're pretending not to be—that they've learned to believe their own publicity. They think that everyone else perceives them as straight and that it can therefore never happen to them.

But you know that famous observation about World War II. When they came for the communists, I wasn't a communist and said nothing. When they came for the Jews, I wasn't a Jew and said nothing. When they came for the homosexuals . . . They never think it's going to happen to them.

MASS: In one of your pieces, you noted that the San Francisco Opera Guild had no gay chapter. You interviewed Terry McEwen, another leading public figure in the opera world who has never said a word about his sexual orientation, about starting one and he seemed willing and encouraging. That was 1982. What has happened since?

HEYMONT: Nothing. You can only start such a thing if people are really interested in it. We made an announcement in our paper, *B.A.R.*, and no one showed up. They were all too busy shopping, I guess. But in fairness, there's another factor. The AIDS crisis has changed vounteerism in the gay community, and certainly that's where much of it should be going. In any event, as I've said, I spoke with this officer of Opera Guilds International who has been trying to organize a gay group in Chicago for a specific event. Alas, you can't force gay people to band together. They have to want to do it. And there has to be someone fairly dynamic who is willing to make all the phone calls, push things around, be a social director and get people to give money. Gay opera people have never understood that they could have certain benefits by doing this. For example, they'd be entitled to backstage tours and other perks of fundraising and volunteerism. But again, gay opera people have to *want* to do this. They have to approach the Guild and say: we want this. That's the only way it ever really happens.

MASS: In one of your pieces, you ask "Could musical works that speak of the homosexual experience, such as *Death in Venice*, be used to raise scholarship funds for consciousness within the gay community?" Aren't we already doing this with gay chorus benefits and gay-themed film benefits (*Maurice, Torch Song Trilogy*) for gay organizations like NGLTF, The Human Rights Campaign Fund, GMHC and The Hetrick-Martin Institute?

HEYMONT: Yes, we're getting there, but we always seem to be doing it under threat, when there is a political or health crisis. Even so, the networking is falling into place. We are now starting to branch out into other areas where people can develop nonprofit foundations and organizations and become more sophisticated about their fundraising. This kind of networking started with such organizations as the original Gay Marching Band, the No on Proposition 6 Campaign, and Harvey Milk's election. Of course, there were things elsewhere, especially New York, and I want to say here that Arnie [Kantrowitz] was a major figure in the gay press in helping us realize that we had value as people, not just as pieces of meat. Please give him a big hug for me.

MASS: I had the same reaction to Arnie's writing. It was so warm and genuine and affirmative. It was the first writing I'd ever read that really made me feel that I was someone who had essential value as a gay man and human being.

HEYMONT: Yes, Arnie's writing told you that you could be a *mensch.* But let's face it, it's taken a long time to get our act together. In San Francisco, there's a much stronger sense of community than elsewhere, to the point that gay and lesbian people have long realized that their money and votes count and that it means power for us as individuals when our money goes into our community. It's keeping the money flowing and understanding that you can use that money to help create things, whether it's an organization like the Hetrick-Martin Institute or the Harvey Milk School, that will help us make something better for ourselves and for the next generation of lesbians and gay men.

Homosexuality and Music III

A Conversation with Ned Rorem

Ned Rorem, the Pulitzer Prize- and Grammy Award-winning composer and author of twelve books, including *The Paris Diary* and *The Nantucket Diary*, was one of the first and has remained the best-known of openly homosexual figures in the world of music. His most recent book is *Settling The Score: Essays on Music* (Harcourt Brace Jovanovich, 1988). The following conversation, which focuses on opera and homosexuality, began in Rorem's living room in New York City on February 15, 1988, and was completed by correspondence in mid-1989.

MASS: Where do you think you stand as an opera composer today?
ROREM: Can one ever know one's own standing? We are not given to "see oursels as ithers see us." All I can provide is facts rather than opinions.

I've composed seven operas, each of them published and available. The first, *A Childhood Miracle* in 1951, was based on a Nathaniel Hawthorne text and was a collaboration with my friend [*Village Voice* film critic] Elliot Stein. It runs approximately 35 minutes and is a virtuosic turn for 13 instruments and six singers. It was first done in 1952, and later televised in 1956 in Philadelphia with Curtis undergraduates. An adolescent Benita Valente starred, and a boy of 15 named Jaime Laredo was concertmaster. Another Curtis student, Plato Karayannis (now head of the Dallas Opera) directed. Then I did a second one-acter affair called *The Robbers* based on a Chaucer tale, and using my own libretto. Marc Blitzstein drastically revised the rather arch text. In 1965 I wrote *Miss Julie*, my only "full-length" opera, though I've never quite known what this term means (isn't a short work full-length?) other than a full-evening's opera. My co-writer was Kenward Elmslie, and the piece was glamorously though unsuccessfully produced by the New York City Opera. Next came *Bertha* and *Three Sisters Who Are Not Sisters* in 1968, both on commission (unpaid) from the Met Opera Studio. The librettos were by Kenneth Koch and Gertrude Stein. In those days, I was still young enough to do things because I liked to do them. Later came *Fables*, five operas in a grand total of 22 minutes, based on Marianne Moore's glittering translations of La Fontaine. In 1965 there was yet another opera, *Hearing*, originally a song cycle on poems of Kenneth Koch, which Jim Holmes, many years later, reworked into a scenario which I orchestrated for an unusual combination of nine instruments.

So of my completed operas, six of the seven are brief, and they all saw the light between 1951 and 1968. It's been twenty years since I've written a new opera. There are still four that are half-done — one based on *The Suicide Club* of Robert Louis Stevenson; another on *The Matron of Ephesus* from a tale in Petronius; a student work in 1946 drawn from Paul Goodman's play, *Cain and Abel*; and, in 1962, to Jascha Kessler's libretto, I all but completed and even partially orchestrated *The Anniversary* for the City Opera before we scrapped it in favor of *Miss Julie*. For completeness, let's include a pop musical called *The Ticklish Acrobat* written in 1957 with Elmslie, but never produced; and a seven minute *scena* I composed just last spring on Cocteau's *Anna La Bonne*. Which brings the wavering total to thirteen, most of them, to some extent, on books of my choice, without any coercion.

I know that you're interested in finding relationships between composers and their choice of librettos, and there have to be such relationships, but I've never really thought much about that.

As to where I stand . . . I would love to write another (and I use the term opera *faute de mieux*). . . . another dramatic piece for singers before I die. Not a cantata, but a staged affair. Whenever I get around opera people, as in Santa Fe or like [philanthropist and leading opera patron] Robert Tobin, who's contributed lavishly to the Met, and the conversation turns to "What shall Ned do?," I get enthusiastic, but it's dangerous to get too enthusiastic about an opera unless you're going to be commissioned. Because unasked-for operas never get done.

MASS: Several years ago you told me that there was a possibility of a commission from The Santa Fe Opera.

ROREM: I did talk to John Crosby [Director of the Santa Fe Opera] at some length in 1985 and he said, "Write me an outline." Robert Tobin was anxious to subsidize it if he, Robert, could also have a say about the subject. If I were them, I'd want to have that say, because more than any other musical format, opera is a collaborative venture. But I'm not very good at collaborating.

MASS: In *The Nantucket Diary* you discuss some of the subjects you've considered for a new opera. You then go on to say, "Probably I'll settle with JH [musician and writer James Holmes, who is also Rorem's life-partner], on a sort of 'Life of Whitman,' or 'Aspects of Walt,' rather like *The Mother of Us All*."

ROREM: Jim [Holmes] and I were extremely enthusiastic, but Robert Tobin felt that Whitman was out of date. Tobin was upset by the AIDS crisis and felt we needed to do something more "timely." What does that mean? Is *Oedipus Rex* timely?

MASS: You say that Tobin was upset by the AIDS crisis. Did he want you to do something about AIDS? Did he have a specific suggestion for a libretto?

ROREM: What he wanted was that it *not* be about Whitman.

MASS: As I recall, around 1985, when you first told me about the possible commission from Santa Fe, you were considering a wide range of subjects, including *Oedipus*. In fact, you asked me if I had any ideas for operas with gay themes. I suggested two possibilities: Mishima's *Confessions of a Mask* and the story of Ganymede. You read *Confessions*, but decided it wasn't right because, among other reasons, it wasn't sufficiently "mythic." Obviously, that was not the reason for rejecting Ganymede, but I don't remember what the reason was. In *The Nantucket Diary* you imply that you also considered *Kiss of the Spider Woman* and an unspecified collaboration with William M. Hoffman. Clearly, the possibility of doing an opera with a gay theme has been an issue you've grappled with.

Has anyone ever written an opera about Walt Whitman?

ROREM: I don't think so. [Theater producer, director and designer] John Wulp wanted me to do an opera on the life of Henry James. I read all five of the Leon Edel books with mixed feelings. I worship James, but operas on the lives of great men are flirting with danger.

Like that movie on the life of Billie Holliday using another singer. The greatness was in the *oeuvre*, not in the life.

MASS: You say that you and Jim were extremely enthusiastic about the idea of doing an opera about Whitman. Have you and/or Jim done any work yet on such a project?

ROREM: No, for the simple reason that I haven't pushed it. If I really wanted to do this opera, if I were ready, I could probably arrange to get a commission. Maybe there's something in me that refrains. Most opera composers always have a new opera up their sleeve. I don't. But I do have enough other work contracted for during the next few years to keep me from brooding too much about an opera.

MASS: In your essay on Joe Orton (from *The Advocate*, 6/9/87), you say that you would love to have had an opera libretto from him. In the absence of a specially conceived libretto, would you, if you had the time, consider setting one of his farces, such as *Entertaining Mr. Sloane* or *What The Butler Saw*?

ROREM: Orton's plays are already very musical, like Edward Albee's, oozing with echoes, rhythms and colors that are so exact in themselves, and with wit so pungent and dependent on time, music could only slow them down. As opposed, say, to Tennessee Williams. The difference between Albee and Williams is that Albee's theater is music already. [Scored] music cannot add to it. It would only detract from the icy aptness of his clipped phrases; whereas Tennessee's writing is all rhapsodic. It's about music but it is not music in itself, which is why Tennessee's plays lend themselves so much more gracefully to opera. I worked with Tennessee on two occasions (providing incidental background music to *Suddenly Last Summer* and to *The Milk Train*). But I wouldn't consider turning any of his plays into an opera now. They don't hold up with the passing of time. They embarrass me.

I read everything that has been published of Joe Orton's in preparation for that essay, but song didn't come into it. When I reread Jane Bowles' *In A Summer House* every five years, I think maybe I should do that. But the last act deteriorates. It's a noble failure. I've also considered Colette's *Chéri*, which would have been ideal for Poulenc. But whenever I reconsider it for myself, it becomes more and more remote.

It's easy to know what you *don't* want to do. In the abstract, I know what I do want to do. Something about myself. I'd need to be inside of the main male or female character if I'm going to live two years with those damn people. Something of Mishima, yes, might work, but not Ganymede, since I'm not interested in children. There's a lot of me in Chéri, and in Leah, his mistress, but the story is dated. Of course, all art dates from the moment it's penned. Beethoven and Stravinsky date well. Tennessee Williams doesn't. Colette dates wonderfully, but *Chéri* isn't *à propos* any longer.

MASS: We were talking about Orton. Charles Ludlum is an artist whose work you've said you believe in as much as Orton's. Did any of his works present themselves to you as possibilities for opera?

ROREM: I haven't seen much of his work. I seldom go to the theater anymore because it's dull and expensive. I go to movies. Ludlum's plays aren't all that suitable for singing for the same reasons that Orton's aren't. They're ironic and crisp and extremely dependent on words and on timing. Wit in opera is not the same as wit in plays. Nobody's going to understand the words anyway.

There's more potential with film. Like every self-respecting American, I was raised on movies. *The Umbrellas of Cherbourg* bowled me over. That was 25 years ago, but it's still the sole opera originally conceived for the movies. In all of its corny glory it truly works. Since then nobody has tried anything else *new* with opera and film. It's an open field. There are, of course, the television and screen adaptations of the standard repertoire, and many of these come off well. I got a lot more out of the TV presentation of *Lulu*, for example, than I ever did from seeing it on stage. Interestingly, George Perle, the world's foremost Berg scholar, told me he really understood *Lulu* when he saw it on the tube, and he adored the subtitles.

MASS: Are you saying that if you were to do a new opera you'd like to conceive it for the cinema?

ROREM: Yes. If I had an idea. I'd want to work with a director like Antonioni, for example; not a director who knows about music so much as one who knows about film.

MASS: Is Antonioni still doing films? (Is he still alive?) In the *Nantucket Diary* you discuss your work with such famous directors as Zeffirelli. But there are a number of leading directors you don't mention, like Visconti, Ponnelle, Caldwell, Felsenstein, Wieland Wagner or Chéreau. Any comments?

ROREM: In 1962 Zeffirelli had never directed anything in America. That's when the Strasbergs reigned supreme. Zeffirelli thought he'd like to begin big, so he hired Susan Strasberg, the world's least talented actress, to take the role of Marguerite Gautier in *The Lady of the Camelias*, adapted by, among others, Terrence McNally. I wrote the score, working every day for a month with Zeffirelli. They put it on as a Broadway play. I wrote about 40 minutes worth of music for four or five instruments filtered through an echo chamber. Romantic, Chopinesque, Frenchish, decadent. It was a horrible experience. Collaborations always are. It lasted four performances. I didn't personally care for Zeffirelli. His vaingloriousness was oppressive.

We were all raised on Visconti's films. When I lived in Rome in 1954-55, he was sort of a god. I met him once or twice at Bill Weaver's. That's in the days when I never knew what to say to idols, so I'd get drunk. I was very impressed. Late one night we all went to a nightclub with Massimo Girotti. Remember him from *Teorema* (which, incidentally, is going to be made into an opera by Michael Torke)? Remember that last scene, when Girotti, virile head of the family, ends up sneaking in and out of a men's room in a Milan bus terminal? Very, very sad. When you recall that in *Reflections of a Golden Eye*, Brando had taken a homosexual role similar to Girotti's in *Teorema*, and then recall these two old icons in their scene together in *Last Tango in Paris*, it was something very special.

I saw the Callas-Visconti *Sonnambula* at La Scala that Lenny Bernstein conducted. Visconti, like all Italians, knew what opera was, and he knew how to cope with Callas. But I once overheard her talking to someone at the little cafe next to La Scala (she was toying with fresh strawberries in mid-February) about how he was on the right track but got off somehow. "Era sulla buona strada," said she in her accented Italian. I heard Callas many times. Now, I don't worship divas, but Callas represents one of the two or three greatest experiences I've ever had in any theater. The others were Mary Wigman, the dancer, when I was in third grade, around 1932, the early Martha Graham, Billie Holliday, Nazimova in Ibsen,

Edith Piaf. All female, needless to say. There are no male equivalents, Whitman notwithstanding. Theater is artifice and artifice is feminine.

I've never seen a Felsenstein production, but I've seen many of Caldwell's things, and so many of my friends have worked with her and just adore her. Let's see. I saw the *Lulu* at BAM. She may be a bit on the gimmicky side. Ponelle?

MASS: I don't think gay men are more involved with divas than divos because "artifice is feminine." I think the reason gay men's stage and screen idols have been predominantly female has mostly to do with our stronger identification with women. (We identify more with Judy Garland and Maria Callas than with Frank Sinatra or Elvis Presley.) For gay men in our time, this identification is a lot more easily expressed than sexual attraction, whereas the opposite is grossly true of heterosexual women. If there were no homophobia, maybe gay men would be more prominent among the fans of the Sinatras and Presleys. Conversely, if our operas, movies and songs were less patriarchal (conceived, written and directed by men), maybe women would be more prominent among the most ardent fans of the likes of Garland and Callas. [Ed. note: These issues are explored in Catherine Clement's *Opera, or the Undoing of Women.*]

Ponelle's the one who did the recent *Manon* at the Met. You know, the one where Manon ends up in a pile of garbage.

ROREM: The trouble with all of those directors: they're trying to breathe life into dead horses. Why doesn't Chéreau coerce his friend Boulez into writing an opera instead of doing the *Ring*? They spend their energies on masterpieces that have long since proved themselves. They're not taking any real chances. The important thing is new music. It always was until our century. Now all we do is these eternal revivals. The so-called "alternative versions" of the *Ring* or *Manon* or whatever, say, Frank Corsaro touches, all deal with updating, so that today's public will find it relevant. They update the costumes, sets, direction, viewpoint—everything except the music. But why not the music too? Why not add a "beat," as someone once did to Bach, adding tom-toms to the *Well-Tempered Clavicord*? Because then it would be a truly new opera. Well then, just commission new operas instead of sprinkling bitter sugar — expensive sugar! — on old chestnuts?

MASS: On this extremely important point, I've heard you say that concert music and opera, as we present and appreciate them here in the U.S., are the only major art forms whose art is almost exclusively of the past. Would you care to say more about this?

ROREM: Movies didn't exist before our century, so they're by definition new. At the theater, nine out of ten plays are by living playwrights. Such plays of the recent past as those of Inge or Williams or O'Neill are called revivals. (Imagine calling a Beethoven symphony a revival, since Beethoven is the rule, not the exception.) The book reviews we read in the *New York Times* are virtually all about vital, breathing authors. The exhibitions in the galleries are nearly all by vital, breathing, painters. (Only in the museums is there emphasis on the past.) This is true of every art except music, where the present is anachronistic and the past is sovereign. For most people, the serious living composer isn't even a despised minority. He doesn't exist enough to be despised. The vitality of contemporary music is something that even cultured nonintellectuals mostly aren't aware of. And I'm afraid that's true of people like Ponnelle and Chéreau too.

MASS: But it's not just the directors. Who shares the responsibility for the mortuarial state of opera today? Is it our critics? Our audiences?

ROREM: It's our managers. There are more gifted young composers around today than there ever were, but there's no outlet for them. No big orchestra will touch them. No opera company or recording company or publisher cares about them. So they are going to have to find their own way as creative artists, just as they will be forced to concoct new sexual rules since the advent of AIDS. They're going to have to do what Britten did in Aldeburgh or Peter Maxwell Davies in Scotland — start their own little groups. Management has a *lot* to do with it. Impressarios are in it for the dough and they lie when they say they're not.

MASS: Herbert Breslin is in it more for the money than the art? I don't believe it!

ROREM: To think that the great Jennie Tourel was required by her manager to go out on those tours in the sticks and sing "My Hero" from *The Chocolate Soldier*, in the face of her nuanced repertoire in eleven languages! And the condescension that her managers forced her into, of singing music that she didn't sing very well simply to pay the bills. Money shouldn't be what dictates. Beverly Sills shouldn't have to say, "I can't afford to take the chance." In every era but ours, one *could* afford to take the chance. Now, it's difficult if Pavarotti can make $100,000 for one concert—three times the amount a composer gets to write a whole opera. Conversely, it's difficult for a manager to ask a Pavarotti to sing a recital of contemporary American songs, or even one such song.

The legitimazation of pop music with its huge public has thrown a monkey-wrench into the situation. With that kind of potential for making money, why would managers want to do anything else? William Parker, for example, the best recitalist in America, has exactly zero recitals lined up for next year. His singing engagements are mainly for foreign language operas. There isn't one singer in America today who can earn a living fundamentally as a recitalist. In Europe, the few who can, like Ameling, Souzay and Fischer-Dieskau, are all over the hill. As a result, the whole sense of how to shape a song is fading. There's no public for it, and that's management's fault. I don't know many managers personally. I don't have much to do with them because they have so little to do with living composers. I sometimes meet them at parties and never fail to say what I think. What have I to lose? With rare exceptions, they are unconcerned with contemporary American music. Yes, Matthew Epstein says he is. Tommy Thompson (who was Donald Gramm's manager) has been terrific. On the whole, though, they don't want their string quartets even playing Bartok, much less Elliott Carter, if it's going to scare away the women's club in Podunk. The dishonesty lies in their saying "*I* want such and such singer to sing this, but the audience doesn't." Now, audiences will take what they get, if it's given to them right.

American singers are the only singers who don't sing first and foremost in their native language. They learn to sing badly in every language except their own, and on the rare occasions that they approach their own, it's by rolling their r's and doing all kinds of Europeanistic things that have nothing to do with English. Imagine a young French singer specializing in every repertoire except

French! When American singers understand what they're singing about, they're terribly embarrassed. The great poetry in English is not really part of the tradition of American song. If you do get a small audience of 300 in a small theater for a recital of songs based on poems by Emily Dickinson or Elizabeth Bishop or John Ashbery, that can be a very heady experience. Managers would like to discourage this, because they don't want audiences of 300. They want 300 million. They're size queens.

MASS: Hmmm . . . I never thought of Cynthia Robbins as a size queen before. And what about our critics? Do you think they could have more influence on this situation?

ROREM: Most of them have their hearts in the right place. But take Andrew Porter, who is arguably the most read critic in the country. He just doesn't have that much influence, judging from all the suggestions he makes that are never taken.

MASS: Somewhere in the new *Diary* you note that John Rockwell wrote his annual piece urging the NYCO or the Met to do *The Mother of Us All* or *Four Saints in Three Acts*. And you ask, why doesn't *he* ask the managers directly?

ROREM: Critics write these things, but nobody listens. Occasionally, a performer might become interested in a piece the critic has mentioned, but that's about it. Critics can stifle or even break a performer's career if it hasn't already gotten off the ground. But they can't really launch a young composer, or do much damage to an old one.

MASS: One more thought about management. Any observations about Terry McEwen? [McEwen had just announced his retirement, for reasons of health, as Director of the San Francisco Opera.]

ROREM: None, except that he's an old friend. His tastes are specific. He once said to me, "I'm not a music lover, I'm an opera lover." [As director of the SFO], he couldn't have been more reactionary.

MASS: Yes. During his tenure there was no emphasis on new works.

ROREM: Yet he did commission, of all people, Hugo Weisgall, who writes very knotty music. When people like Terry finally decide to do their good deed, they'll be damned if they'll call on someone "accessible," like Carlyle Floyd or Tom Pasatieri.

MASS: Terry McEwen is widely known in the gay community to be gay, though he has never been openly so in interviews. Respecting that opera was McEwen's business and that he was a professional, I think it says something about the minority status of gay people in the music world that he was the officially closeted homosexual director of the opera company of the city with the world's largest (proportionately) and most politically progressive gay community and audience during the era of gay liberation and the AIDS crisis. For New York, I think similar observations could be made about such leading musical figures as Stephen Sondheim.

We touched on McEwen's tenure as director of the SFO and the issue of new commissions. To some extent, we've been exploring the status of opera in America. How would you contrast the place of opera in America with that in Europe?

ROREM: Almost without exception, opera in Europe has been written by what we call experimental composers, from Monteverdi through Wagner to Nono and Berg, by chromatic composers, composers breaking or inventing the mold, starting new musical as well as theatrical systems. One of the reasons this has been so is the subject matter, which in Europe has always been rather short on humor and high on horror. Murder, incest, rape, you name it, from *Poppea* to *Lulu*. Except for Mozart—and Mozart was not necessarily, fundamentally an opera composer—I think this obtains. The Europeans were fundamentally opera composers—experimental, nondiatonic.

The reverse obtains in America. We don't have much of a history of opera, but what we do have is by plain diatonic composers. The operas that have lasted are the two operas by Virgil Thomson, which are possibly the best by an American, maybe Deems Taylor's two operas, Aaron Copland's one, Barber's two, the several by Douglas Moore, Blitzstein, Menotti. All of this is music with no accidentals. White-key music, as we say.

Look at the operas in this country that work. They aren't by Elliott Carter or John Cage. They're by Philip Glass and John Adams and it's all nonmodulatory, super-simple music.

Doesn't this reflect a difference in the psychology of Europe and America? Is that why jazz is an American rather than a European thing and why a lot of our opera, like Gershwin's *Porgy and Bess*, stems from that kind of music? It's something to think about. Our opera themes aren't psychotic themes.

MASS: What about *Lizzie Borden*?

ROREM: But *Lizzie Borden* was never a hit. I'm talking about our most successful operas.

We don't even have a failed opera by, say, Milton Babbitt. We do have madness, however, in the tradition of Martha Graham. There is no new music being written for so-called modern dance today, but there used to be. For every new score that's used, now, fifty are based on pre-existing music. Except for Martha Graham, who's deliciously psychotic. She once commissioned a hundred different composers. But them days is gone forever.

MASS: On the subject of utilizing pre-existing music, I want to ask you something about your hypothetical Whitman opera. You've set a lot of Whitman to music already. How would those compositions that you've already created figure in with the new one?

ROREM: It's always tempting in a case of this sort to want to cheat, to re-use something you've already composed. Yes, I have set a lot of Whitman to music. I've found, though, that when you cheat in that way, it never works. I might be able to use a tune or two, but I doubt that I could take intact a song written 30 years ago and put it into the opera. Unless the opera were a mere garland of songs and were in a sense my biography as well as Whitman's. But there's a difference in kind between a song and an aria, between something that's sung in a theater and on a recital stage. There's a difference in scope and intimacy.

For example, Whitman wrote the following:

"Stranger, if you passing meet me and desire to speak to me, why should you not speak to me?
And why should I not speak to you?"

(The answer to the poem's question, by the way, is: because you might get a sock in the jaw.)

I set that to music for piano and voice. It takes the same time to sing it as to say it. Now if I were to rethink that and put it into an opera, it would need some sort of introduction and postlude, some-

thing to get the piece onstage and off. Would I use the same music?
Maybe not.

MASS: Are there many examples of composers who take the text
and rework it with lots of different versions?

ROREM: Usually, opera composers are not song composers. For
example, Verdi and Menotti aren't known for their songs, and
Schubert and Faure aren't known for their operas. There are exceptions, like Virgil Thomson and Britten and Poulenc.

MASS: And Richard Strauss.

ROREM: Yes, but for every exception . . . People always used to
say, "Ned, you write such great songs, you were born to write an
opera." It doesn't necessarily follow. Song is a self-contained experience of two or three minutes. It's a distillation. A song is conceived on preexisting poetry that is unaltered, or should be unaltered. Operas are based on prose that often can't stand alone. When
they try to write operas, song composers write visual song cycles
and then cross their fingers. Opera composers are more involved
with dramatic thrust. It must be worth watching as well as hearing.
Arguably, Wagner fails. But Menotti, who is no Wagner, does not
write boring operas . . . at his best.

MASS: Did you see *Juana La Loca* or *Goya*?

ROREM: Before I saw *Goya*, I read the frightful reviews and sent a
letter of condolence to Menotti, who is an old acquaintance and
who was my teacher when I was a 19 year old at Curtis. About 10 or
12 years ago I wrote an essay in his defense, against Henahan who
had given him short shrift in a way that seemed undeserved. Henahan smirked about Menotti's moving to Scotland, more or less saying good riddance and isn't it silly that Menotti should take himself
seriously. Well, I don't think that's very nice or right since Menotti,
whatever he may be "worth" in retrospect, singlehandedly put opera on the map in America.

Anyway, when he got my letter about the reviews of *Goya*, he
phoned in tears, saying, "Oh, Ned, you're the only one who understands!" in that Italian way, and "Let's get together soon," etc.
Then I saw *Goya* on the television and, well, I should never have
sent that letter. The Menotti situation is a sad one. *The Medium* and
The Consul are unflawed in their way. His music is corn, but it's
inspired corn. Like Tennessee Williams. After those early plays,

everything went downhill. *Goya* missed the boat at every turn. Domingo was valiant to learn that thing by heart.

Years ago, around 1946, Menotti said in my presence that he would like to write a homosexual opera. One didn't say gay in those days. He wanted to do something on Proust, which, God knows, would certainly tempt me. But it can't be done. Like Kafka. It's too personal.

MASS: If you *were* to write a new opera, would you write it with a specific singer in mind (e.g., the way Menotti wrote *Juana La Loca* for Sills and *Goya* for Domingo or as Barber wrote *Antony and Cleopatra* for Price)?

ROREM: It's hard to explain why the least difficult aspect of writing an opera is the music and the most difficult is finding a proper book and honing it into singable shape. What you're asking about is really one of the last considerations. To come up with a good idea about Whitman is simply the tip of the iceberg. You get the idea but *then* what? Sometimes a perfect pre-existing text falls in a composer's lap. Lee Hoiby took *Summer and Smoke* and used it intact, after Lanford Wilson dolled it up a little. Barber did the same with *Antony and Cleopatra*. These operas are literally the play. *Dialogues of the Carmelites* is exactly the Bernanos filmscript plus a few set numbers from Catholic liturgy. If the right property existed now and didn't need to have much done to it, and it were in public domain, I'd grab it, whether it was old or new.

In the case of Walt Whitman, the work would need a point of view, which I still don't have. Once you get the point of view, the work should let him speak for himself through his own words, while trying also to be a biography.

As for a specific singer, I would coldly decide the role's going to be this or that kind of a voice. Sometimes it's interesting to go against type-casting. It'd be interesting to do Whitman as a black countertenor.

MASS: My first thought was that this would have been the perfect vehicle for the late Donald Gramm.

ROREM: But Donald's dead now. He was the most intelligent and persuasive male singer we've ever known. I would have entrusted the role to him, but that's now idle conjecture.

MASS: In *The Nantucket Diary*, you repeat a question someone asked you about which singers do you admire. You then go on to list a number of wonderful American singers, many underappreciated, about whom you say wonderful and interesting things. There were several prominent ones you didn't mention. Teresa Stratas, for instance.

ROREM: Don't forget that a lot of the diary entries you're talking about were written years ago. Well-known singers change quickly.

Fifteen years ago I was a different person and the singing situation was different. I was the sole composer in the U.S.A. one thought about when American song was mentioned. That's not the case today. I'm not complaining, simply stating a statistic. They sing songs by Bolcom now and they still sing Barber a lot, but they don't sing my songs much, which makes me wistful.

Stratas? I've seen her in *Lulu*, in *Mahagonny* and in the movie of *Traviata*. I don't care for her record of Kurt Weill; it's too slick and slavic, but she's otherwise pretty interesting, though no more so than Migenes-Johnson.

MASS: Did you see/hear her Mélisande?

ROREM: Yes, years ago, and I liked it. It was too slow, but that was Levine's fault. I heard Von Stade do it on the radio the other day and I like her too. Cool and mature. *Pelléas et Mélisande* is my favorite opera. Of course, Pelléas and Mélisande are really silly children. Bruce-Michael Gelbert recently quoted me for having once used that naughty word "gay" to describe Pelléas on the grounds of the text. There *was* something up between him and Marcéllus, whom he never gets to see again. But it's another one of those cryptic, dangling themes that's introduced by Maeterlinck, dropped, and never resumed. So Pelléas decides he's in love with Mélisande, but I think he's telling the truth when he says they've never sinned together. They were just pals.

Von Stade lent an unusual dimension to Mélisande, probably because of the darker sound of her mezzo, but also because of her less babyish (babyish the way Bidu Sayão used to do it) point of view. . . . Mélisande is the escaped last wife of Bluebeard, or so Mary Garden used to contend, justifying her crazed performance.

MASS: I remember when I read Mary Garden's biography I got the very strong impression that Garden had fallen in love with Lilly Debussy.

ROREM: Why not?

MASS: In *The Nantucket Diary* you say that "the most valuable composers are apolitical and aristocratic (Wagner, Ravel, Stravinsky), or bourgeois and bearish and pseudo-political (Bach, Beethoven, Debussy), or just straightforwardly religious members of the status quo, like all those before the Industrial Revolution." Please elaborate.

ROREM: Art can make political statements, but it cannot have political effect. Art is not moral, it is something else. It cannot change us, but it *can* reinforce our convictions and help us get through life. If I were able to make a political statement as an artist, I would. If I were able to write a song that could make people march away from war, I would. The way to stop wars is not to fight them. Art is created in leisure, not in the heat of battle. Art won't make a Democrat out of a Republican and it won't make a peacenik out of a warmonger, as the Nazis, who were very sensitive to music, have proved. And it won't make a nice person out of a bad person, as Wagner, who was a great genius and misguided rascal, has also proved.

I've written only one "political" piece, which is "War Scenes," drawn from Whitman's Civil War diary, but that could just as easily have been about The Trojan War or the Viet Nam. It's about the horror of war in general. I'm moved by Britten's *War Requiem*. Who isn't? It's political yet enduring; but, again, he's using timeless words rather than timely ones.

MASS: You're acknowledging that something timely *can* be just as timeless as something ancient or mythic, but you're skeptical about the prospects for anything very topical enduring as art. "Imagine *As Is* as an opera!" you once quipped. Hence your skepticism about doing a "gay" opera. Perhaps that's why, up until your current setting of one of Paul Monette's *Elegies for Rog* for the New York City Gay Men's Chorus, you had never scored anything with explicitly gay or other "political" content. I think it's sad that the only conceivable contribution of the Santa Fe Opera (the management of which has always had gay people in its highest ranks) to the AIDS crisis ended up being Penderecki's *The Black Mask* (based on Nazi collaborationist Gerhard Hauptmann's racist, 1929 soap opera about the second wave of the black death in seventeenth century

Europe). Why couldn't a new opera about real people of our time (but no more than the extent to which *Figaro* and *Lulu* are explicitly of their times) have made just as strong a bid for artistic propriety?

[Ed. note: At its premiere in San Francisco in May 1989, *Least of My Children* by Donald Briggs and Loren Linnard became the first opera to deal explicitly with the AIDS epidemic, and there are several operas-in-progress that are about AIDS, including one based on a text by Sarah Schulman commissioned by the Houston Grand Opera.]

Did you see *Malcolm X*?

ROREM: Yes. In a Philadelphia tryout. I certainly wasn't against it in principle. Malcolm X was a powerful figure, a hero, but also an abstraction. You can humanize a hero but not until enough time has passed for the hero to become a symbol, an invention, like Julius Caesar or Henry VIII. Real live heros don't go into the street singing.

MASS: Had enough time elapsed, according to your criteria, for this to work? That is, was *Malcolm X* a success, and if not was it because it was "too political" or "too timely?"

ROREM: No. The main problem was that it was unbalanced. The whole first section was completely improvisatory and fell flat. But as a tragedy it worked.

MASS: What about *Mahagonny*?

ROREM: Brecht was a political man and a less important artist than Kurt Weill. Weill succeeds in spite of his propaganda content rather than because of it. Music, insofar as it's propagandistic, can never persuade. Insofar as it veers from propaganda, it can work. *Malcolm X* became a tragedy about a hero, but Malcolm X himself is too remote now for even me to quite remember. A speech *by* Malcolm X is far more jarring than an aria *about* him.

MASS: But in addition to the general human interest in Malcolm X as a tragic human being, the hero's main concern, racism, *is* timely, just as the fate of capitalism, the principal subject of *Mahagonny*, remains timely. So *Malcolm X* and *Mahagonny are* political, rather the way *Figaro* was. *Figaro* was literally revolutionary in its views of contemporary class relations, and it dealt with everyday people and everyday life in contemporary Europe and was based on a play by a living playwright. It incited people to riots. What you're saying is that the long range value of, say, *Figaro* transcends the class struggle in France that stimulated and permeates it. Everyone can agree with that. What I'm emphasizing, though, is that some great, timeless works like *Figaro* were originally as topical as some of the contemporary works—operas about Viet Nam, racism, sexism, homophobia and AIDS—you're so certain would be too propagandistic, too timely, to endure.

But even when an artist's themes are ancient and mythic and don't appear to be political, they often are, as in the case of Wagner. I was thus intrigued by your generalization that Wagner was apolitical.

ROREM: The Wagner case is a healthy example, like that of Rock Hudson dying of AIDS. Hudson showed that even a national idol can have AIDS. Wagner showed that a great artist can also be a son-of-a-bitch, even wicked. It's necessary to demythologize the Hollywoodian notion of artists as "good people." I'm always moved when strangers tell me I've touched their lives by my words or music, and what a good person I must be, because I'm not. If they knew the real me!

MASS: Some writers characterize *Lulu* as a "feminist opera." Are they bad?

ROREM: Bad? The use of words like homosexual, negro, black, gay, depends on how old you are, what part of the country you're from, and to the class of people you hang out with. The word feminist didn't exist during the 1930s when Berg wrote *Lulu*, at least not with the same resonance as today. Negro was a noble word when I was a kid, in an extremely radical milieu. Now that word is banned and we're supposed to say black, which used to be a "wrong" word. Well, Paris is worth a mass, so I say gay now and black too, though I never used to. Like friends who change their names when they become famous. Sooner or later you get the hang of it.

MASS: Do you think gay liberationists like myself are misguided in regarding the Countess Geschwitz, the first explicitly lesbian and homosexual and feminist character to enter the international repertoire, as a source of gay and feminist pride? Or is she no more interesting or pertinent to gay or feminist history or to the so-called heritage I'm claiming of gay people and women in music and opera than, say, Mohammed, "Der Kleine Neger" in *Der Rosenkavalier*, is to the musical heritage of black people?

ROREM: You've criticized me for talking about groups of people, like Jews, as though they weren't individuals. But you are inclined to talk about gay people as a group. I'm willing to talk about gay people as a group if it helps the situation. I don't think that homosexuality is a very interesting subject, *except* politically, just as heterosexuality is not a very interesting subject. As you well know, homosexuals are just as boring as heterosexuals. Homosexuality is interesting only insofar as homosexuals are a persecuted minority. (Of course, that's pretty interesting.)

We can make the past what we want to make of it. We can put motivations into Berg's works, and we might even be correct on one level, although he may have been quite unaware of what we think he was thinking. One can write doctorates about *Lulu* until the cows come home. The Countess can be interpreted in many different ways, unsympathetically as well as sympathetically. Finally, she is only what the music tells us she is.

MASS: You must think, then, that I was likewise misguided in expecting our music critics to have said something about why the Countess might be especially interesting to today's opera going public, with its large numbers of gay and lesbian persons, during this era of gay liberation struggles and AIDS. Incidentally, George Perle, who has characterized lesbian sex as "naughty," wrote me that he knows of no criticism, neither at the time of the writing and premiere of *Lulu* nor today, that engaged this question, period. I don't think he sees the pertinence of the Countess to today's audience and to our time as any more worthy of comment than you or Peter G. Davis do.

ROREM: George was being naughty himself to have used such a characterization. Of course, all sex is naughty, which is why it's fun. Now, when you say critics, you're talking about nongay as well as gay critics. I recently read Ed Sikov's comments about Lehmann-Haupt's review of the Oscar Wilde book [by Richard Ellman] in the *Native*. Sometimes people point out homophobia where I don't see it, but in this case I did.

I was interviewed recently by somebody in Philadelphia for a straight magazine. In the galleys, the interviewer said something about "cheery" homosexuals. I wrote him back that I thought it was homophobic to stereotype a bunch of people as "cheery." He changed the reference, but reluctantly. By the same token, I'm not looking for homophobia all the time. Lehmann-Haupt would doubtless deny that he's homophobic, while being more careful in the future.

MASS: Like your good friend, John Simon, who graduated from his interview with you, in which his homophobia is the principal subject addressed, to become the film critic for William F. Buckley's *National Review?* Lehmann-Haupt has been homophobic many times in the past and there have been repeated complaints in the gay press. I myself have written him letters.

ROREM: Did he ever respond?

MASS: No.

ROREM: The disappointing thing is that someone like Norman Mailer, who's smart and, I gather, rather well read, is homophobic. It would be so much more interesting if he weren't. Most of our star heterosexual writers are inadvertently homophobic — Styron, Updike, Mary McCarthy . . . But going back to the question of critics, I think you're asking them to discuss something that's not pertinent in a review. It might be in a Sunday article.

MASS: In a little review in the *New York Times* of *Albert Herring*, Donal Henahan, of all people, suggested that perhaps Britten identified with the character as a homosexual and that it's possible to see the opera as a kind of "coming out" story. *That's* the kind of *timely*, pertinent observation about something of interest to lesbian and gay persons that we almost never get in mainstream music writing, even when the critic is gay.

ROREM: But Henahan's point had to do directly with Britten and the opera. With *Lulu*, you're asking critics to talk about social issues in their performance reviews.

MASS: When the social issues are pertinent and interesting, yes, that's precisely what I'm asking them to do!

When the Waldheim affair broke, the *New York Times* published several op-ed pieces (by Anthony Lewis and others) urging James Levine to cancel his performances in Vienna and Salzburg, the way Toscanini did in protests to the Nazis and Fascists. Not only didn't

Levine cancel his performances, he never publicly responded to these challenges. Was he wrong?

ROREM: During the Second World War I was almost a conscientious objector because my mother wanted me to be. But at the army exam, I arranged to get rejected, not as a C.O. but as a 4E, on the basis of nearsightedness and flat feet. A year later I again had to go through that same sordid business of the induction exam, so I got a letter from my psychoanalyst, who explained that I was "not sufficiently mature" to be in the army. (The army, as we know, is made up only of mature people!) I felt, and my parents agreed, that since the army is immoral, why be "moral" about staying out of it? I didn't want to be a conscientious objector. My sister's husband was a conscientious objector, and it was hideous. I'm not of that fiber. I have music to write. I don't like to throw stones . . . During the 1950s when I was living in Europe, and people talked about the cold war and collaborationists—did you know that so-and-so went to bed with German soldiers during the occupation?—I kept my mouth shut and listened. Who am I to say what they should or should not have done, since I was not in their place? Nobody has asked me to go to Austria. If I had been asked to go to Austria and my friends had asked me not to, I would certainly have thought about it. If I were Jewish, I don't know what I would do. I know people who have gone to South Africa. Will Parker, for example, gave recitals there but told his friends to keep quiet about it. Edward Albee, meanwhile, refused to allow his plays to be done there, which is sort of pretentious. It doesn't accomplish anything, unless it gets a lot of publicity. I can't presume to speak for James Levine. But Lenny Bernstein conducts in Vienna, and he's not exactly a fascist.

MASS: In *The Nantucket Diary* you quip that you are a "gay pacifist," as opposed to being a gay activist. Actually, you're not the only prominent composer who is known to be both homosexual and pacifist. Britten and Tippett are two others. Do you know of any straight composers who are similarly, outspokenly pacifist?

ROREM: Sexual orientation and pacifism are not related, certainly not in my case. I was born a pacifist and raised by convinced Quaker parents, both of them ardent heterosexuals. Britten, on the other hand, came to his pacifism by conviction. Probably, the same

10 percent of pacifists are homosexual as the 10 percent of taxidermists or horseracers are. I don't think there are any real generalities that can be made here. It has never occurred to me that homosexuality and pacifism have anything to do with each other. Pacifism is far rarer than homosexuality and unlike homosexuality, pacifism has to do with intelligence. Pacifism used to be a dirty word. It's become less so since the 1960s. Also, with regard to your quoting of me, the opposite of pacifist is not activist. Pacifist has to do with peace, not with passivity. So it's a false play on words.

MASS: In your essay on "Women In Music" in *Setting The Tone*, you ask the question, "Why have there been so few women composers?" If you've given the answer somewhere, I've missed it. Beyond your belief that art is ineffable and follows no rules, do you have a theory?

ROREM: They've all been discriminated against. It's that simple. There are more women poets because there's less "manual" labor, less dirty work, involved in being a poet than in being a composer. It's hard to raise children and still spend twelve hours a day orchestrating.

But *all* composers are discriminated against. I don't think female composers today are any worse off than male. If I had to name twelve living composers who interest me, four or five would be women: Thea Musgrave, Betsy Jolas, Barbara Kolb, Louise Talma, Miriam Gideon . . .

MASS: You've pointed out that I speak about gay people as a group. I do, to some extent, even though that group, like all groups, is unquestionably made up of a wide diversity of individuals. But as you've also acknowledged, most of my generalizations about gay people are affirmationally defensive of gay people as a minority. Your observations about Jews, by contrast, are often negative stereotypes about the entirety of a people. You once asked me if I thought you were anti-Semitic. I said then that I didn't think you were. I'd like to continue to believe that you're not anti-Jewish, Ned — and I know that many of your best friends and at least one of your principal patrons are Jewish — but a number of entries in *The Nantucket Diary* challenge that belief.

For example, the last entry of 1973 (p. 51) concludes as follows: "I've never read *The Diary of Anne Frank* ([Meyer] Levin's book

[*The Obsession*] concerns her rape by those presumed monsters who denied him use of his own theater adaptation), but while hearing him kvetch one wonders if [Otto] Frank did not himself author that diary. Could such a document—an intact work of art—have just been left like that? And many a brokenhearted poet has keen financial instincts.''

Now, how is this different from the sick jokes that were circulating about Marilyn Klinghoffer conspiring with the terrorists aboard the Achille Lauro to murder her husband so she could collect the insurance money? In any case, hasn't the authenticity of *The Diary of Anne Frank* already been proved beyond a reasonable doubt?

ROREM: You're making a comparison that I didn't make. I don't know the Achille Lauro details. Nor do I see anti-Semitism in what I wrote. I *do* believe there's too much objective distancing in the Anne Frank book to convince me that she wrote it, such as after-the-fact generalities about the Holocaust that she couldn't have known both because of her age and when she lived. In any case, why is it anti-Semitic to believe this? Or am I obtuse?

MASS: In transcribing your remarks here, I've capitalized Holocaust, mindful of your observation in *The Nantucket Diary* that you're tired of hearing about the six million. From now on, you want to hear about the 20 million or not at all.

We touched on the subject of sick jokes. On page 407 you state categorically that ''Jews did invent the sick joke.'' Certainly, it's legitimate to talk about Jewish humor, as you do in several places, but Ned, is there any real basis for this allegation? I mean, is it something you could prove, or even develop a consensus on?

ROREM: I was quoting Paul Goodman, who was Jewish. I should have credited him. By sick joke he meant the joke of despair—when all is so hopeless there's nothing left but laughter. He even wrote a play about it, *Jonah*, which Jack Beeson (a gentile) made into an opera.

MASS: That's what seems so fascinating and contradictory about you, Ned, is your willingness, habitual and often zealous, to generalize about every group one could think of *except* homosexuals.

ROREM: That's mostly because when they themselves generalize, they get ungrammatical. [laughter] Every time I pick up *The Native*, I read something like ''gay people don't like lavender but we do like gin.'' It should always be ''*We* gay people don't like lavender, but. . . .'' etc. In their zeal not to be thought of as standing apart from their brothers and sisters, they forget to scan their written phrases, even Ed White who should know better.

MASS: Let me ask you about one more of these statements. On page 412 of *The Nantucket Diary* you say, ''Jews, more than Catholics or American WASPS, seem to feel a loathing for homosexuality.'' In view of the exhaustive history of Catholic and Puritanical tortures, witch burnings and other Inquisitional persecutions of homosexuals (which has no counterpart in Jewish history, whatever the Old Testament prejudices and whatever the prejudices of Jewish fundamentalists and neoconservatives), and especially with regard to the current positions and statements of the Catholic church, is this statement really tenable?

ROREM: My understanding of Jewish upbringing is that the notion of homosexuality is offensive biblically to Jews, whereas it doesn't even arise in the New Testament, much less in the Koran.

MASS: I often wish you would tell us more about the gay lives of many of the important people you discuss, especially those who are still officially in the closet. The reason I wish you would do so is that it's in the interests of clarity as well as truth. Here's an example of what I mean. On page 196 of *The Nantucket Diary*, you note that you attended a recital by Eleanor Steber at the Waldorf Hotel, where you ran into socialite musicologist Joseph Machlis, who whispered to you: ''It's like running into your best friend at a whorehouse.'' Now, that's *very* funny. But it's a lot funnier knowing that both of you are gay. Since Joe is still in the closet, however, this part of the humor (and the psychology it exposes) is lost on the vast majority of readers. By the way, in *The Nantucket Diary*, you mention a documentary for television about gay composer Charles Griffes. It was to be produced or directed by Roger Englander and hosted by you. Do you know if it dealt with (or was to have dealt with) the composer's homosexuality?

ROREM: As narrator, I wrote my own script from this documentary. Naturally, I mentioned Griffes's policeman boyfriend, but CBS cut the reference.

MASS: Generally speaking, do you think your being gay has had any impact on your progress as a musician and writer?

ROREM: I don't know. You've pointed out that I've written pieces on Sappho and Whitman and Stein, but Whitman is the most used poet, internationally, by composers. In Japan his words are set to music, and by heterosexuals — Kurt Weill and Hindemith and Roger Sessions — right and left. It's not his homosexuality but his universality that has made him beloved throughout the globe. The first Whitman I used was in 1946, a pacifist poem, but also quite homophilic. I used Sappho the same year for choruses, but Sappho and Gertrude Stein are not exactly unknown and their publics are not queer publics, except for the classical ten percent. Also, you overlook the fact that if I've done these three, I've done approximately 150 other poets, 90 percent of whom are, or were, straight, though some were drunks, Roethke for example. These issues don't arise when I'm composing, except, maybe with the *Calamus* poems and *The Whitman Cantata* which were made for special occasions. I will sometimes, because of the commissioner, use something that's a bit gayer than something else, most recently the setting of Paul Monette's excruciating AIDS elegy for the Gay Mens Chorus. But on the whole, I set whatever speaks to my condition, of love or hate or hunger. Too many nongay American bards have uttered universal feelings that strike home — Wallace Stevens, William Carlos Williams, Robert Frost, and so on — for me to restrict myself. Music cannot be defined as having any sexuality, although words, especially the prose of a libretto, can.

MASS: Ned, with all due respect may I suggest that what you can't see is how negatively defensive you are, like most homosexual artists of earlier generations but in striking contrast to your colleague Lou Harrison. You're saying, yes, such and such person may be homosexual, but that has no meaning or importance, except for the fact that we are a persecuted minority. Bill Hoffman is similarly defensive about being called a gay writer. By contrast, Toni Morrison is proud to be thought of as a black writer, just as Isaac Bashevis Singer is glad to be called a Jewish writer. Morrison sees clearly that being a black writer does not mean that she's not also a woman writer and an American writer and a great writer. It's the same with Lou Harrison. Being gay is something affirmative. He's proud to be a gay composer and interested in talking about what that might mean. He doesn't feel threatened that this means he won't be thought of as an American composer who is also great and timeless and universal. Am I being bad again?

ROREM: You say I'm defensively negative, but how can I win when you're making the rules? I'm not defensive. I'm simply defending myself. I will not, and neither will Lou Harrison, compromise my friends, especially those of an older generation (those happy few!) who have their own set of perfectly decent standards. If I've done so in the past, I regret it.

MASS: The standards of older generations of closeted gay composers may have been decent and sympathetic twenty, even ten, years ago, but they're not now. They obscure the truth and abet homophobia. You keep saying that artists and composers are more discriminated against in our society than gay people. Ned, are artists routinely, daily, mugged, maimed and murdered for being artists the way homosexuals are for being homosexual?

ROREM: Jim has told me I must stop going around saying that. What I should say is that *I* have suffered less for being homosexual than for being an artist. I did suffer to some extent during childhood, when I was called a sissy, but my primary identity is as a musician. I do what I do best. I could never do what you and Larry Kramer and Andrew Humm are so nobly doing.

MASS: But that's what's so funny about you. You do! As Bruce-Michael Gelbert recently suggested, you're like Katharine Hepburn, a living champion of women and feminist goals who vigorously denies having anything to do with women's liberation.

ROREM: I think Gelbert's constant chiropractic bending of anything toward gayety is at once touching and burlesque. It distracts from the business at hand: his often perceptive, often caring, criticism of music.

MASS: I have the opposite reaction to Bruce-Michael. I think he communicates gay perspectives that are legitimate for the audience he's writing for (and often for a more general readership), and that he does so naturally, richly and professionally, without eschewing the caring, objective criticism of music that may or may not be of overriding interest.

You refer to Parker Tyler in your writing. Tyler wrote about homosexuality and movies. Did it ever occur to you, in the course of

your friendship with him, that someone might write about homosexuality and music?

ROREM: Parker didn't write about gay people in movies. He wrote
about gay movies, yes, somebody could write about gay music, but
they'd have to be able to define it first. A movie is definable. Music
is not. You're comparing genres that aren't comparable. Still, I'm
not saying it can't or shouldn't be done.

MASS: I think the following statement by another very outspoken
gay American artist might well apply to you: "Do I contradict myself? Very well then I contradict myself. I am large. I contain multi-
tudes." Am I wrong?

ROREM: Of all of the silly statements Whitman ever made, that's
the most irresponsible. Even poets should not give themselves a
loophole by saying they are so complicated that they think all sorts
of different things. Of course, they do. . . . But the contradictions
need to be organized and then frozen into art. For people to use their
complexity as an excuse for laxity is too easy an out. I don't approve of it, not for Walt Whitman, not for me nor anyone else. In
the guise of being contradictory, evil things can happen.

Sexual Topography

A Conversation with James Weinrich

[Ed. note: The concluding dialogues of this collection are engaged in many of the same debates about sexual identity that preoccupied earlier dialogues. In discussions of sexual identity, we have evolved from the vocabulary of nature/nurture to that of essentialism versus social constructionism, but with no more empirical certainty of either interpretive orientation in 1989 than in 1979. In 1979 Masters and Johnson were stating their belief that homosexuality is "a learned preference." In 1989 D'Emilio and Freedman are saying what is essentially the same thing. In between, there has been a rise and decline in popularity of the belief that sexual orientation is a biological essential that is relatively impervious to social learning. This belief peaked with the publication of John Boswell's *Christianity, Social Tolerance and Homosexuality* in 1980 and the second Kinsey/Bell, Weinberg and Hammersmith study of homosexuality, *Sexual Preference*, in 1981, and has ebbed ever since, mostly under the influence of social constructionist historians. Whatever one's interpretive orientation, the work of social constructionists such as D'Emilio and Freedman has established with certainty that the sexual revolution of our time has consisted of bits and pieces of numerous larger and older sexual revolutions and is destined to become an increasingly small cluster of details in an infinitely bigger picture of change. Conversely, it is clear that as long as sex remains, as D'Emilio and Freedman put it, "a source of both deep personal meaning and heated political controversy," so will questions of sexual identity.

At the start of a new decade, a younger generation of observers of sex researchers, historians and independent scholars is endeavoring to find ways to transcend earlier dialectics, utilizing some of the same methods of categorization that empiricists, scholars and theorists of earlier generations have found useful.]

James D. Weinrich received his Ph.D. in biology from Harvard and is assistant research psychobiologist in the Department of Psychiatry at the University of California, San Diego. He is a certified sexologist, a member of the American Psychological Association, and has published widely in scientific journals. The following interview took place by correspondence during the summer and fall of 1988.

MASS: The dust jacket of *Sexual Landscapes* states that you are currently assistant research psychobiologist in the Department of Psychiatry at the University of California, San Diego. What is a psychobiologist and how did you come to be one?
WEINRICH: A psychobiologist is a biologist with a special interest in the psyche. I started my graduate training at Harvard thinking I wanted to be a mathematical biologist—a kind of ecologist who models populations with mathematical equations. Second term of my first year, however, I took a course in animal behavior from Robert Trivers, and suddenly I realized why I had always been interested in the psychological articles in *Scientific American* all these years! By June, Trivers had become my thesis advisor.
MASS: You are a certified sexologist. Sexology is a relatively new field. How many certified sexologists are there and what, generally speaking, are they doing (e.g., research, teaching, sex therapy)?
WEINRICH: Sexologists are certified by the American College of Sexologists, which is affiliated with the Institute for Advanced Study of Human Sexuality in San Francisco, which is itself licensed by the state of California to grant advanced degrees in sexology. I don't know for sure, but I imagine that the number of people so certified numbers in the low hundreds.
MASS: What did the process of certification involve?
WEINRICH: Filling out a form, sending a curriculum vitae, writing a small check, and having my qualifications looked over by well-

established sexologists such as Wardell Pomeroy (coauthor of the Kinsey studies).

MASS: How international a field is sexology? (e.g., Is there sexology in the U.S.S.R.?)

WEINRICH: There is a department of sexology at the university in Prague, but not in the U.S.S.R., as far as I know. Sexology is a very international field—one which the U.S.A. leads in several areas, but not all. The Dutch and the Scandinavian countries are much better at public AIDS education, for example.

MASS: In general, how is sexology faring today and how will it evolve? (e.g., Will it remain independent? What will be its relationships to—how will it meld or conflict with—such other established and newer disciplines, specialties and subspecialties as psychiatry, psychobiology, psychology, sociology, sociobiology, gynecology, etc.?)

WEINRICH: Sexology is doing increasingly well, academically speaking—and AIDS is one of the reasons, alas. AIDS cannot be ignored by humane people, and even in relatively repressive regimes many people can discover that you need basic sexological knowledge to fight this disease (as well as, of course, enormous amounts of applied research into treatment and education).

Sexology is also doing well because of the baby boom generation, which fed on a certain amount of sexual openness, and which is finally taking the reins of power. So academics who don't call themselves sexologists nevertheless are finding that every now and then they can do what would have been peripheralized as a "sex study" and even let their tenure committees know about it. And purer sexologists are finding that their ideas are not considered as foreign to mainstream departments as they used to be.

That means that sexology will remain usually not as a separate department, but as a topic-oriented program: like the biologists who study eating in any species that eats, rather than the biologists who study birds and only birds.

MASS: How and why did you select the metaphor of *Sexual Landscapes?*

WEINRICH: My publisher asked me for a brainstorming list of titles, and that was one of them (the subtitle was completely her idea, and an excellent choice). As I thought about those two words, it struck me that I liked the metaphor, and I added references to the metaphor on my next editing pass throughout the book.

MASS: Speaking of metaphors, let's jump ahead to the Richard Green study of "sissy" boys, which you discuss in your chapter, "Families of Origin." Green has written that the metaphor for his study is a pair of identical twin boys, one of whom turned out in young adulthood to be more "masculine"/heterosexual while the other seemed more settled in being "feminine"/homosexual. The one striking difference in the background of these boys is that the more butch boy was raised exclusively by the father (who is characterized by the mother as "a dyed-in-the-wool conservative") during a prolonged period of early childhood. During that same time period the less butch boy was ill and exclusively cared for by their mother. Green believes that "the greater degree of homosexual orientation in the previously 'feminine' twin demonstrates the influence of gender-role behavior on later sexual orientation." What do you think of Green's metaphor?

WEINRICH: First, I'm not convinced that it's really a metaphor in the literary sense; how can a pair of twins be considered a figure of speech referring to the study as a whole? But let's not be picky; I'd like to concentrate on what Green's twins mean to basic sexology.

Green favors the notion that it was the fem boy's affiliation with the mother and the butch boy's affiliation with the father that caused the former boy to be more gay, although he is careful (in a fashion typical for Green) not to seem too much of an advocate of it, and may well honestly believe there are other reasonable interpretations. In my opinion, there are indeed two other reasonable interpretations — interpretations that do not imply as strongly as Green seems to that it was this identification process that was the actual proximate mechanism causing the later difference in sexual orientation.

The first is a small but important modification of Green's position: that it was the fem-to-be boy's childhood *illness* that triggered a mechanism that made him disproportionately likely to be gay. The other is that far from being quite different from each other on sexual orientation, the twins really have the same sexual orientation underneath it all, and that the apparent differences merely relate to which twin chose to team up with which parent in what is clearly a very argumentative family. Careful readers will see that both positions may be true, and Green does point out that the illness may have contributed to the identification process.

In support of the first position are several studies, including Green's own, that suggest higher levels of early-childhood illnesses in sissy boys, as well as a sociobiological theory that suggests that illness can increase the probability that a nonreproductive (i.e., homosexual) strategy will maximize an individual's "inclusive" (evolutionary) fitness.

In support of the second position is the remarkable fact that in spite of the differences Green stresses in his description of the twins, and in spite of the differences they themselves stress in their interviews (sometimes to the point of the-ladies-doth-protest-too-much), the two are also similar in remarkable ways. For example, both brothers have more heterosexual experience than most homosexuals have, and more homosexual experiences than most heterosexuals have. Both are torn between satisfying their homosexual desires (allegedly stronger in the fem twin) and worrying about social approval. Likewise, denial is strong in both twins. The butch twin apparently used the tradesman's I-only-did-it-for-the-money-and-I-didn't-do-it-at-all-when-I-could-just-take-the-money-and-get-away-with-it excuse for his homosexual escapades (apparently at the gay bar, "Numbers," according to a remark that made it into the transcript). The fem twin, on the other hand, denies the strength of his heterosexual impulses: for example, Green points out to him that he is the brother who first gets a woman pregnant (she gets an abortion). And it is the fem twin who beats his butch brother into marriage (and a second pregnancy, which miscarried).

MASS: In "Families of Origin," you relate that you once questioned Green about his study in an open forum. You asked him what "nonmasculine" boys who are not "sissies" grow up to be? "Green replied, with a wry grin, that some of them grow up to be sex researchers who study what happens to sissy boys!" You then say, "And suddenly, his reports all make sense . . ." Are *you* being wry here?

WEINRICH: Not really. My editor just didn't want me to make unsupported allegations, no matter how tame, about people who have not yet publicly told the story of their childhoods. I have never asked Green about his childhood, but I think it is reasonable to guess that he was nonmasculine and not sissy (like many pre-university boys). The culture of childhood often fails to make that distinction. So many nonmasculine boys are teased and called "sissy" when in fact they do not show overtly feminine traits of the sort that could get them referred to a study like Green's. Of course, the culture of adulthood often fails to make that distinction too.

MASS: How do you distinguish "nonmasculine" from "sissy" boys? Hasn't Green been doing this? Have other researchers?

WEINRICH: As far as I know, no one has developed for children the type of scale now popularly used with adults: a scale that differentiates psychological traits by sex and gives subjects a separate score on each. Adults can rate themselves high, for example, on both "strong" *and* "sensitive," and thereby raise *both* their total "masculinity" and "femininity" scores. That is, the test does not assume by its scoring structure that those two are opposites. I don't know anyone who uses a similar procedure with children. No one has separated "nonmasculine" from "sissy" boys—except in the sense that the sissies in many of the studies are really extreme, clear-cut cases of high femininity and low masculinity.

MASS: In the same chapter you make an extremely important point. "It is, after all, a stereotype in our culture that homosexual men are effeminate. Putting aside the scientific merits of a study like Green's, what are the philosophical consequences of conducting such a study? Why did a proposal to study sissies get submitted in the first place, and why was it selected for government funding?" What, in your opinion, are the answers to these questions?

WEINRICH: I don't know the answers to those questions. I only have hunches and the beginnings of answers. I presume that sissies were more interesting to government funding agencies than tomboys were or than prehomosexual butch boys were because it is the effeminacy that rubs most people the wrong way. Sissiness is seen as more of a problem than those other phenomena are. Why sissiness is seen as a problem is itself an unsolved puzzle. But note that sissies get it from all sides: from their peers in childhood, from teachers who try to suppress effeminacy, from many gay men and lesbian women who don't like queens, from bars that insist on "butch" behavior. . . . The list goes on and on. Closely related, of course, is the presumption that male homosexuality is more of a problem than female homosexuality — although *that* puzzle is one I address at length in *Sexual Landscapes*.

MASS: How might the Green study have been designed or redesigned to incorporate associations between male homosexuality and masculinity?

WEINRICH: Frankly, it would have been difficult. The usual 10 percent figure cited for the average level of homosexuality in the male population at large includes a lot of closet cases. The percent of those willing to say they are gay on most sorts of questionnaires is much lower, probably only 2-5 percent. Roughly half of those will turn out to have had sissy childhoods (perhaps more, if there is significant selection bias), so probably only 1-3 percent of a sample of boys will turn out to be gay and masculine enough in childhood to fall into the category suggested by your question. Given that men with a non-sissy childhood probably take years longer to come out, you're looking at a very low yield for a general population followup study.

Sissy boys were considered for prospective studies because this "yield" of adult homosexuals was expected to be higher — as indeed it was: approaching 100 percent in some studies. To do a study beginning with masculine boys, you'd have to guess, and guess well, about the traits that might presage a homosexual outcome in a masculine boy. Frankly, I'd look for subjects on the junior high school tennis, swimming, and wrestling teams — although I'll admit, wryly, that this is only one step away from a personal prejudice.

MASS: It may be just a coincidence, but now that you mention it, I'll bet I wasn't the only "team member" (as we used to say) on my high school swim team.

In this chapter you make a stimulating and I think provocative observation. You suggest that "the boys who are sissies typically lose much of that femininity in adulthood, that gender nonconformity for most gay men is a memory, not an actuality. It is a fond memory for many of them and a painful one for others, but not one that insistently intrudes upon the adult men's own behavior." What I've always wondered is how much gender nonconformity is *suppressed* by adult gay men. That is, if we weren't so internalized in our sexism and homophobia, if gender nonconformity in adulthood weren't so stigmatized and dangerous, maybe we adult gay men and lesbians would have a lot *more* gender nonconformity in our lives. What do you think about what I'm saying? Has the fading of gender nonconformity in gay and lesbian adulthood ever really been studied?

WEINRICH: I think you may be right here — and, indeed, this "fading" has not been studied (if only because prospective studies in general are so rare).

MASS: In an interview for *The Advocate* (with Stuart Timmons 3/29/88) as well as in your book, you state your belief that gay and lesbian persons *tend* to have certain talents, to gravitate towards certain occupations and activities. In the interview, you cite tennis as one example. You then go on to say that you "try to find the most important first-order approximations, even if they are stereotypes [because] most stereotypes have a grain of truth in them." What is the grain of truth in the phenomenon of gay and lesbian persons in tennis, as opposed to, say, their relative absence from (or nonvisibility in) the world of golf? An answer that occurs to me is that golf is more a phenomenon of the suburbs and countryside than of the city, where tennis is probably as common as in the suburbs. Since gay people tend to be more visible, more self-accepting — if not always openly identified as lesbian and gay — in urban than in suburban environments, and since tennis is more accessible than golf to city people, you'd *tend* to find more gay people playing tennis than golf. But this is very circumstantial. It doesn't suggest that there's anything about tennis, about the mechanical sport itself, that would attract gay people. Are you suggesting otherwise?

WEINRICH: Let me begin with a technical point. I have been led to believe that lesbianism among women golf professionals is legendary, and I don't know a thing about homosexuality on the male side.

The first-order approximation is that gay men tend to be less interested in sports than straight men are, and that lesbian women tend to be more interested in sports than straight women are. So at this level, I would predict disproportionate lesbianism in women's golf and tennis, and disproportionate heterosexuality on the men's side of those sports. The same generalization applies, to a first order approximation, to occupations.

The second-order correction, then, is to find sports that gay men disproportionately choose in comparison with straight men (such as, apparently, swimming and tennis); gay women will presumably continue to predominate simply because of their first-order interest in sports in general. Your explanation seems to be trying to make tennis a gay sport for both sexes, whereas mine only needs to "explain" the tennis part for men. And alas, despite some of my most strenuous efforts, a reason for the interest in tennis escapes me.

Likewise, there are some professions that are disproportionately "gay" for both sexes. I strongly suspect that computer programming is one of them. It is masculine-typed but not butch. The same phenomenon (but not the same explanation) seems to be true of librarians and teachers. An acquaintance suggested that these are distinctive professions in that they are ones that everyone can aspire to, in contrast to doctoring or lawyering, which are much more difficult to get into. Bright kids even from poor families can much more easily aspire to teach or deal with books.

MASS: In your chapter "Sexual Arousal: Ten Unsolved Problems," you note that "some people think that transsexualism is what happens when someone is too gender rigid to admit his or her homosexual impulses. . . . This explanation has never satisfied me for it makes a prediction that turns out to be wrong. As social options for women grow, this theory predicts that we should be seeing relatively less female-male transsexualism because fewer women would feel that they are not feminine if they are attracted to women. But in fact we've seen more f-m transsexualism, not less, as feminist beliefs have become more accepted in society."

Let me suggest an alternative view. Although feminist beliefs are currently more widespread and accepted in and for adult society, they haven't yet had much impact on childrearing. That is, the current generations of babies are still growing up with a lot of the same inculcated, sexist beliefs as their parents, even as their parents begin to espouse and attempt to practice nonsexist beliefs. It's a little like "the sexual revolution" of the '70s when liberal attitudes suddenly gave us license to practice our stammering and stuttering sexualities. In this "liberated" environment, we saw more rather than less paraphilia because the society was more tolerant of sexuality in general, but it would require (at least) several generations of this greater social tolerance before we'd see the impact on the children, where real change could be expected to begin. As *these* children become adults, we might then begin to see a substantial decrease in paraphilia.

In the case of transsexuals, the increase in f-m transsexuals might reflect their greater survival, visibility and access to research rather than a genuine or absolute increase in their numbers. Regarding the impact of feminist and nonsexist beliefs on the phenomena of trans-sexualism, it would seem to me that it would be just as pertinent to consider what has happened to the other major category of transsexual, the male-female transsexual. According to feminist theory, in a less sexist society, wouldn't you expect to see *less* m-f transsexualism for the same reasons you'd expect to see less f-m transsexualism, and might we not be seeing *more* m-f transsexualism for the same reasons I'm suggesting (above) we're seeing more f-m transsexualism?

WEINRICH: First, it is misleading (though only slightly so) to say that feminist beliefs "haven't yet had much impact on child-rearing." Whether this is so depends upon the community and the particular institutions in it. What would be accurate is to say that feminist beliefs haven't yet had much impact on *children's culture*, which modern socialization theory undervalues and underestimates. Adults seem naively to assume that children's culture can easily and straightforwardly be shaped by adults, whereas certain aspects of children's culture have clearly been shown to be remarkably continuous over time. Adults remain unaware of the extent of children's culture and of its importance.

But now for the substance of your suggestion. I am not so much making a point about the actual number of transsexuals as I am casting doubt on one common class of explanation: the notion that individuals' choices are almost always explainable as reactions to their society's social practices, rather than to factors that are best understood as coming from within the individual. Socialization theory and social constructionism are very important, but in some disciplines they are oversold. The idea that the number of transsexuals *merely* reflects the attitudes of the society that calls people transsexuals is just one example of this very common point of view. If there were no change in the number of m-f or f-m transsexuals, this fact would be just as damaging to the notion that their numbers ought to be decreasing.

MASS: In your chapter, "Meet The Gender Transpositions," you state that "in order to avoid a thorny sexological debate, I will reserve the term 'transvestites' for heterosexual cross-dressers." What is this "thorny sexological debate"?

WEINRICH: Some sex researchers want to use the terms "transvestite" and "cross-dresser" as synonyms. But by custom, and with some empirical support, another group wants to say "transvestite" instead of the thorny phrase "classic, fetishistic, heterosexual transvestite." That's all.

MASS: I understand that homosexual drag queens are different from heterosexual transvestites in that the latter are sexually, fetishistically aroused by women's clothing. But are there homosexual transvestites? That is, are there homosexual men and lesbians who are fetishistically attracted to the clothing of their sexual objects? (Might some leather and uniform fetishism sometimes be this kind of phenomenon?)

WEINRICH: Leather and uniform fetishism among men might be considered homosexual *vestism*, if you get my drift, but male fetishists usually are not crossing the gender boundary when they put on leather or uniforms. Accordingly, they should not be considered *trans*vestites. Female leather fetishists may be (it depends, of course, on the exact item worn), so the question with them would be: are they sexually aroused by the act of doing so, or are they doing so merely to arouse their partner or to make it easier for them to fantasize about a scene in which they will become aroused by the scene (and not by the actual feel of the clothes)?

MASS: Did you ever really solve "the transvestism puzzle: Fetishistic heterosexual transvestism is not rare in men, but it seems not to exist in women. Why?"

WEINRICH: Strictly speaking, no. But we can construct a solution by combining two other explanations: why transsexualism is rare, and why female-to-male transsexualism is rarer than m-f transsexualism. Ray Blanchard has shown that fetishistic male transvestism and m-f transsexualism are two different expressions of what we might presume is the same underlying mechanism. For example, some transvestites seek transsexual operations as they get older, and (according to Blanchard) all gynephilic (woman-loving) m-f trans-sexuals probably have been fetishistically aroused by cross-dress-ing. And to get the fetishism in there, you'd need to be imprinted at some point to cross-dressing stimuli, a process that is apparently facilitated by testosterone. Accordingly, to be a fetishistic hetero-sexual female transvestite, you'd need to get a very lucky dose of a lot of things that are rare for women.

MASS: One of the puzzles you address is the question of why we don't see more homosexual exhibitionists. One theory you don't consider is that male homosexual exhibitionism is simply too dan-gerous. The straight male exhibitionist risks arrest and prosecution when he exposes himself to women. The gay male exhibitionist would risk probable life-threatening physical violence in addition to arrest and prosecution if he exposed himself to other men. So per-haps male homosexual exhibitionists do exist and would be more visible, (less closeted, if you will), if the dangers weren't so ex-treme.

WEINRICH: Let me first quibble with your details, then disagree with the general thrust.

There are gay men who are not deterred by life-threatening physi-cal violence as they cruise public areas like the bushes and the parks. I don't see how exposing oneself sharply increases the proba-bility of attack; it is, after all, only one step more extreme than fondling oneself to silently indicate one's desire to another man. Gaybashers don't need excuses to bash, although they often give them.

More importantly, the point of view you summarized is one that presumes there is logic to people's sexual turn-ons. There is, but it is not so cut-and-dried. After all, a transsexual subjects him- or herself to enormous risks (complications from the operation, etc.), yet will (stereotypically, at least) stop at nothing to get what he or she wants (namely, the operation).

For example, one fellow in Maryland threatened to castrate him-self if the doctors at a well-known hospital there wouldn't approve him for the operation. When he was refused, he actually cut off one testis and then showed up in the Emergency Room. They sewed him up and sent him home while he raved that he'd cut off the other one if they didn't approve him. They didn't, and he did, and this time, as they were tut-tutting to themselves in the E.R., he threatened to cut off his penis. For an organ so laden with blood vessels, this was regarded as a much more "serious" (i.e., immediately life-threatening) threat and he was finally taken seriously (which is, of course, not to imply that they should have passed over his earlier threats).

So avoidance of danger really isn't an explanation, is it?

MASS: I guess not, but then why don't we see more overt female exhibitionism? I understand that women (like men) can be exhibitionists in all kinds of subtle and less subtle situations, but I'm talking about the exact counterpart of male exhibitionism, such as women in raincoats flashing nude bodies on busses and in elevators.

WEINRICH: One of the best hypotheses to explain male exhibitionism is to see it as a so-called "courtship disorder" — an interference with the typical courtship sequence as engaged in by men. Women play a different role in courtship (both socially and biologically), and so when something goes wrong with the process you expect different kinds of disorders to be common: not disorders of what turns you on (with erection or vaginal lubrication) but disorders of what you fall in love with (irresponsible people, for example). Women who love too much, women who fall in love with those who will hurt them — in popular culture these disorders go on and on. I suspect they do in real life, too (as opposed to popular culture).

MASS: In the conclusion of your chapter, "The Periodic-Table Model," you note that for many gay men, lust and limerence may be simultaneous impulses. It seems to me that there's a discrepancy between your thinking and that of John Money in that Money sees (or used to see, in the early 1980s) lusty attraction as a phase of limerence, which is in turn a phase of pair-bonding. By contrast, you seem to see lusty attraction and lusty sexuality as phenomena that may exist apart from limerence, and which may or may not coexist with limerence. Have I got this straight?

WEINRICH: Yes, but Money was thinking in more ultimate-cause ethological terms and I was thinking in more proximate-cause terms. In practice, some people can separate their lusty and limerent impulses. In the long run, however, many people discover that their lust has turned into limerence.

MASS: In your chapter on courtship theory, you state that "some homosexuals go through a promiscuous phase soon after coming out that they interpret as 'catching up' on what heterosexuals were doing in high school. Courtship theory suggests that this promiscuity has another function, namely, that it helps them learn at least one, maybe two sets of courtship signals and also how to apply them to other members of their sex."

So in this view the legendary "gay promiscuity" that reactionaries are always talking about is not a phenomenon of sexual compulsivity or, to use John Money's term, polyiterophilia. Even so, aren't you glossing over the reality of how dysfunctional a lot of this promiscuity is?

WEINRICH: I said "another function," not "a different function." It is always difficult, in this dichotimizing society, to remember that something as multifaceted as promiscuity serves more than one function. I'm sorry I didn't see that the word "another" is ambiguous: it can mean "a different" as well as "an additional." I meant the second.

MASS: Like C. A. Tripp and David McWhirter, you seem to be implying that gay men may need to have both phenomena going on simultaneously in their lives and that this need not represent any kind of pathology. In the McWhirter study of gay male couples, gay men who were not monogamous were actually found to be "happier," "more stable," "better adjusted" and more successful in maintaining long-term relationships than those who were monogamous. This seems roughly congruent with your own views. But doesn't this contradict the findings of Bell and Weinberg? In their study, *Homosexualities*, didn't they find just the opposite, that the "closed-coupleds" (those who were in monogamous relationships) tended to be the "happiest," "best-adjusted," etc.?

WEINRICH: I don't have an explanation for this discrepancy, except to point out that Bell and Weinberg's study was cross-sectional—a "snapshot" of a group of men at the time of their interviews, and didn't follow the men up over time to see how long their relationships lasted. The McWhirter and Mattison study, on the other hand, was of a large number of couples who had been together for long periods of time.

MASS: So where does this leave us? Beyond the certainty of some variability in patterns of gay and lesbian relationships, are there alternatives to heterosexual monogamy that are more realistic general models for gay and lesbian relationships?

WEINRICH: The characteristics of heterosexuality in general and heterosexual monogamy in particular are a function of the nature of heterosexuality (and of other things), which in turn has been affected by the role heterosexuality plays in the transmission of genes from generation to generation (and by other things). If homosexuality has different effects on this transmission, and if it has been around for more than just a few generations, then evolutionary theory predicts that what is evolutionarily natural and what turns out to be enjoyable for homosexuals may well be different from what heterosexuals have found for themselves over the generations. One of the strengths of kin selection theory within sociobiology is that, properly applied, it helps us to understand why monogamy might serve the interests of certain societies at certain times and why it might not serve those or other interests at other times.

Homosexual behavior in early humankind served many functions — quite different functions in different societies, and rarely the same functions as heterosexuality served. We need more and better research about those functions in order to understand what modern gay and lesbian relationships ought to be.

MASS: In your chapter on courtship theory, you state "if courtship signals are neither automatic nor completely learned, but rather something intermediate, then prehomosexual kids will find themselves needing to learn a language — the language of gay life — that no one around them is speaking." You then state that you don't know anyone who is really looking into these childhood questions. Should Green be doing this as part of his work? That is, do you think the Green study might have been modified to be more affirmative of "the language of gay life"?

WEINRICH: I'd rather not focus, with 20/20 hindsight, on what a researcher ought to have done, unless there was plenty of evidence available at the time that she or he should have done something differently. But let me give you a wish list.

I wish we lived in a society where we could prove with certainty, to Left and Right alike, that investigating childhood sexuality is a worthy undertaking, and that direct genital-measurement studies (plethysmography), for example, could not possibly hurt the development of the children studied. We could then prospectively study girls and boys from early childhood to young adulthood (and beyond) to address questions like the stability (or lack thereof) of sexual arousal patterns, their relationship (if any) to a family's early rearing environment, etc.

I wish we lived in a society that supported scientists in long-term research, rather than insisting that results be produced in synch with promotion- and tenure-committee review cycles.

I wish we lived in a society that put its money where its mouth was and devoted much more basic-research money to sexual questions, so that we could let a thousand Richard Greens flower and contend. Which of those Richard Greens I'd like the best I don't know yet.

MASS: In your chapter "Limerence, Lust and Bisexuality," you quote C. A. Tripp's observation that sexual attraction to men and sexual attraction to women are not opposites and are not necessarily incompatible. A number of your statements imply a real belief in bisexuality. You point out that bisexuals get flack from both straights and gays, both of whom believe that a bisexual is *really* one or the other. I've met plenty of bisexually active men, but every one, without exception, has, in fact, turned out to have what I would call a primary homosexual orientation. Using your paradigms of lust and limerence, their lusty needs are entirely satisfied by men but their limerent (as opposed to their social and cultural) needs were much less clearly being satisfied in the heterosexual marriages they were all in.

Dorothy Tennov said she didn't rule out the possibility of "bilimerence" in people, but it was a phenomenon she didn't observe. Is it a phenomenon you've observed? At this point in time, is there any substantial research demonstrating genuine bisexuality in adults (by "genuine," I mean lust *and* limerence, as opposed to mere behavior, in the same person for both sexes)?

WEINRICH: The very fact that you have to define a term — "genuine bisexuality" — to make your question clear reflects the fact that the discussion of bisexuality has yet to emerge from the early stage of arguing about definitions. I try very hard to walk that thin line between being accepting of people's self-descriptions and having a healthy skepticism about everything that people tell me. Gay men must keep in mind that the sample of bisexual men they meet is a biased one. There are indeed a great many men whose bisexuality fits the pattern you describe. That does not mean that there aren't others who call themselves gay but who are "really" bisexual "underneath it all." So what's an appropriate definition of "really bisexual"?

I strongly suspect that bisexual lust is very rare among men, and I frankly don't know how common it is among women. Tennov notwithstanding, bisexual limerence is another matter. If one takes the John Money view that lust usually precedes limerence, then Tennov's not finding any bilimerents may merely reflect that her subjects didn't distinguish their lusty phase from the first phase of limerence. I strongly suspect that some kind of bilimerence exists among women, and may very well exist among men. But suppose that some bisexuals come to me and say (as some have) that they know that they fall in love with women but get lustily aroused by men, and let's say I believe them (as I tend to do). Is that not a genuine kind of bisexuality? Why use a term like "genuine," which implies that other kinds are not genuine? After all, we'd immediately rush to our word processors to start the attack against the notion that only penis-in-vagina sex is "genuine" sex, wouldn't we?

In short, I believe in some kinds of bisexuality and disbelieve in others. Homosexuals tend to disproportionately sample the cases that come to be gay, and bisexuals tend to disproportionately learn about the ones that don't. All of us should try to overcome these biases, difficult though this may be.

MASS: In the "Discussion" of this chapter, you state that you see the gender transpositions as "partly biological and not necessarily pathological." What do you mean by "not necessarily pathological"? Are you implying that in a significant number of cases they *are* "pathological" and if so, what do you mean?

WEINRICH: I am fudging—deliberately—the question of whether some of the gender transpositions in and of themselves constitute pathology. After all, only a few years ago did we pathologize one of them (homosexuality *per se*), and who knows what the future will bring? There is quite a bit of evidence that transsexualism is, more often than not, clearly associated with other mental disorders, but what about the cases when it is not? What about those transsexuals who walk into your office with what clearly appears to be paranoia or schizophrenic thinking, who snap back into the normal mold (for better or worse) once they accept the goal of living in the role of the desired sex for a year or more? — e.g., those transsexuals who get a job, because they know it'll help them get the money and the approval for the operation. Analogously, there are many homosexuals who act self-destructively and/or crazily until someone comes along and validates their homosexual feelings — e.g., teenagers who act out or get themselves fat, gay men who continue unsafe sex because they feel at some level they deserve to get AIDS, etc.

MASS: One of the most valuable concepts your book clarifies and popularizes is that the three components of gender identity — core gender identity, gender role and sexual orientation — aren't necessarily related. For example, in your chapter on the gender transpositions, you point out that some m-f transsexuals remain sexually attracted to women after their operations, even though some "gate-keepers," as you call them, believe that true m-f transsexuals can only be attracted to men. You're pointing out that the desire for sex change may be independent of sexual orientation, that it's possible to be a m-f transsexual and still be attracted to women (preoperatively as well as postoperatively). That's absolutely fascinating and very believable. Is there any important research with transsexuals that you've become aware of since writing your book that either strengthens or complicates this perspective?

WEINRICH: Yes, some that strengthens and some that complicates. Ray Blanchard and his associates at the Clarke Institute of Psychiatry in Toronto have continued to nail down their position that m-f transsexualism comes in basically two flavors ("androphilic" and "gynephilic," or man-loving and woman-loving). This has been done in a series of clever questionnaire and plethysmographic studies. Along the way, taxonomic zeal got Blanchard to claim that female-to-male transsexualism was always woman-loving; that is, that genetic females who wanted an operation to turn them into men who loved men didn't exist. In a recent conversation, he admitted to me that this is probably not true, and that he accepts as counterevidence (1) a case he himself has published about and (2) seven cases reported by Eli Coleman and Walter Bockting.

MASS: I was similarly fascinated — and often seduced — by your efforts to distinguish what you call "soft science" from hard science. In your chapter "Soft Science, Hard Knocks," you complement historian Paul Robinson on some of his insights re Kinsey in his book, *The Modernization of Sex,* which is so highly critical of contemporary sex research. Very effectively, you expose the soft science in some of *his* arguments. But I was surprised that you didn't engage more of the specifics of his criticism, re Masters and Johnson, for instance. Why didn't you?

WEINRICH: I just wanted to write about my own stuff, that's all. I loved his book, but I wasn't writing a review of it or of its topics.

MASS: Speaking of Masters and Johnson, you seem to be quite uncritically accepting of the findings of Masters and Johnson's comparative study of the love-making techniques of homosexual and heterosexual couples. Are you similarly accepting and affirmative of their studies of "homosexual dissatisfaction" and "homosexual conversion"? Since everything you have to say about them in your book is relatively affirmative and uncritical, I'd assume, if I'd never heard or read anything about them except what's in your book, that Masters and Johnson are ethical and scrupulous researchers who are anything but homophobic. Am I being hypercritical of them? Of you?

WEINRICH: Of them, no. Of me, yes! On page 172, I rather tackily describe their study of homosexuality, only "for completeness," and I hope it is not hard to read between the lines to see how I pointedly avoid saying anything nice about it. In fact, when their homosexuality book came out, I wrote a highly critical review of it (which was never published).

MASS: Incidentally, what did you think of Masters and Johnson's designation of "ambisexuals"? Are you comfortable with this category or would you have characterized these people differently?

WEINRICH: As I recall, Masters and Johnson's "ambisexuals" are men and women who enjoy plugging holes (whether these be their own or others'), and don't seem to care much about which sex plugs them. I haven't met these subjects, so I don't know if I would characterize them differently.

MASS: In your chapter on "Plethysmography" you conclude, "Of course, the fact that these transposed transpositions are stigmatized by society at large explains some of the interest in them, but we sexologists are allowed to be interested in spite of this bias. . . . Yes, a scientist interested in the size of Jewish noses is suspicious, but a scientist interested in the genetics of Jewish migrations is not (although both scientists may have their research used by anti-Semites)." I take it from what you're saying here that despite their potential for political abuse, studies such as those by Masters and Johnson on "homosexual conversion" and those by Richard Green on "gender reinforcement therapy" are justified in the interests of sexology and science.

WEINRICH: Absolutely not! I meant in that passage to refer only to the studies I cited on plethysmography.

The question to ask about Green and Masters and Johnson is, is their work analagous to research on the sizes of Jewish noses, or is it analagous to research on the genetics of Jewish migrations? I think that Green's early (and long discontinued) studies of gender reinforcement therapy were unfortunate, and arguably crossed the line in the direction of noses. But not by much; it's a judgement call.

If Masters and Johnson were asked this question, they would tell you (judging from other answers I've heard them give) that they'd be happy to try to revert or convert a heterosexual towards homosexuality, but that no such person has ever applied to them for such therapy. They would imply thereby that they are intellectually just as interested in converting heterosexual to homosexual as the reverse. I won't call this response fatuous, although I won't complain if you do. Within their own politically sometimes very naive world view, they have not crossed the line from migrations to noses. I won't call this response fatuous, either, although I won't complain if you do.

MASS: When you say that imprinting is a likely explanation for sexual orientation or preference, aren't you saying something very similar to what Masters and Johnson say in *Homosexuality in Perspective* — that sexual orientation is a *learned* preference?

WEINRICH: Learned? Learned how? Under what conditions? And with what degree of forgetability? The learning that M and J propose for their homosexuals does not jibe with the kind of learning that goes on in imprinting.

Ethologists have shown that responses that appear to be the most highly "genetic" or "inborn" are in fact the result of a very subtle interplay between a biological predisposition to learn something and an environment that with high probability provides the thing to learn. Some birds learn in infancy an archetype that they will find sexually attractive as adults. Typically, the environment has provided an adult bird of the same species for the infant to plug into the space reserved for the archetype. So, yes, its object choice is demonstrably "learned." But it isn't learned in a way that can be converted or reverted in a couple of weeks in St. Louis!

MASS: One subject you don't discuss teleologically in your book is "pedophilia," though you do make the interesting points that there are bisexual pedophiles as well as homosexual and heterosexual pedophiles, and that pornography has reduced the incidence of child molestation in Denmark. Do you have any broader, Weinrichian thoughts about why pedophilia exists and what purposes it might be serving in the bigger picture?

WEINRICH: Temporarily blinding myself to all reality other than what I learned as a biologist, I have to point out the importance of puberty in these matters. We live in a society that claims that the ages from 9 to 16 for girls and 11 to 18 for boys are vastly different from the older ages, whereas I as a blinded biologist see only continuity. Where I see discontinuity is at puberty (9 to 12). Whatever attracts someone to a member of the same or the other sex is a matter of degree and not of kind after puberty, so I would tend to apply models to this postpubertal "pedo"philia that differ only in degree and not in kind from the models I use to explain sexual attractions among those recognized by society as sexually immature.

Adults who are sexually attracted to *pre*pubertal children would have to be explained by a theory rather different from those used to explain sexual attractions among adults.

MASS: In your chapter, "Homosexuality in Animals," you discuss how odorphobic we are in our culture " — and then some of us have the nerve to claim that odors have no effects in human beings . . ."

Is there any new or conclusive research on pheromones in human primates that you can tell us about?

WEINRICH: Alas, no—although I have assurances that such evidence will be out Real Soon Now. We'll have to wait and see.

MASS: I recently saw a documentary about the outer islands of Indonesia, which are among the most remote, unspoiled and "uncivilized" places in the world. The people who made the film were the first white men to set foot in these villages since the only other nonnative visitors in the early 1800s. In one section, they showed several homosexual transvestites (persons your book would call drag queens, even though that somehow doesn't seem an appropriate term for non-Western-civilization gay cross-dressers). As characterized in the documentary, these people had a respected, shamanistic role in their society, very much like the berdaches of Walter Williams's study, *The Spirit and The Flesh*. Since writing your book, have you become aware of any new information regarding berdache phenomena in other cultures or in our own? Are lesbians as prominent as male homosexuals in berdache phenomena, historically and today? And if not, why not?

WEINRICH: Lesbians are not as prominent in these phenomena, but we'll never know if this is so because of an underlying real difference, or if this simply reflects the fact that the explorers were always men. Speaking of which, were any of the people in that modern expedition women?

MASS: No. They were all men.

I was intrigued by your discussion of the applicability of kin selection to homosexuality. If gay people help the survival of their kin, then it's possible to see the gay and lesbian community as a phenomenon that's ultimately, unconsciously, much more interested in the survival of many disparate and sometimes conflicting kin groups than in the nongenetic, circumstantial kinship of the gay and lesbian community. Do you know what I mean?

WEINRICH: Yes, I know what you mean. I was scheduled for brunch once with a famous beat poet when he was in Cambridge for a poetry reading. I dreaded it because (this was long before I woke up to the literary world) I thought that this young scientist (me) would have nothing in common with this older poet (him), and that I would be deadly uptight having to talk with him alone for minutes and minutes. Talk about pearls before swine! He finally got me to talk about my work, and I described an early version of kin selection theory. "That's very interesting," he said, "because my heterosexual brother loves having children — lots of them — but can't support them all to the extent that he'd like to. And I'm not into having children. So I support his." I suspect that this kind of story is more common than would be suggested by the stereotype of the cocained-disco-bunny-clone.

MASS: I keep hearing that in today's world there are something like ten eligible women for every available man. If true, does this superimpose onto some bigger picture of homosexuality in our time or vice versa (that is, does homosexuality fit into some bigger picture of what's happening to the world's populations generally and that would explain this apparently diminished male to female ratio)?

WEINRICH: That depends upon the age at which you take the measurement. The late Marcia Guttengag wrote a fabulous book about the effects of sex ratio on human social structure (*Too Many Women?*; Sage Publications, Beverly Hills). She claimed that we are now at a historic high in the U.S. for the number of marriageable women per marriageable man, because our historic male predominance of immigrants has substantially abated.

There is probably no ultimate significance to this ratio, but as an independent variable it affects many things. I can't see any significance to its relationship to homosexuality, however, because the relationships proposed ("too many men" causes more male homosexuality, for example, or "too many people" causes the same) are either in the wrong direction or rely on group-selection arguments in order to make sense. Group selection (the notion that evolution sometimes proceeds to benefit the group as a whole at the cost of individuals' fitnesses in the group) is rejected by most modern evolutionary biologists.

MASS: Like John Money, you keep stressing that the eternal nature-nurture dichotomy is a false one, and the fact that so many social scientists still implicitly endorse it is unfortunate. Can you give some examples of prominent or popular social scientists (especially with regard to writings about homosexuality and sexuality) who are still bound up in this framework? Do you think this is generally true of gay historians or gay radicals or feminists, etc.?

WEINRICH: I won't name names, but I will tell you how to recognize the leopard by its spots. For example, people who tell you in the first sentences of their speeches that they are social constructionists will, as the night follows the day, have several later sentences in the form of:

"Phenomenon X *is not* caused by Y [usually something biological] but *is* in fact caused by Z [a social construction]."

or

"We now know that phenomenon X is really a social construction and *is not* a matter of Y [something more deterministic]."

Interactionists, on the other hand, say something like the following:

"Phenomenon X *is not only* caused by Y but *is also* caused by Z."

or

"We now know that phenomenon X is both a matter of social construction *and* Y [something more deterministic]."

In my opinion, it's perfectly OK for someone to concentrate on social causes of things: to say, for example, that in order to reach a complete understanding of X you must include social factors. But it's usually not OK to say that these social factors are so important that other factors can be ignored, or are objectively uninteresting. Everyone has to limit their interests somehow, and it's OK for people to say that *they* are not interested in those other factors. But let's all be upfront about our prejudices.

In December 1987 I was on a panel with a social constructionist. She took my talk about interactionism in sexual orientation research to be nothing more than a "pre-social-constructionist" view—a vague, cross-cultural sort of analysis. Pointing to obvious similarities such as the fact that essentially all human beings have two arms, reckon kinship, speak a language, etc., she actually claimed that studying differences among cultures was objectively more interesting than studying similarities! I gently reminded the audience of my example of coal and diamonds, which are objectively made *both* of the same substance (carbon) and quite different substances (ultrahard, transparent rock vs. soft black chunks). They are clearly made both of the same thing and of different things in an ineffable way that defies western dichotomizing. Of course, obvious similarities are boring to study as are obvious differences. What interactionists are saying is let's look for the subtly fascinating similarities *as well as* the differences, instead of just the latter.

What I did not say—because such linguistic oneupspersonship only comes to me the day after it is ever useful—was that my position is not pre-social-constructionist but *post* socialconstructionist!

MASS: But social constructionists, at their best, are saying something more substantial than what you're implying. They're saying that we don't have any proof of most determinist hypotheses and that, indeed, many of them are not borne out by historical analyses.

For example, in their new study, *Intimate Matters*, social contructionist historians John D'Emilio and Estelle Freedman acknowledge that same sex intimacy and desire have existed over time, but feel that anything that we today might call a "homosexual identity" is a phenomenon of capitalism and modern times. They would not acknowledge the existence of a "sexual orientation" that is somehow "primary" or in any way "predetermined" (genetic), and the bottom line of their argument is that there's too little *evidence* (proof) that such an identity or orientation has existed over time. Any comments?

WEINRICH: Historians who argue as you describe D'Emilio and Freedman arguing should pay more attention to how scientists formulate null hypotheses; too much caution spent trying to avoid false positives does not justify endorsing what is probably a false negative. Have such historians really grappled with Boswell's and Chauncey's work in *Salmagundi* ["Homosexuality: Sacrilege, Vision, Politics," Fall 1982-Winter 1983, No. 58-59]? Those I have read have not. Have they really fairmindedly tried to find *personality traits* that are objectively characterizable and enduring, but which are not picked out and enshrined by many cultures? Not as far as I know. Have they subjected the cross-cultural evidence to careful scrutiny, in order to distinguish patterns of variability in the cultures themselves from apparent variability in the anthropologists/reporters' theoretical perspectives? The more you learn about the *details* of various cultural arrangements, the more the *range* of human behavior seems standard. That one observer stressed the cross-dressing while another saw only the homosexual behavior and a third was fascinated with spiritual leadership while a fourth stressed intergenerational requirements should not blind us to the task of finding underlying similarities if they exist. This is so, even if there isn't enough evidence — *yet!* — to "prove" some similarity.

MASS: I was really impressed with your last chapter's section on Responsible Sexual Freedom. I would agree with you that in her discussion of the baths controversy in her essay on "The Castro" (from her book, *Cities on a Hill*), there is a failure to understand, as you put it, how "being up front about sex got confused with being irresponsible about it . . . The point of view Fitzgerald didn't describe in enough detail is the one that says that instead of blaming *sex* for AIDS, one should blame *particular sex practices.*" I think this criticism is likewise applicable to Randy Shilts's book, *And The Band Played On*, and Larry Kramer's play, *The Normal Heart*. Any comments?

WEINRICH: I have not seen nor read the play, and I have not read enough of the book (nor seen the miniseries!) to comment intelligently.

MASS: In summing up, you say that "the best reason for sex-educating your children — and everyone else's children — is the same as the best reason for doing sex research. *Preventing people from doing so is living a lie.*" Generally speaking, I agree, and I know exactly what you mean here. Since these are your closing thoughts, however, I wish you'd added a proviso or three about the serious potential for abuse of sex education and sex research. Or do you feel you've done that adequately elsewhere?

WEINRICH: Let me be insufferably superior for a moment. I went to a college that had the honor system, and even before then I had never heard my parents lie, even about trivial matters like whether I was young enough to get a kids' discount. I am telling the truth (!) when I say that I have only told a few little white lies in my life, and that I cheated on a few exams in high school and none at all in college. And let me make it clear (especially to some people out there who can't seem to believe that a biologist like me ever believes that anything is environmentally determined) that I see no reason to invoke genes to explain my honest upbringing.

Call me old-fashioned, call me insufferably superior, but that's just the kind of boy I am. I have not learned, on a gut level, the value of a lie, and I only recently learned the necessity for telling a "careful truth" (as Sargeant Foley on *Mary Hartman, Mary Hartman* once put it).

Accordingly, it just doesn't come naturally to me to imagine that badness could possibly come from the truth. I know it can, and that I should enlarge the scope of my imagination, if only for my own protection. And so I am fascinated, and sometimes stunned, when people assume that things (as I characterize them in the conclusion of my book) as "spectacular, . . . astonishing, to be lied about and denied regularly.

I did not omit discussion of the ways in which sex research can be misused. I did sometimes tone down specific examples of it, because I am uncomfortable with direct attacks (unless I am responding to direct attacks on myself), and because I have seen that some early offenders have come around and become quite creditable when their own inquiring minds led them to experiments that turned out differently than they had anticipated. (Such converts are, incidentally, extremely useful, both substantively and tactically.) Of course, I would prefer that everybody got things right the first time. Of course, I would have preferred that one plethysmographer hadn't started out by trying to prove that his aversion therapy for homosexuality really worked. Of course, I would have preferred that one gender researcher who showed that homosexuality often shows its roots in early childhood had not first tried to therapize sissy boys into gender conformity. I think it's awful that the femininity of one of the boys, whose femininity had overtly disappeared in therapy, popped up in drawings his mother found under his mattress: drawings of beautiful women, torn in half and hidden by the boy.

But that plethysmographer's recent research has shown that Paul Cameron's bizarre fantasies about the "homosexual" molestation of children are deeply flawed and untenable, and that research was done in the most respected scientific way—empirically. And that gender researcher often uses such horrifying examples in his talk, to illustrate the dangers of the kind of therapy he once espoused. Given our limited resources, I think it is far better to spend our time attacking (and defending ourselves against) our remaining enemies. In a political context in which the truth matters, even though truth and power are not the same thing, it is, after all, the truth that set some of them free.

Homosexual As Acts or Persons

A Conversation with John De Cecco

John P. De Cecco, Ph.D., is Professor of Psychology and Human Sexuality and a member of the American Psychological Association, the International Academy of Sex Researchers, the Gay Academic Union, and the American College of Sexologists. Since 1975, he has been Director of the Center for Research and Education in Sexuality (CERES) at San Francisco State University. In 1978 Professor De Cecco became Senior Editor of the *Journal of Homosexuality* and is currently Series Editor of the *Journal*'s research monograph series on homosexuality.

MASS: In your recent interview for *Paidika, The Journal of Pedophilia* (Winter 1988), you reflect that "Medicine is embarrassingly involved with sexuality. I think that at one point it was an adventure, a huge expansion of institutional power; I think today it's terribly embarrassed and would like to get out of the business if it could." The "medicine" you're referring to here is mostly psychiatry, is it not? And if so, do you think psychiatry *really* wants to get out of the business of sexuality, especially homosexuality? I get less of a sense of medicine/psychiatry *wanting* to get out of the business of sexuality/homosexuality than of a tactical retrenchment — to some extent, at this moment in time — for largely political reasons. As Ronald Bayer, author of *Homosexuality and American Psychiatry: The Politics of Diagnosis*, concludes in his "Afterward to the 1987 Edition" (Princeton University Press):

> Organized psychiatry having officially withdrawn at this moment from its commitment to a medical perspective on homosexuality, what remains uncertain is the form that the social response to homosexuality may take in the next years as social

distress rises with the mounting toll taken by the AIDS epidemic.

I would say that Bayer is simply revealing his own, negatively neutral (and therefore homophobic) biases with such phraseology. Otherwise, at the very least, he would have put the word "medical" in quotations here. But as you and I have discussed in our correspondence as well as in print (see the next question), the most recent work of pyschiatrists like Richard Green is anything but progressive, and certainly doesn't make a case for medicine and psychiatry getting out of the business of sexuality and homosexuality.

Is there some conflict in your positions? That is, do you believe on the one hand that medicine wants to get out of the business of sexuality, but on the other that it's actually doing just the opposite? Also, do you think I've misread Bayer?

DE CECCO: The conflict is not mine but that waged by medicine against its wayward child, psychiatry. By "medicine" I refer to our cathedrals of knowledge, the medical schools, which still pretend that obstetrics, gynecology and pediatrics are all their students need to learn about sex. Sex beyond reproduction and the care of the newborn, in their judgment, is not science and therefore not medicine. They will include a little urology and proctology, mostly to insure that penises properly erect and ejaculate in the performance of the "primal," procreative act upon which, according to St. Thomas Aquinas, the protectors of the "right-to-life" and the Moneyesque sexologists, mankind's fortunes ultimately come to rest.

Medical science, which has replaced the sacerdotal cassock with the white laboratory coat, preaches theories of sexuality that St. Thomas Aquinas would call plagiarism. It teaches that sex outside of reproduction is so unthinkable that it best be domiciled in psychiatry, whose special medical mission is to deal with those who depart from the biologic norm by talking and/or drugging them back into the fold of the civilized and married. As you keenly observe, psychiatry, in oedipal rivalry with its parent discipline, wants to hold on to the business of sex because after "relationships," sex may be its most profitable line. People who have enough leisure time to worry about "sexual dysfunctions" (in the current jargon) are invariably those who have the money to pay stiff consulting fees. By contrast, those with déclassé ailments, such as schizophrenia and paranoia, are generally poor.

Throughout its history psychiatry has been on a collision course with most of medicine. This conflict stems from the unshakeable but usually unspoken conviction of the medicalists that there is *real* medical science which can treat *real* ailments with the promise of physical immortality. The medicalists regard psychiatry as a bastard of medicine and as witchcraft — particularly in its most ethereal form, psychoanalysis — which deals with "the mind," an entity that hovers between Descartes' pineal gland and Jung's archetypes.

Within some departments of psychiatry there exist cells or soviets called "sexology" or "human sexuality" programs, some of which function as faceless units. Several are headed by psychiatrists but they are usually staffed by clinical psychologists with humble Ph.D.s who often call themselves "medical psychologists." Because they lack medical degrees, the latter often outdoctor the M.D.s in attributing all unChristian sexual behavior and desire to hormonal or brain abnormality. As vassals of the medical establishment — for tenure, promotions, research funding and a state of academic grace known as *scholarly recognition* — medical psychologists must periodically renew their oath of fealty to it.

Medical schools have tolerated but hardly relished sexology programs and they sink them at the first budgetary opportunity or they hurry tenured professors like Money into retirement. These programs try to mask or sanitize their presence by such misleading, pseudoscientific or innocuous appellations as "psychohormonal unit" or "andrology clinic" or "department of family practice and community medicine." For example, a few years ago, major medical schools axed their sex-change programs for transsexuals when the market in people requesting that their genitalia be re-sculpted shrank more rapidly than the testicles of hormonally treated males in their quest to discover the mysteries of femininity. The other reason was the fear of litigation by those who post-operatively began to miss the ol' cock or clit and found out that life as either sex has its own sweet frustrations.

As medicine has attempted to become pure biological science, psychiatry's existence and the bastard's bastard offspring, sexology, have become intolerable embarrassments. The *coup de grace* was delivered in 1973 when the psychiatric profession *voted* (mind you), in a moment of unscientific pique, whether or not homosexuality was a disease. The fact that psychiatry was not a science and, indeed, that sex, as Foucault was to show, is medical politics, was broadcast to the world. What had been a thorn in the side of medicine, which was so energetically trying to project the image of hard, no-nonsense science in order to attract more and more federal research funding, then became a metastasized ulcer that had to be excised (the surgical metaphor is most apt since surgeons rule the medical establishment).

The institutional medical response to this exceptional moment of professional honesty was twofold. Psychiatry, never to be forgiven for the kind of damage it has visited upon the parent discipline, has been gradually converted by medical schools into a branch of pharmacology and neuroscience, with the intention of replacing psychotherapeutic voodoo with the magic of drugs (the witch doctors' potions) and brain surgery. Sexology, as absorbed by psychiatry, also has had to become more physical, so that sexual disorders psychoanalysts once attributed to maternal smothering, paternal neglect or arrested development were now recast as disorders of sex hormones and malformed "sex centers" in the sub-cortical brain, processes and locales clearly outside the realm of thought and will but well within the domain of "medical science."

Ronald Bayer, if he had recalled Machiavelli, would have known that in the art of politics (as in every phony negotiation), behind apparent concession (which must appear an irreparable loss to the sacrificing party at the time it occurs), there is a gain that can be surreptitiously revealed after the gullible "winning side" is convinced of victory. Psychiatry was not depathologizing homosexuality. It was merely supplanting the psychoanalytic theory that it was a disorder of love—an erroneous "object choice"—with the neuroendocrinological theory that it was a "gender disorder." It was also dethroning the old fogey psychoanalysts against whom younger psychiatrists, eager to spread their own scientific truth, had long harbored aggressive, hostile wishes, unchecked by superego surveillance.

Some of the very people who were arguing with compassion and selfless altruism for the declassification of homosexuality as a pathology, such as John Money, Ph.D., and Richard Green, M.D., were the very same players who behind the political scene were sponsoring what may be generously called "research" which would provide the physical basis for new listings of "gender disorders." An astute Machiavellian could even imagine them urging wavering psychiatrists about to cast their ballots for immutable scientific truth to go along with declassification, promising that when the *bottom line* was written, much was to be gained and little lost in money and clients. Money and Green, who appeared as the intrepid liberal allies of the gay psychiatrists and psychologists, now have blossomed forth with books that frankly view homosexuality as a biological abnormality. Green, in his *"Sissy Boy" Syndrome* book, even adds the old psychoanalytic theories so that he has not conceded a thing. Both allow that *some* sissies are capable of genuine monogamous love, just like straights, and *for that reason* should not be listed as lovesick; only gendersick. Bayer's comment is not homophobic, but for a student of medical politics, it betrays a shocking naiveté.

MASS: I was really fascinated by the "Adversaria" exchanges you sent me from the *Journal of Sex Research* (February 1987). They begin with your commentary, entitled "Homosexuality's Brief Recovery: From Sickness To Health and Back Again," which is a powerful critique of the psychohormonal surveys of Heino Meyer-Bahlburg and the longitudinal studies of Richard Green. Their work, you argue, amounts to a repathologization of homosexuality. Meyer-Bahlburg, at least, responds and that response is printed in the Adversaria. But there's no printed response from Green. Why is that?

DE CECCO: I was told that he was busy studying for his bar exams, but I don't believe that was the only reason because of an incident that occurred after *"The Sissy Boy" Syndrome* was published. When his appearance on the local ABC channel in San Francisco was being arranged so that he could promote his book, I was invited to join him because of my reviews in the San Francisco Sunday *Examiner-Chronicle* and the *Advocate.* When he was informed that I was also to appear, I was told by the show's producer that he threatened to cancel, an opportunity I would have welcomed since there was much I could expose about the book that hardly required his appearance. Since he was the star, however, I was out. In my place, they scraped up a "gay" clinical psychologist who wasn't announced as gay and who is in fact in and out of the closet about as often as one visits a rest room. The firmness of Dr. Gay Psychologist's "unshakeable conviction" (which can be decoded as "I'm totally ignorant of the research but therefore I'm free to believe") that people are "born gay" shook even Green. (Green, by now, was presenting himself as "eclectic" and "open" to *all* pathological theories of homosexuality, including his own creation that sissy boys are often exceptionally beautiful babies whose mothers gaze at them too much.) As the proverbial "sissy boy," I thought I showed more macho than Green, but not in every interpretation. Clint Eastwood has taught the nation that a macho man is a man of few words, mostly monosyllabic. Green carried that one step further: he wrote nothing at all.

It's always difficult to decipher the motives of a person whose writings appear to be filled with contradictions. I have described how he had vigorously argued for the depathologizing of homosexuality at the same time that he had been engaged in biomedical research to prove that it was pathological in origin. As a graduate of Yale Law School, he has now decided to defend sexual liberty. Yet the theories of homosexuality and gender that he endorses are patently homophobic and sexist. As Money's student, he shunned psychoanalytic theory, but later, as the protégé and colleague of psychoanalyst Robert Stoller, he subscribed to it. While he did not have the time to prepare a response to what was a serious challenge to his work, he did continue his editorship of *Archives*.

Everyone has the right to change her or his mind, but in Green's case, it looks as if he never made his up. Therefore, any challenge to a position he takes at any given moment in time stands to expose his underlying confusion. By remaining silent and avoiding all challenges he will have the support of sexologists, like Timothy Perper (the implacably "scientific" girl-boy watcher), who believe that they are truth-seekers, dispassionately guided by The Scientific Method, and the guardians of what Money recently called "the immutable and irreducible" sex differences. In that pontifical posture, they place themselves above controversy. After all, true sexologists don't argue. Science is not disputation or personal vendetta, as was demonstrated so convincingly in the scramble between Gallo and Montaigner for the title of Father of HIV.

People in my position who challenge their fellow sexologists are not playing by the club rules, which allow the faggots and dykes to join, even occasionally to become president, to share the travel budgets, receive awards and achieve *true scholarly recognition*, but with the tacit proviso that they know their place as normalized freaks.

MASS: In my "interview" with him in 1987 for *Christopher Street* (issue 110), Richard Green answered what I regard as the most important of my questions as follows:

> Mass: You were one of the principal supporters of the 1973-74 American Psychiatric Association declassification of homosexuality as a mental disorder. In the gay community, you are less widely known as a principal architect of a more recently characterized — in the third edition of the Diagnostic and Statistical Manual of Mental Disorders (DSM-III) — "psychosexual disorder" called the "gender-identity disorder of childhood." Since most reputable studies, yours included, concur that gender nonconformity in early childhood is the strongest predictor of homosexuality in adults, is psychiatry wittingly or unwittingly in the process of trying to redefine homosexuality as a mental disorder of gender identity in childhood? In other words, DSM-III might permit most adult homosexuals to be considered "normal," but it would be classifying a significant percentage of those same persons, during their childhoods, as mentally disordered. Is this correct?

> Green: The nuclear component of the gender identity disorder of childhood is the child's strong wish to be the other sex. Cross-gender behaviors (e.g., preferential cross-dressing, male or female role-playing) reflect that painful discontent. To the extent that children mature beyond that early pain, they do not have a mental disorder, be they heterosexual or homosexual. To the extent that they retain it, they have a diagnosis: transsexualism.

Do you think this is a satisfactory answer?

DE CECCO: Well, at least you got an answer. But are we much better off? I suspect the "pain" he refers to is his rather than the child's. It is generally true that men who have spent their boyhood and adult years packaging every gesture, spoken word and thought, so that it all neatly fits the current version of machoism, evince acute *pain* when they see other men cooking, "camping" or dressed as drag queens. I think one study showed that their penises and testicles shrivelled.

Middle class parents who want their children to be able to some-day know the familial joys of raising their own children — in a heav-ily mortgaged home and paying spiraling costs for shoddy educa-tion — can, with the assistance of psychiatrists such as Green, convince the boy who prefers dolls to trucks that the *pain* is his, not theirs. Has it ever occurred to Green or the mortified parents that the imaginative child, girl or boy, can invent more life around a doll than a truck?

Green's reference to "nuclear component" is to remind you that you are now in the Holy Temple of Science. What indeed could be more scientific or macho than *nuclear*, as in fission, fusion, and bombs? What could be freer of moral or political nuance? As Money's disciple, Green gave an answer that merely echoes that Moneyesque split between gender identity (which sex the person *feels* he or she really is) and that person's actual biological sex and social behavior. It is a bit of 19th century nonsense invented by Ulrichs and Hirschfeld which Money now offers as his claim to apotheosis. As is so often the case in psychiatry, the diagnosis cre-ates the disease which in turn creates its sufferers — people always looking for ways to explain their boredom and failures in ways that relieve them from any responsibility. It is Moneyesque post-En-lightenment dogma that what one feels to be the truth or fantasizes about the self is more intimately who that person is than what that person actually does. It is a doctrine that is ultimately destructive of moral responsibility which weighs the consequences of acts. It is acts that make biography and history and actions speak louder than words.

MASS: In your Adversaria statement, you point out that while gay rights advocates succeeded in getting American psychiatry to dis-continue its classification of homosexuality as a *mental* disorder, whether or not homosexuality was a *biological* disorder went unaddressed. As you put it, "An unforeseen consequence of not also opposing the classification of homosexuality as a biological disorder, we now discover, is that the door has been left open to its being treated as a physical abnormality."

In his response to your statement, Meyer-Bahlburg presents the example of left-handedness.

> It is not listed as a mental disorder . . . although scores of neurodevelopmental researchers are looking for pre- and perinatal brain "abnormalities" that might explain why a minority of people develops left-handedness. It seems unlikely that left-handedness will enter a future version of the DSM, even if a partially biological etiology should become established. Left-handedness is a particularly pertinent example because left-handers share with homosexuals a minority status. Historically, also, left-handedness was seen as a negative characteristic and, until about the middle of this century, much pressure was exerted to forcefully change left-handedness in children. [Ed. note: Also like homosexuals, lefthanders have, historically, been tortured, murdered and otherwise persecuted for being who they were.] I conclude from these examples that there is no "inevitable" path from findings of some physiologic, including endocrine, abnormality affecting a certain aspect of behavior to the classification of such behavior as a "mental disorder."

First, did you notice the absence of quotations around the word abnormality in this last paragraph (in contrast to the use of quotations for this word in the preceding paragraph, with regard to left-handedness)? Conceding that this may be nit-picking, I note that you did not explicitly address Meyer-Bahlberg's example of left-handedness in your rejoinder. Would you care to do so now? That is, what's wrong with the analogy between homosexuality and left-handedness?

DE CECCO: You don't think for a moment that Meyer-Bahlburg doesn't believe that being queer is abnormal, do you? The analogy of left-handedness is tiresomely invoked by his whole biomedical crowd to convince the naive that inquiry into the physical causes of homosexuality is motivated by nothing more than pure, sublimely scientific curiosity. However, whenever the topics selected for investigation are forms of stigmatized behavior, the history of science demonstrates that research is ultimately used to justify present oppression of a group or even to eradicate the abominable behavior or its practitioners or both. As you pointed out, this was indeed true for the left-handed.

Meyer-Bahlburg claims that research on left-handedness continues with great gusto. Well, I haven't seen six books on its causes this year, but there will be at least that many volumes on the causes of homosexuality published in 1988. The research on black IQs has disappeared with the research funding once it was clear that it was intended to provide black children inferior education. Research on hysteria in women became less scientific once we realized that it was intended to keep women securely domiciled and out of board meetings and law offices. Tragically, the Nazi eugenic studies which were to provide the scientific knowledge to keep the Aryans pure and to exterminate Jews, who were perplexingly bright, sophisticated and successful for a people who belonged to an inferior race, could not be stopped in time to save millions of victims. Although biomedical research into the causes of homosexuality is a methodological shambles, it continues even though researchers like Meyer-Bahlburg have been saying for years that it is going nowhere but is still "promising." For what? For faggot and dyke extinction.

Why not turn a nonpromising inquiry into a perfectly neutral investigation of the biomedical causes of monogamy, a "condition" which requires a monumental propping-up by partners, church, government and the media just to make it possible for it to limp its way to the end of the 20th century. Incidentally, the word for *left* in Latin is *sinister*, which just happens to mean evil, exactly what they believe homosexuality to be in the depths of their compassionate hearts.

MASS: The concluding piece of these Adversaria is by Timothy Perper, Associate Editor of the *Journal of Sex Research*, and is called "Enough is Enough: Reflections on the Views of De Cecco and Meyer-Bahlburg." In it, you are characterized as "the unilateral voice of social determinism" and Meyer-Bahlburg as "epitomizing the view that biology alone can shape behavior." In your intelligently reasoned, politically conscious and often impassioned belief that the constant redefinition of feminine and masculine metaphors will "lead to the erosion of such nominal categories as 'heterosexuals' or 'homosexuals,'" is this in fact what you've become—a social determinist or, in today's parlance, a social constructionist?

DE CECCO: Timothy Perper does not want to be distracted from the wordless world of the singles' bar, where he can endlessly watch female and male yuppies cruise each other while he counts the number of eye contacts, leg spreadings, shrill laughs and ass, leg, crotch and tit glances that are exchanged. He can then compare such behaviors with the mating dances of subhuman species and convince himself that what looks like an interest in pure fucking-for-fucking's-sake is indelibly marked by an inescapable reproductive heritage. He has never tried to replicate his studies in lesbian or gay bars, where, if discovered, someone might think he was queer. Also, the glint of progeny is conspicuously absent from the eyes of denizens of lesbian and gay bars. I'm sure he would prefer not to trouble his tidy, empirical brain with any conception of sexuality beyond the biological or—to include the seventies vogue—sociobiological. Even a little challenge to the sexological establishment is too much for the science-priests. After all, my article was the only time I know that the APA's partial declassifying of homosexuality as pathology was exposed as a political sham.

Since I have only one voice, any specific use of it has to be "unilateral" or at least unison. In a sociobiological brain-washed mind like Perper's, the two "determinisms" do not have equal status. For Perper, to be called a biological determinist is much better than to be labeled a social determinist. Biology is seen as a "hard" science (it's actually considered a soft science by physicists) and what he calls the "social" comprises the "soft" sciences—leaving unspecified the effete, sissy humanities such as history, philosophy, literature, religion and the arts (which Money, the sexological philistine, calls "spookology").

It's true that I have temperamentally preferred the soft to the hard areas of human knowledge because I think it is in the former that I find some hope of discovering the range of humankind's imagination, weirdness, idealism, treachery, ingenuity and so on. Actually, *soft*, in this application, turns out to be much more variegated and complex than *hard*, just as the strength in femininity is more subtle and complexly interwoven with other personal attributes than crude masculine aggression. But "soft" is not for steely macho minds that count the number of times eyes focus on crotches and cleavages and still don't know that the mating instinct is not what drives yuppies to singles' bars.

Biology makes its contribution to sexuality through the body which, with greater or lesser charity, it bequeathes to each of us. No culture I know has been without its corporeal standards of beauty and power. In the sexual realm, whether you are tall or short, endomorphic or ectomorphic, have blue or brown eyes is responsible for what university students in singles' bars now call "chemistry" — sexual and personal attraction.

Since no one seems to be able anymore to resist a noun for an adjective in the *ist* game, I would call myself an "interactionist": neither culture alone nor biology alone determines the shape of our preferences or experiences. However, it is not rash to assume that most people grow beyond initial childhood tastes and behaviors. Otherwise, most of us would still be eating pablum and strained fruit. Now that I think of it, sex as presented by Money, Perper and Green really never gets beyond the bland consistency of boiled cream of wheat. Preferences as attributes of individuals are very much the result of personal experiences as bounded by culture.

MASS: Doesn't the social constructionist position, in its purest form, deliver us right back into the hands of psychiatrists like Green and sex researchers like Masters and Johnson who believe that abnormal — or variant, if we insist — social learning is responsible for much if not all homosexuality?

DE CECCO: In its purest form, social constructionism, as represented by both Michel Foucault and Jeffrey Weeks, is as ideological as biological determinism. To assert that sexuality is merely historical or social invention leaves out both biological endowment and what individuals contribute to their own sexuality over a lifetime. We are born with the biological capacity to engage in sexual acts with either sex, and that hardly seems unique to particular historical periods or cultures. Although each culture has its own standards of who is attractive, the fact is that these standards require a body that most people regard as a biological given, except perhaps in Beverly Hills, where bodies are reconstructed as if they consisted of papier mache.

Alone, neither social constructionism nor biological determinism respects individual liberty. Alone, each becomes a tyrannous ideology that depicts individuals as clay, molded entirely by external or internal forces. Although individuals of Money's stripe would reduce individuals to sexual robots, the fact is that human beings do have motives and intentions that direct behavior toward or away from particular goals. To their credit, social constructionists such as Foucault and Weeks and feminists such as Vance and Millet have made pellucid that sex is politics whether in religious, legal or scientific drag.

MASS: In the Adversaria, you make this statement: "As symbols for evolving, complex social phenomena, it will not be possible in the foreseeable future, given the present status of the neurosciences, to determine their ['masculinity' and 'femininity'] "true" relationship to biology and perhaps forever impossible to connect causally to such an amorphous, rapidly evolving phenomenon as human sexuality." When you say "given the present status of the neurosciences" and "perhaps forever impossible," aren't you leaving the back door open, as it were, to the possibility of establishing the very relationships to biology you're otherwise so dubious about?

DE CECCO: Those remarks were an act of charity for particular biomedical colleagues in our sexuality program, who I now realize are convinced that all dykes and fags are braindamaged. As Ruth Doell (Biology — and she is a rare exception) and Helen Longino (Philosophy) have argued, as soon as individual motives and intentions enter the picture, there is no possibility of predicting adult behavior from prenatal or childhood states. Between some prior biological neural condition and the manifestation of particular behavior so many things have occurred in the individual's life that there is no way to establish a direct route between the two. Individuality is not something that science in either its natural or social forms can explain or predict. So determinists, unhappy in the realization that sexual behavior is beyond the control of medicine or society, in fact beyond any *control,* conveniently remove the biggest fly in their theoretical ointments by pretending that people qua individuals do not exist. Skinner called them "black boxes" and we would all be in boxes, munching on scientifically dispensed food pellets if he had managed a cabinet post in the Reagan administration.

MASS: You are essentially a social constructionist in the sense that you believe, in essence, that there's no such universal as "a homosexual" or "being gay." At the same time, you're urging that future research on homosexuality move away from the traditional, politically motivated comparing of similarities between homosexuals and heterosexuals towards greater acknowledgment and exploration of difference. That is, (from the *Paidika* interview): "I think the idea of the gay identity limits the study of homosexuality . . . Much research that came to me . . . was an effort to prove that homosexuals were "normal," but by criteria applied to heterosexual society, and there was nothing unique to homosexuality itself . . . If inquiry into homosexuality is to be open, we must resist ideology, we must resist the normalization as well as the pathologization."

Do you see any conflict in these positions—that is, between not really believing in a gay identity and urging that future research on homosexuals be more open to differences between homosexuals and heterosexuals?

DE CECCO: It would be more accurate to say that I am not an essentialist, since I am uncomfortable with the political agendas of both the biomedicalists and the social constructionists. The differences are not between "heterosexuals" and "homosexuals," which at best are political abstractions. What I fear is the normalization of homosexual behavior, which otherwise stands as a challenge to heterosexualism—the belief that all sexual behavior should be procreative or at least not preclude the possibility of babymaking.

Now that the republic has returned to religion and robber baron economics, that normalization proceeds unabated. Gay Liberation at the close of the eighties now proclaims that gay people can combine love with sex, they can "marry" their own kind (even in a gay ceremony in a gay Christian church), can have their own life-time mortgages and can even have and raise children. They can pay for all this because they can have and are "mature" enough to keep jobs, pay taxes, perform civic duties and so on. Gay people, so eager to assert in the seventies that gay was good, in the eighties have become "guppies" — gay yuppies.

What was lost in this process of claiming special human status and becoming house dykes and faggots was respect for forms of homosexual behavior and relationships that stood as critiques of heterosexual monogamy: engaging in sex only for its own pleasure; learning to enjoy several partners, including one-night stands; enjoying the independence of living alone; living alone yet not being lonely; centering one's life around something other than one's home, a lover and possessions; ending relationships without suicide or murder; maintaining them, if you had to have them, with ample autonomy for both partners; living *without* children, including surrogates such as pets, plants, and even a ceramic kiln; devoting time to a variety of books, ideas, people; living abroad; and so on. These are not differences between heterosexuals and homosexuals. Yet they are not options usually open to devotees of romantic bliss and the nuclear family.

MASS: Returning to the question of future research on same sex intimacy, in an interview for *Radical History Review* (Winter '88), historian Martin Duberman made this observation: "A lot of interesting new material on being gay is coming through a historical prism. It's no longer being argued in terms of psychology. All the interesting questions of [sexual] identity are [now] being approached through historical documentation." I take it you'd pretty much agree.

DE CECCO: I am not sure what Martin means by the words "being gay," but among the materials that are sent to me as editor of the *Journal of Homosexuality*, the historical articles, along with the anthropological, seem to be the most revealing of the many political and cultural contexts within which homosexual behavior has occurred, how it was socially regarded, how it was regulated and how it was associated with shifting gender boundaries. In addition, the biographical, literary and philosophical articles are documenting the variety of ways homosexual behavior has been a part of individual lives. The fact that the biomedical view or even the idea of gay identity are products of recent history rather than universal truths will become more convincing as more of these articles are published.

MASS: In the *Journal of Homosexuality* ("Controversy Over the Bisexual and Homosexual Identities," Winter '84), Lilian Faderman discusses "The New 'Gay' Lesbians." Faderman believes that some lesbians choose their sexual orientation, that their sexual preference is less often a matter of an involuntary sexual object attraction that has been present since earliest childhood than of political choices. This is in marked contrast to how most gay men perceive their sexual orientation. Have you come across any new research on lesbian identities that's tending to confirm, contradict or otherwise complicate Faderman's observations?

DE CECCO: Isn't Faderman merely saying that women in our culture, whether heterosexual or homosexual, prefer to establish an emotional bond before they add sex? And isn't your question merely saying that most men do the reverse—try to build an emotional bond upon sexual attraction? That most gay men qua males appear to be driven by sex (since lust is supposed to drive all males)? That lesbians qua females are motivated by love rather than driven by sex? Of course, these are gross stereotypes and like any stereotypes they begin to crumble under the scrutiny of individual lives. It is possible to generalize that women are driven by romance and men by sex, but I've seen the reverse of this so often with male romantics and female viragos that I think such generalizations will always end up in the trash can. Lesbian publications like *Off Our Backs* enjoy popularity because they describe women lusting after women, just as men do. Don Clark, the grandfather of gay clinical psychology, has been writing about gay male romance even longer. Before all that, Tennessee Williams showed that women could lust after men.

MASS: In the *Paidika* interview you mention "lesbian pedophilia." Is there any literature or other confirmation of the existence of this phenomenon?

DE CECCO: Of course, there is nothing new under the sun. Only if we knew more about ancient harems and medieval convents. Three lesbian communes in California once published a newsletter boldly called *Kinder Kunt*, which advocated woman-girl love and sex. I've never seen the publication, but I understand it folded when the communes began to argue bitterly over the permissible crossing of sexual boundaries; e.g., that between mother and her own daughter, and prepubescence and pubescence. Marjan Saxe of The Netherlands is researching such relationships for *Paidika*, so we should learn more in a year or two.

MASS: You discuss feminist opposition to pedophilia and theorize that many of these persons are stereotyping all men as aggressive and exploitative in much the same way women have been stereotyped as weak and subservient. You surmise that most feminists can't conceive of men in nurturant roles. I've had a similar impression. For example, in her guide to childrearing, *Growing Up Free*, former *Ms*. editor Letty Cottin Pogrebin draws a sharp line between encouraging parents to nurture their lesbian and gay children and endorsing any kind of intergenerational, sexual relationships. In her view, as in that of most prominent gay and lesbian community observers, such relationships cannot be other than exploitative. *Growing Up Free* is nearly ten years old. Even so, I don't think we're wrong to generalize about feminist views of pedophilia any more than we're wrong to generalize about those of lesbians and gay men. They remain overwhelmingly negative and disapproving. But there are a few gay male writers and spokespersons who aren't pedophiles who believe and who have publicly stated their belief that pedophile relationships (like S-M relationships) suffer from misunderstanding and discrimination. Are there likewise feminists who are more open-minded on this subject and who have been publicly so?

DE CECCO: Well, yes. Marjan is one and Gayle Rubin, Pat Califia, Carole Vance and Susan Bright are others. Even Germaine Greer and other seasoned feminists have condemned the wave of hysteria over child abuse that makes it impossible for a teacher to embrace a crying child or a parent to kiss a pubescent son or daughter.

MASS: In the same interview, you generalize that "from what I know of pedophile relationships, they are supremely nurturant, in a way that should make most parents crumble with shame. The children respond so well to the care in pedophile relationships because they are getting what they want, their desires and their needs are getting met. The fact that these relationships are seen as only sexual is a way of hiding the inadequacies of biological parents."

What is the basis of your knowledge here? Beyond anecdotal reports and individual testimony, has there ever been any even remotely objective research on pedophilia? Beyond the theoretical benefits you so persuasively articulate, do we actually know that many of these relationships *are* "good" for these children?

Also, when you speak of "pedophile relationships," are you talking about children of all ages? In your view, I would imagine, "pedophile," like "homosexual," "gay" and "lesbian," will resist rigid classification. Even so, is there anything like a provisional definition of pedophile or pedophilia or pedophile relationship that you're comfortable with? And if there is such a working definition(s), are there comparable names and definitions for the youngsters in such relationships?

DE CECCO: Yes, there is an increasing number of sources. One is the study by Theo Sandfort in The Netherlands. He interviewed twenty-five adolescent boys who were having relationships with adult men. The boys apparently cherished both the men and the relationships. Another is a study that was submitted to the *Journal of Homosexuality* before I became editor. It involved interviews with adult men who recalled their teenage relationships with older men. They reported that the experience was valuable because it started them down productive career paths and made them better husbands and fathers. There is also the historical evidence in Edward Brongersma's new book, in O'Carroll, and in the *Nambla Journal*. German novels published in the 19th and early 20th century, and recently translated by Hubert Kennedy, seem too authentic to be pure fiction. *Paidika* will be publishing much more. If censorship would be lifted, the doors of safes and rented lockers would fly open and a ton of pedophile material would be published.

The answer to the question about the permissible age of the child is based on a prior ethical question: Would the experience be in the child's own best interest? That is, would it be pleasurable for the child and make the child happier in some general sense of its life fulfillment? In answering this question, among others, the child's voice should be heard since it is its welfare that is at stake. That voice is usually ignored or silenced by those who *know* what the child needs better than the child does — always the conviction of the powerful for imposing restrictions on the powerless. I think that the individual who is attracted should also be heard since genuine attraction to a person as an individual is often accompanied by a keen sensitivity to the other person's desires and welfare.

Yet children are easily exploited and adults easily exploitive; even the reverse is true since modern western society forces both groups to live in entirely separate domains. If adults were all ethical characters who would forego sex when there was the slightest possibility of harm to the child, no matter how much time and material benefits had been showered on the child, I think the decision could be ethically left to the child and the adult. Since high ethical character is generally in short supply, it is often necessary for third parties to step in. It would be desirable if these were parents or others generally responsible for the child's welfare. In the absence of responsible guardians, the government must have that authority, but it should be exercised without prejudice to the possibility of consensual sexuality between the adult and child.

Even with these ethical and legal precautions, my position is a far cry from those who believe that children are never "sexual," never attracted to adults, or that any sex between child and adult is inherently harmful to the child and exploitive by the adult. These are prejudices that resist both factual support and ethical analysis. Regarding the issue of a "pedophile identity" . . .

MASS: You say that we must find a way to look at pedophilia that frees it from the confines of identity. Just as you've shifted the emphasis of your inquiry from gay persons to their relationships, you imply that the same shift of emphasis would illuminate not only pedophilia but the larger context of childhood sexuality. "Maybe the inquiry should be framed differently," you propose. "In other words, it's not going to be an inquiry into pedophilia *per se*, but an inquiry into childhood sexuality and the roles that adults play in that, including the sexual role. We've maintained this preposterous stance in Western society that the adult has no part in that, or that the part is simply that of an observer, and yet in almost every other aspect of children's lives the adults are participants as well as observers. . . . If you narrow the inquiry to "pedophiles," to the adults, you're going to deflect it away from the children, and you're going to deflect it away from the broader examination of the sources of heterosexual oppression and prejudice."

Is *Paidika, The Journal of Pedophilia*, the start of such a process of inquiry? What can you tell us about this publication?

DE CECCO: It is my belief that we will come to understand homosexual desire and acts, whatever the age of the partners, when they are described within the context of the individual's life, and that life within its social context. The idea of "sexual identity" reverses that process by establishing a social category through which the individual's life is perceived and interpreted. In effect, the individual's entire life is subsumed under that person's sexual desires and acts. Although this may be appropriate for a few individuals, it is rarely true in history. Even today, outside gay political enclaves, it is not a sensible portrayal of the lives of most people who prefer their own sex. The idea of a homosexual identity emerged in the early 18th century from the very prejudice that it is now intended to fight. Instead of removing homophobia, it congeals and targets it. If "identity" has not turned back homophobia and, as Alfred Kinsey feared, has intensified it, it is folly to adopt the idea as a political strategy to fight the fear and hatred of other forms of forbidden sexuality, such as pedophile relationships. Finally, if what we seek through "sexual revolution" (your optimistic phrase) is greater freedom of sexual expression, to fight heterosexualist ideology with homosexualist ideology (which is what the "identity" notion finally boils down to) is self-defeating.

The editors of *Paidika*, Joseph Geraci and Don Mader, are very bright and dedicated men. Joe is particularly gifted at framing issues and finding writers and materials to research and write about them. The publication is supported through subscriptions, which means that they end up donating many hours of labor and even some of their money, particularly now that it has come under the scrutiny of American customs. They try to guard against advocacy and simply publish reports of persecution by authorities of both adults and children and document how such relationships have existed in other historical periods and have been institutionalized. Unless such evidence is published, it would be most difficult to have a public platform for explaining pedophile relationships.

I accepted the editors' kind invitation to join their board because I am interested in broadening inquiry into homosexual behavior, indeed, to understand the extraordinary prejudice toward it as growing out of encrusted assumptions about sex, marriage, children, love, ethics and so on. Since pedophilia at the moment seems to be at the heart of the sexual debate, it's intellectually important to be where the action is. I also admire their courage, a rare commodity in the academic world, which will be the last to recognize the importance of their work.

MASS: You sympathize with the need of pedophiles to organize, to have a subculture, and you touch on the situation in Amsterdam, where, as you put it, "there's this whole emigré group of men who have been run out of their countries because of the so-called abuse of children." Are most or all of these persons homosexual? Are there any organizations of heterosexual pedophiles, and if not, why not? Can you tell us more about Amsterdam? Generally speaking, what's going on there, not only with regard to pedophiles, but with regard to other sexual subcultures and sex research?

DE CECCO: Who else do they have to talk to but each other? They are refugees, incidentally, from the great industrial "democracies" — Britain, Australia, Canada and, of course, mostly from our dear republic, all governments which have managed to institutionalize a waspish fear and morbid preoccupation with sex. Among those I occasionally met, most preferred to have sex with boys, usually adolescents, although one or two of them liked teenagers of either sex. Some like boys around the age of ten. A few of the older men are from distinguished Dutch families, which demonstrates that a preference for boys must be human if it is shared by the rich and powerful. All are educated, some superbly, and some were former members of the clergy and helping professions.

Historically, Holland has been a haven for dissenters, including our own Pilgrim fathers. The Dutch also have an inherent suspicion of centralized authority, so that some cities have been able to manage considerable legal autonomy, and Amsterdam leads the way for laws that pertain to both sex and drugs. I believe the legal age of consent in Holland is now 16, but there have been legislative attempts to lower it. There are businesses which advertise that they provide boys and young men, especially for British and American tourists. Restrictions on publishing and distributing fiction and photographs about boys are much less severe than in most other countries. The COC, the gay political organization supported by the government, has not always been pro-pedophilia, but now appears to be more supportive than ever.

Unfortunately, all this freedom is now threatened by pressure from other countries, chiefly our own bastion of democracy, and threats have been particularly strong from the office of the Attorney General, especially when it was occupied by Edwin Meese (who everyone agrees is a man of unblemished moral character). There have been police raids on the two gay bookstores in Amsterdam, once to close a show comprised of photographs of teenage Puerto Rican boys (without erections, they are much more amply endowed than Dutch boys their age, and this may have elicited a cross-cultural penis-envy) and on two occasions to confiscate shipments of a German magazine which contained nonpornographic photographs of nude boys. There appears to be an effort to choke off the exporting and importing of all pedophile materials and to make it economically impossible to continue their publication. They will probably try to drive *Paidika* out of business.

There are other, less visible forms of forbidden sexualities in Amsterdam, particularly those that choose leather as their emblem and, of course, a flourishing business in female prostitution in the red light district near the central railroad station. There women stand behind large windows and look like undraped mannequins. Male prostitution is confined to the central station and a few bars near the Amstel River. None of the sex scene has the gusto of New York City or San Francisco. But then American energy grates on Dutch nerves.

MASS: You were the principal investigator of a large-scale study of discrimination based on sexual orientation, for which I was interviewed by Sal Licata on the subject of the prejudice and rejection I experienced when I came out during interviews for a residency in psychiatry. What has become of this research? Was it ever published? Will it be?

DE CECCO: That "study" was my first experience in researching homosexuality under government funding and university auspices. It was followed by two additional grants, to study aging and jail rape. When the grants were made, I believed in the Enlightenment doctrine of progress through reason and knowledge and in the university as the great citadel of free inquiry. I paid a high price for my political naivete.

Under the guise of protecting human subjects from revealing information that could damage their reputations, the university officials appointed a real homophobe (a heavily veiled Socratic lover of young men) who had a law degree, although he had never practiced law, to chair the committee that was to monitor all aspects of the research. The administration's chief concern was to avoid getting sued by a disgruntled interviewee. Although those of us who were doing the research certainly knew what it was like to be victims of homophobia, we were still not to be trusted with the responsibility of guarding our fellow victims from further suffering.

The grant to study aging passed the committee's surveillance with less difficulty than the other projects, partly because the Robespierre of Supreme Reason and Justice was attracted to one of my male co-investigators. The study of jail rape turned Justice Personified into a raving maniac because he was sure that our research would lead to someone getting raped, a scene he would have salivated over. He finally was removed from the committee but, only after he had shackled the research and consumed vast amounts of time and energy.

In the meantime, the federal government kept the research under surveillance. The committee that funded the discrimination and aging studies, led by some old New Deal liberals who really believed in individual liberty, was easier to deal with. The woman who supervised the rape research, however, was a real ball-buster. She decided what she wanted us to find out before the first bit of evidence was gathered: that black and white gay men were raped in jail by straight white men. As it turned out, inmates reported relatively little rape—they were more interested in drugs and release than sex. Those who did have sex were doing it in the so-called Queen's Tank, a "protective" dormitory reserved for self-identified gay inmates, and there it was mostly consensual. Finally, most of the rapists were black and most of their victims were white—all findings that did not fit her belief that all white men are chauvinist pigs who rape white women. Gay inmates, in her unprejudiced mind, were really fairies, misgendered women. Since black men were oppressed, in her twisted liberalism, they could never be victimizers. When Ms. Ball Crusher realized that the evidence did not fit her man-hating, fashionably anti-racism ideology, in reverence for the goddess of Scientific Truth, she had the research funding cut off "in the national interest." In girth, she could cover a good portion of the nation's geography and perhaps thought she was the nation.

Reports were dutifully filed with the government, of course, and some methodological research reports on these studies were published. Actually, two book-length manuscripts were prepared but never published, to my assistants' and my own great disappointment, because they could not tell how little we learned about the topics investigated, nor what we had really learned. It was a regrettably costly price to pay to learn about the politics of government funding for "objective" research in the social sciences and how easily university administrators collapse under the slightest challenge by federal authority.

MASS: I've heard a lot of arguments for gay academics coming out of the closet, but none as cogent and persuasive as the one you gave in your interview with Arthur Lazere (*New York Native*, 9/21/87):

> What they have done . . . is to overidentify with the establishment. Some have become extremely conservative forces on campus. It's a self-image thing. They've created themselves in the image of the academicians that they think everybody ought to be. To say they are homosexual, they think, somehow reduces their credibility. In their minds, it gives them less stature.

> Whatever stature closeted academics achieve is built on quicksand. Since many of their colleagues, more often than not, have already guessed that they are gay, their inability to be honest about it is to consent to the judgement that there is something inferior about them. *If they lie about their lives, what assurance do their colleagues have that they don't lie in their work* (italics mine)?

I think that says it all, but in fairness, have you ever received a challenging response to this argument from a closeted gay academic? (E.g., "I'm a social constructionist who, not unlike Jeffrey

Weeks and John De Cecco and Gore Vidal thinks labels like 'homosexual' and 'gay' are too delimiting. In view of the real complexity of my identity and my (admittedly mostly same-sex) relationships to others, and in view of the fact that today's 'gay identity' is really just a byproduct of patriarchy, coming out as 'gay' or 'homosexual' seems to me to be just as big a lie as not doing so.'')

DE CECCO: The grim fact is that "coming out" does weaken or destroy general public credibility and esteem not only for academic work but also for the achievements of artists, writers, scientists, public servants and so on. Eventually, some of these people have the immense talent and dogged persistence it takes to overcome the homophobia, but I suspect that most feel that they must be supremely successful to attain the same level of recognition occupied by mediocre but "normal" competitors.

Married colleagues will distrust single (unless divorced) colleagues and envy them, even when the latter incarnate St. Francis of Assisi and Florence Nightingale. The driving curiosity of the married about *why* their single colleagues don't pairbond, to use the current sexological substitute for the Judeo-Christian *wed*, must ultimately be fed, if only because the enslaved are obsessed with both hate and envy for the unencumbered. Once the appetite for marital gossip about the unwedded is whetted, it is relatively simple for matrimonialists to distinguish eventually among the single those who are "gay" from straight sex addicts and straight celibates (the possibility of gay and celibate is usually precluded since everyone knows that all fags have an insatiable appetite for sex and new partners).

You're really damned either way—coming out or staying in. The advantage of "staying in" is that your work *might* be judged for itself, regardless of your sexual preferences or gender adequacy. If, however, colleagues have "figured you out," judgements about you and your work will inevitably be affected, whether or not you remain silent. Since all of my work deals broadly with homosexuality, "coming out" has ended the transparent questions about why *that* topic. Also, I have to confront less homophobic shit, which I presume is saved for "good boy" meetings and conversations occurring when I'm not around.

MASS: How do you feel about being called "the grandfather of gay studies," as you were dubbed in the *Native* interview?

DE CECCO: Well, it completes the family metaphor — gay brothers and lesbian sisters and gay community composed of the gay pair-bonded. If you have a family, then you must have relatives, including grandparents. I suppose longevity as editor of the *Journal of Homosexuality* and age in a world of rapid burn-out and early death qualify me for the position of gay grandfather. Actually, I feel more like a grandmother who has presided over at least a temporary academic home for numberless students and authors, some of whom are still speaking to me. In truth, I find the family metaphor far cozier than the reality of my relationships with some prima donna gay scholars.

MASS: In his review for *The Advocate* (6/21/88) of the anthology you edited, *Gay Relationships*, Patrick Franklin sneers: "DeCecco may be valuable too — in keeping psychologists running at their usual pace of about a decade behind the times. With the aid of *The Male Couple's Guide to Living Together* by Eric Marcus, perhaps a new sample of committed gay couples will help therapists realize that gay partners are a solid fact of life and are, increasingly, here to tell the world about it." This statement more than implies that durable gay relationships aren't acknowledged in your book or that there's some sort of bias against gay and lesbian couples therein. But this is grossly untrue. Have I misunderstood this reviewer or did he completely misunderstand and misrepresent *Gay Relationships*?

DE CECCO: The anthology was intended to be a summary of available psychological research. His appraisal of psychologists is far too generous. I think they *never* catch up with the times or, more precisely, with the lives of the people they say they have studied. Because psychology tries so hard to ape the natural sciences, the complexity of people's lives, their mixture of impulses, feelings, attitudes, perceptions, thoughts and actions are reduced to simple-minded attributes that can be "measured" in isolation from the whole. Relationships, of course, are even more complicated because you have at least two people involved. Most research psychologists are not interested in getting to know their subjects as individuals. That would distract them from their roles of scholar-squirrels, as Vidal aptly describes them, scratching around for data and plugging them into computers, which have replaced the deity as the ultimate source of revealed truth about the human condition.

At the same time, what are more simple-minded than guides for living, as if one's journey through life can be charted like a tour of Egypt? People who have acquired some wisdom about humankind and society are the last to offer advice or, having provided it, respect the judgment of the person refusing it. It would be hard for me to decide whether the bigger scam is psychological research on love and relationships or guides for attaining durable, committed monogamy. "Durable" is a terrifying word when applied to relationships. It's better used for material objects such as tires and shoes. And "committed" is best applied to prisons and mental hospitals.

MASS: What do you think of psychologist Dorothy Tennov's concept of *limerence* and its application to sexual orientation? Limerence, which Tennov defined as the state of falling and being in love, and as lovesickness—featured prominently in the gay couples studies of Bell and Weinberg and McWhirter and Mattison. Limerence for one sex or the other has been seen as a relatively simple and very effective means of designating sexual orientation. Whichever sex you fall in love with, that's your sexual orientation. If it's the same sex, you're homosexual or lesbian. If it's both, you're bisexual. How has this concept of limerence meshed with your concepts of sexual identity? (Did you feel that limerence was subsumed under other categories, such as interpersonal affection and/or erotic fantasies?)

DE CECCO: I am instinctively suspicious of neologisms, especially when coined by people such as those named in your question (to which we can add John Money, who manufactures them faster than the Japanese produce computer chips), whose prose, even when doctored by armies of anonymous copyeditors and ghost writers, are barely salvageable for the reading public. If *limerence* derives from *limen*, meaning *threshold*, then it makes little sense to describe a state of rapture that involves more than merely entering through a doorway. It is like diving blindly into the deepest part of an unmarked swimming pool. If it derives from *lime*, as in *limestone*, then it fails to evoke the intended image of passion and emotional turbulence, although, in that case, it could be applied to monogamy that endures long after the partners have forgotten why they got married. I suppose the word's etymological origin is best attributed to *limerick*, the name for a poem that makes *no sense*.

People who live their lives with some modicum of self-awareness no more blindly "fall in love" than they "fall" without awareness into snorting cocaine, imbibing alcohol, puffing tobacco, overeating, having sex, making money or working weekends. Any human behavior can become habit but not without intention and conscious practice. Why one adopts one habit rather than another can no more be attributed to a single factor in one's background, such as sexual orientation (whatever that is), than why one prefers Michelangelo to Picasso. Habits once formed, especially those with physiological repercussions, are no easier to break than they are to form and sometimes harder when their abandonment leaves the individual with a mental vacuum. Because habits become fixed does not mean that they are not acquired through time and often with singular dedication.

There are indeed people who cultivate the habit of falling in love. For many of them, having a lover is more important than who the partner is, including gender or character. Sometimes, it is enough just knowing that one has a lover—even though the person is a continent away, an occasional voice over the phone. People who habitually "fall" in love believe that they are themselves more lovable than those terrible "loners" who are incapable or fearful of *warm, enduring, intimate, passionate* love relationships.

The biomedicalists of sexuality, such as those named in your question, love to invent neologisms that reduce the human experience to reflexive emotional states and behavioral responses over which no one has conscious control. They then attribute feeling and conduct to body chemistry and electrical brain functions, which presumably comprise the person's essence. In the latest edition of Money-on-Money, he actually refers to limerence as *glue* that binds we sexual robots together. If we get glued to the "wrong" robot, it takes about two years to get unstuck. I should imagine it would take Money much longer, especially if he were to adhere to a robot much like himself.

MASS: Your inquiry into homosexuality and sexuality led you to view sexual identity as increasingly complex and variable from individual to individual. This view was roughly congruent with but was more sophisticated than that of Bell and Weinberg in their study, *Homosexualities*, which was contemporaneous with the work you were doing on the multiple determinants of sexual identity in the early 1980s. I recently attended a panel on "Gay Sensibility" that seemed to me to be very wrong-headed. Most of the panelists were prominent social constructionists; yet, ironically, here they were, looking to identify some essence of a gay sensibility in our time and over time. No one thought to emphasize the certainty that there could only be gay sensibilities, plural, like homosexualities.

Have I misunderstood something or is the discussion of gay sensibility precisely parallel to that of homosexuality—i.e., there ain't no such singular phenomenon?

DE CECCO: A pathetic search, indeed. While the biomedicalists are expatiating on the physical essence of homosexuality, the culturalists of homosexuality are rhapsodizing over its spiritual essence. In either case, they are trying to build a case for a special genus of humankind, the former group to prove its biological freakiness, the latter to show its cultural superiority. Of course, my sympathies are more with the culturalists. One can understand the natural reaction of people who practice a form of behavior that has been condemned and grossly punished for centuries to claim that they have powers that make them, as a group, superior to their persecutors.

Both claims are foolish and dangerous. The biomedicalist conception logically leads to attempts to eradicate homosexuality, but the sensibility group provides the ideological basis for the rule of the witches, priests and eunuchs. Of course, with American electoral politics bent on keeping the rich rich even at the price of sinking the nation's economy, who knows which tyranny of the three would prove to be the most disastrous?

MASS: One of the more impressive refutations of essentialist explanations of homosexual and bisexual identities is anthropologist Gilbert Herdt's data on ritualized homosexuality in Melanesian societies. That there is ritualized homosexuality in these societies, however, seems to me to be a separate issue from the question of sexual identity. In other words, there may be "homosexuals" in this society who are quite distinguishable by their erotic preferences, even if everyone's sexuality is more fluid and even if everyone is engaging in ritualized homosexuality. If this distinction is discussed by Herdt in his commentary for the *Journal of Homosexuality* (Winter 1984), I missed it.

Let me put it another way. If I had been reared in a less homoerotophobic culture, I may have been more fluidly bisexual. But it's difficult for me to conceive of not having the attraction for men and the distinctive ability to fall in love with them that has been with me since I can remember. Very much in synch with the findings of Bell and Weinberg in their second study for the Kinsey Institute, *Sexual Preference*, I *feel* my sexual orientation to be very primary and immutable, even while there is fluidity in my sexuality.

Have I misunderstood Herdt's analysis? Do you think I am otherwise misinformed or biased?

DE CECCO: There is faint possibility in rigidly organized tribal societies such as the one Herdt studied, in which all aspects of sexual behavior are ritualized, for individuals to develop their own preferences or to become aware of preferences that fall outside the prescribed ones. Some tribal societies have provided alternatives for individuals who don't fit the general cultural prescriptions (e.g., the berdache), but even those niches have fixed requirements. Such restriction of personal freedom and awareness, I imagine, is the crucial difference between tribal and civilized societies.

American youth *feel* they were born to love rock, hamburgers and country. One can hope, although the quality of American education and life in the republic dim the prospects, that as youth are civilized, their tastes will be refined into more complex appreciations of music, food and international politics. Because of the great American fear and ignorance of sexuality and the specific societal prohibitions against experimentation, most people are stuck with their original sexual menus.

If our diets remained at the level of our sexual development, the whole nation would be eating Kentucky Fried Chicken. Most people lack either the opportunity or will or are too fearful to try new forms of sexuality. There are also what Vidal calls Cautionary Tales that keep our sexuality domiciled, at the price of mounting ennui, within the familiar and safe. It is impossible to know how broader and bolder experience would refine the choice of partners so that it would not stop at mere gender. I would hope that new amalgamations, like French sauces, would be far more ingenious than deep-fried chicken.

MASS: Correct me if I'm wrong, but what you're implying is that if people with circumscribed sexual preferences, say for one sex in favor of the other, could just overcome their fears and have more experience with other, untried forms of sex — with the opposite sex, with different color and different age people, with different acts — many or most of them would probably expand the range of their sexual *preferences* (as opposed, merely, to their experiences). Their sexual preferences would evolve, so to speak.

But John, what about all of those "bisexual" men and women who *wanted* to be heterosexual and who got married and who were at best functional but never comfortable or happy in their marriages because the only people they had ever really been attracted to were partners of their own sex? With the vast majority of these people, it wasn't a question of the kind of opportunity or availability or practice or experience or overcoming of fearfulness that would reveal us all, in sexological (à la John Money) and social learning theory (à la Masters and Johnson) paradigms, to be happily-ever-after bisexuals (among other -als and -iles). No one wanted that kind of learning-and-experience model to be true more than these people in these miserable marriages or more than attendees of sex therapists like Masters and Johnson and Helen Singer Kaplan. But it didn't work out that way. Instead, they continued to be drawn to who and what they *felt* they were *attracted to*, in their fantasies and throughout their lives, regardless of what the opportunities were and regardless of their levels of courage and fear and regardless of what society said was right or wrong, sophisticated or chic, normal or not. (Unlike rock music and hamburgers and the American flag, same sex relations were never promoted as normal or good or healthy and made easily and cheaply and safely available to adults and certainly not to young people. In our culture, on the other hand, wanting to get married and have kids and a mortgage is a lot like liking hamburgers and feeling patriotic. Nevertheless, all the *soupçon*ing and exposure in the world, to say nothing of all the "persuasion" — to the point of aversion therapy, prison sentences, physical violence and the loss of jobs and children—did not change the preferences of these persons.) After leaving their failed marriages, these people haven't gone back or on to bisexual lives. They've returned to or tried to find what they felt they always wanted—sex and love (I'm trying hard not to use words like committed and durable and pair-bond) relationships with persons of their own sex.

But maybe I'm wrong. Do you know of any studies or historical or anthropological findings that suggest or demonstrate that sexual *preferences* (as opposed to behaviors)—who and what people *feel* they are attracted to and what they *want* to do sexually—are easily or even not easily changed? That they do, in fact, "evolve"? And if so, does this mean that Masters and Johnson, Helen Singer Kaplan and Lawrence Hatterer were right in their assumptions and not necessarily unethical in their practices of "converting" homosexuals after all?

DE CECCO: Sexual taste is a part of gender experience and cannot be expected to change independently. In modern western patriarchal society, particular gender boundaries pervade everyday life—in connubial roles, the rearing of children, the division of labor and the distribution of money, property and power. They dictate gesture, dress, posture, movement and modes of speech. Personality traits like assertion and yielding are assigned on the basis of gender. And they dictate choice of sexual partners. As individuals cross gender boundaries, as young people are doing in dress, vocabulary and mannerisms, and the boundaries appear less sacrosanct, then I believe they will be able to do so in the more charged area of sex. After all, it is not our prospective partners' biological sex *per se* that attracts us but their particular expression of the sex or sexes we like. Notwithstanding the claims of Christians and psychoanalysts railing over the sexual compulsiveness of fags and dykes, we are not attracted to just *any* man or woman. People who think about what specific qualities attract them sometimes discover that it is an idiosyncratic admixture of the feminine and masculine—the demure weightlifter with the high voice, the wispy southern belle who rules with the sharp tongue, a male with an oversized cock who does what he is told. The increased tolerance homosexual behavior had achieved before the AIDS epidemic was partly the result of more and more men and women crossing over into each group's gender domains. Much reticence to engage in homosexual acts, after all, stems from the belief that they are unmanly or unwomanly—that they will cause one to fall from genus, the original meaning of *degenerate*.

Regarding your tormented lesbian wives and gay husbands, I have known men who gave up heterosexual marriages for homosexual marriages without a decent interval separating the two relationships. They apparently prefer marriage and, after they add the kids, it appears that the conjugal state and the family is at least as important to them as the gender of their partners. There are others who simply want to get out of all marriage. By declaring their homosexual essence, they can permanently get rid of unwanted spouses and children. Undoubtedly some married because they hoped it would bridle or eradicate their homosexual behavior, but most people who marry expect that there will be curtailment of their sexual activity and a shift away from sexual to family interests no matter how many sex manuals, toys and Masters-and-Johnson miracle two-week cures they incorporate.

Surely in Mediterranean and South American countries maintaining a marriage while engaging in homosexual affairs is hardly an exceptional occurrence. The marriage, after all, fulfills traditional obligations, including having children, safeguarding property and establishing oneself in the extended family, while the homosexual affairs may be the exciting sexual practice. There is very little psychological or social pressure to give up one type of relationship exclusively for the other largely because sexual behavior is not inexorably tied to sexual identity. Although the married person may prefer the homosexual over the heterosexual, such marriages can be a source of affection, stability and comfort so long as jealousy and possessiveness can be avoided. Arrangements are personal and pragmatic.

I've never known anyone who married to "cure" himself or herself of homosexual behavior although I've heard their number is legion. If there are such people they belong to a class of doctrinaire idiots who prefer the miracle conversion (from whatever to whatever) to learning as one lives one's life. Even in the midst of the ultimate revelation of the real "me," one feels that they are conforming to the currently voguish truth as a way of winning approval from others that they cannot provide for themselves or that gives them control over fellow ideologues. Even after their conversions, they appear to be self-deceived, childish and untrustworthy—even silly. Who can know that what they *really desire* today is what they will *really want* a few months or years hence?

Your question assumes that there is a Platonic essence of sexual desire that stands solitary and immutable within the individual psyche and that it is immune to experience—it can shape experience but is not shaped by it. This notion was taken over by Krafft-Ebing and Freud and rendered as libido or sexual instinct. Both Foucault and Weeks have shown that the idea of an irreducible sexual desire is a social construct developed by medicine in its effort to take over from church and state the patroling and normalizing of sexual behavior.

Desire may not arise in personal and social vacuums and behavior *may* change with personal insight and the circumstances of one's life. People live with relatively little understanding of themselves as individuals and of their society. They also try to arrange living conditions that guarantee stability and even guard against change. They lack the basis and opportunities for learning and so they learn very little. One would not expect such people to be harbingers of change or the basis for the argument that people cannot change.

I also believe that people should not be changed by others and perhaps cannot be in any profound or durable way. At some points in his career, Freud believed that psychoanalysis illuminated character and personality but did not change them. One merely learned to live realistically within the confines. It did afford insight into who you were and how you became that person. Changes that do occur in people's lives should occur from within that life free of ideological pressures, particularly from those liberators who would hand them to us on *their* silver platters. There is little one can do about people seeking out miracle workers or the presence of miracle workers themselves. The latter invariably become obsolete as knowledge replaces ignorance and prejudice or when new ailments are invented, such as sexual addiction, by new miracle workers edging their way into the therapeutic market place.

MASS: As your work so dramatically illustrates, we're moving away from temporal concepts of "homosexual" and "gay," just as we've moved very far away from simplistic preconceptions of what it means to be male and female. That social constructionist views are at least largely valid is beyond dispute. But let me pose an essentialist question. Let's grant that all men and women are, first and foremost, persons — individual human beings. Even the most radical constructionists, however, would probably concede that there have always been "men," just as there have always been "women." Even from a strongly social constructionist point of view, it would be theoretically possible to write a book entitled "Men Throughout History" or "Women Throughout History." Do you think, when a lot more data is in, that there could ever be a legitimate study of "Homosexual Men and Lesbian Women Throughout History"? And if so, wouldn't this really be saying that like "men" and "women," in one form or another, "homosexual men" and "lesbian women" have been here throughout history?

DE CECCO: I hope we are spared such historical nonsense, but I fear it is inescapable because the temptation of the oppressed to fight back by claiming and "documenting" some transhistorical essence will be irresistable as the homophobic and sexophobic madness spreads. It is always the way victims screw up their collective courage and try to convince their persecutors, intent on annihilating the creeps, of their "immutable and irreducible" (to borrow a strenuous phraseology) presence on the planet.

The division of the human race into males or men and females or women is biology. When historians make sex differences the basis of their investigations, they usually end up like the sociologists, explaining the inevitability of the status quo. They become the Darwinians of social progress.

I see little difference between Adam Smith turning to the past to prove the presence of the Invisible Hand and gay and feminist patriotic historians pretending to document the inevitability of the gay bar, lesbian coupledom and women's monopoly of nurturance. This is history in the service of ideology. History that respects the complexity of evidence and the uniqueness of the past can free us from such political madness by showing how befuddled, ambitious and greedy leaders destroy civilizations through the tyranny of ideology.

Homosexuality is behavior or acts, not people. Many people prefer sex with partners of their own sex. Many enjoy both sexes. Most prefer the opposite sex. These all represent human capacities. In themselves they require no more explanation than why most people prefer monogamy, many polygamy and some celibacy. The conversion of the word *homosexual* from an adjective for describing acts to a noun for lumping together individuals was the result of the social and political efforts of those who preferred their own sex to resist ecclesiastical, secular and, later, medical encroachments on their sexual activities. They transformed their sodomitical status or abnormal mental condition into a human species as a way of identifying fellow victims and fighting homophobia.

I entirely agree with Gore Vidal that homophobia is madness and that to fight it by claiming to be a subgroup of humanity created by biology or constructed by history is also madness. Insistence that there is a gay genus that is different from the rest of humanity requires that it be assigned a unique set of characteristics which usually pertain to gender (sissiness for the males and butchness for the females), even though, in the first instance, it was homosexual *acts* that this identity was intended to exonerate. Yet the major characteristics of the genus are identified as deficits, a nonprocreative, sinful and criminal sexuality, a male effeminacy, female butchness.

Ironically, for the genus to win general social acceptance as a part of humanity, it is necessary for the deviants to appear ''normalized,'' like the rest of humanity. The contradiction is inescapable and it torments the organizing committees of the Gay Freedom Day parades, which must allow the screaming libertine drag queens and dykes on bikes to join the soberfaced gay political and business leaders, gay fathers and lesbian mothers, trying to show the public that homosexuals can be as Stoic as heterosexuals.

I recall a quotation which appeared in a moving essay on Tennessee Williams by Gore Vidal that was published after Williams' death:

> He never tried, consciously at least, to make sense of the society into which he was born. If he had, he might have figured out that there is no such thing as a homosexual or heterosexual person. There are only homo- or heterosexual acts. Most peo-

ple are a mixture of impulses if not practices, and what anyone does with a willing partner is of no social or cosmic significance. (from "Tennessee Williams: Someone to Laugh at the Squares With")

MASS: Let me just add here that Gore Vidal no longer publicly identifies himself as "bisexual" and has never, to my knowledge, publicly identified himself as homosexual or gay. But this reticence, you're quite sure, is merely consistent with the depth and sincerity of his convictions about the true unimportance of sexuality. If this reticence is also in the interests of advancing Mr. Vidal's literary and political careers, that's merely a coincidence. It's not, you're quite sure, a case of our old friend, the closet.

DE CECCO: Larry, your ideological fervor dazzles! How can you require the man to martyr his reputation for a cause he does not believe in? Vidal believes that *the homosexual* was created as a way of fighting homophobia — a countermadness to combat a madness. He believes that *homosexual* as an adjective fits the facts of people's lives and of history better than as a noun. I think he also believes that the treatment of sexuality as an incandescent presence pervading life is the result of a legacy of Judeo-Christian guilt — an overreaction in response to oppression.

He has spoken out against homophobia on several occasions; for example, in his essay *Sex Is Politics* (1979) in which he attacked Bryant's Save Our Children campaign, in *Pink Triangle and Yellow Star* (1981) which pointed out the fag-baiting of particular Jewish journalists, and in the essay on Tennessee Williams (1985). Even after the successful appearance in 1948 of *The City and The Pillar*, the first American novel to deal sympathetically with homosexual behavior, he had difficulty getting published. But that did not discourage his publishing *Myra Breckenridge* (1968) and *Myron* (1974).

Vidal has hardly feared controversy. He has been one of the most astute and forthright critics of American politics in which paranoia, megalomania and greed have been allowed to endanger the economy and ruin the nation's reputation abroad. His mordant criticism would have been inevitably discounted or perhaps not even heard if he had "come out": it would have been another complaining voice from the ranks of Gay Liberation.

Incidentally, when queried in an interview on whether he preferred females or males, he responded, "I've always been too embarrassed to ask."

Dialogue of the Sexual Revolutions

A Conversation with John D'Emilio and Estelle Freedman

John D'Emilio is associate professor of history at the University of North Carolina at Greensboro. He is the author of *Sexual Politics, Sexual Communities: The Making of a Homosexual Minority, 1940-1970*. Estelle B. Freedman is associate professor of history at Stanford University. She is the author of *Their Sisters' Keepers: Women's Prison Reform in America, 1830-1930*. D'Emilio and Freedman are co-authors of *Intimate Matters: History of Sexuality in America*. Our dialogue took place in Jonathan Ned Katz's home in New York City on September 9, 1988.

MASS: As you know, the working title of the collection that will conclude with this interview is *Dialogues of the Sexual Revolution*. It's a provocative title because, as I've come to realize and as your book makes clear, there is no singular, unitary movement or period of time that everyone agrees should be called "the sexual revolution." As you put it in the Introduction to *Intimate Matters*:

> For the modern period, new research refines the notion of a sexual revolution. Some scholars push its origins backwards in time, before the 1960s or even the 1920s; others question whether a sexual revolution ever occurred, arguing that modern sexual ideas simply restated nineteenth century concerns about family stability. In this view, birth control, for instance, did not challenge the existing order but merely gained acceptance as a means to strengthen marriage through family planning.

At the conclusion of my interview with him, sexologist John Money proposed a definition of the sexual revolution, which he also calls the Birth Control Age, that dates its onset "with the Philadelphia Exposition in 1876, where the first rubber condom was displayed to the world." (The interview with Money was originally published in *Christopher Street*, 9/80, and is contained in *Homosexuality and Sexuality: Dialogues of The Sexual Revolution, Volume I,* the complementary collection of interviews and conversations I conducted between 1979 and 1987. Money's definition of the sexual revolution was originally published as a manifesto in *Forum Magazine*, 7 (6): 62-64, 1978.)

Do you think the phrase, *the sexual revolution*, still has legitimacy, as Money used it, or do you think, as you infer but do not insist upon in *Intimate Matters*, that there was and is no such singular, characterizable agglomeration of social and cultural developments; that what everyone has been calling the sexual revolution during the last twenty years has really involved a much more complex series of "sexual revolutions?"

FREEDMAN: One thing that struck me about Money's definition was the great weight he puts on technology. As a historian, I would take issue with the implication that technological change creates social change, as opposed to the concept that social change facilitates technological change and *then*, in turn, more social change.

Birth control is a good example. Between the Philadelphia Exposition of 1876 and the 1930s contraception was in use, but it was not socially acceptable. It really took several major social changes—a radical birth control movement, for one, but also women's entry into the paid labor force, the need to reduce family size, and the economic depression of the 1930s—to change the law and popular attitudes. In addition, the diaphragm was probably more important than the condom in terms of family planning in the twentieth century.

As for assigning a discrete time frame of a decade or a generation to the sexual revolution, even Money's quote isn't doing that. I don't think we're really in great disagreement about what we mean by the sexual revolution, since none of us is talking about the last twenty years. We're all talking about long, historical processes.

D'EMILIO: In this definition, Money emphasizes birth control technology as the key to a process that starts in the 1870s and extends through the 1960s. In this sense, the sexual revolution would be more analogous to the industrial revolution than to the French or the Russian revolution. One can trace the beginnings of the industrial revolution to economic changes and technological advances in England in the second half of the eighteenth century. If one then looks at Western Europe and the United States a century and a half later, in the 1920s, one would have to say, "My God! There has been a revolution!" This is what we call the industrial revolution. It's about one sphere of life, the technological, but that sphere has affected everything in our lives—where you work, how you work, where you live and what you do for a living.

I think the sexual revolution is similar. For a period of about a century and a half, in this country, we've been experiencing continuous change around sexual values and behaviors. By the end of the 1960s, when the phrase "the sexual revolution" became popular, there had been profound change in many areas. In this sense, there has been a sexual revolution—a very, very long process in which the place and influence of sex in our society have changed.

FREEDMAN: I think we would agree that the key factor of change has been the change in the meaning of sexuality in its relationship to reproduction in the family. That's the theme of our book. Money is citing certain kinds of contraception as important, but the larger context of that importance is that already, *before* 1876, a drop in birth rates was occurring. People were finding their own ways and means of contraception. But the overall change does have to do primarily with the separation of sexuality and reproduction. To go back to the sexual revolution/industrial revolution analogy, they're more than analogous; in fact, they're deeply related. What you can say about the bigger picture, in fact, is that the economic transformation of Western society into a system of capitalism gave rise to both a change in the organization of economic life and a change in the organization of sexual life, from a family-based economy to a wage-labor system of industrialization, and to the separation of sex and reproduction and ultimately the "sexualization" that our book discusses.

D'EMILIO: Using the sexual revolution as a term to describe a short period of time such as the 1960s and '70s doesn't really hold much water when you look at a larger time span. But there were reasons why this phrase exploded into our consciousness in the

1960s. Some very specific things were going on then that seemed to bring together a slow process of change. I can think of three elements: the birth control pill, which in fact represents the culmination of a century of change around contraception; the massive reduction in the level of censorship in this country, which occurs in a very short period of time because of Supreme Court decisions, but is also the result of two generations of pressure created by the expansion of a commercialized sexuality; and the fact that the baby boom generation is coming of age so that there's a large population bulge among a group of people who are not married yet, but are sexually mature. You put those three things together and you have what looks like a sexual revolution. But all of them — birth control, the changing behaviors of youth and the public visibility of sex — were happening for a hundred years.

MASS: So far as I can ascertain, the phrase the sexual revolution was first popularized by Wilhelm Reich in his historical and visionary analysis, *The Sexual Revolution,* which was published in 1936. In the most literal sense, Reich used the phrase to characterize the events that occurred in Soviet Russia during the first few years of the economic revolution. But like Money, Freedman and D'Emilio, he's really speaking about a much larger historical process.

> What we are living through [he stated in the preface to the third edition of this book (1944)] is a genuine, deep-reaching revolution of cultural living. It takes place without parades, uniforms, drums or cannon salutes; but its victims are no fewer than those of a battle in the civil wars of 1848 or 1917. The senses of the animal, man [sic], for his natural life functions are awakening from a sleep of thousands of years. The revolution in our life goes to the roots of our emotional, social and economic existence.

Reich didn't have a rigid, temporal definition of this movement, but he did have a strong sense of its objectives. Among the most important of these, he believed, was the liberation of childhood sexuality, a battle he felt was essentially unprecedented:

In what way this prohibition can be brought about it is impossible to say today. *But the necessity for legal and social protection of infantile sexuality can no longer be doubted.* [from *The Sexual Revolution*]

Do you have any thoughts about Reich's belief in the protection and liberation of childhood sexuality as a kind of bottom line of revolutionary sexual change?

D'EMILIO: Well, I do find it interesting that he's making these observations as early as the 1930s. One of the more surprising results — at least it surprised me — of looking at the 1970s and 1980s very closely was that I noticed that fears about the young seemed to be the glue that held the various New Right moral campaigns together. If you examine the rhetoric of the campaigns against abortion, pornography, gay rights, sex education and other such issues, you'll find fears about the autonomous expression of sexuality among youth as a motif that runs through all of them. Anita Bryant, for instance, called her antigay campaign "Save Our Children." The right-wing anti-pornography campaign in the 1970s began with the issue of kiddie porn. In the nineteenth century, conservative moralists focused on the purity of women as their key symbolic concern. That won't hold water in a post-Freudian world. So, now, the line that's being defended is the "innocence" of youth. I don't know whether that makes it the bottom line of revolutionary sexual change, but it certainly is the bottom line that the right seems to be defending.

MASS: In her critique of *Intimate Matters* (*Tikkun*, 7-8/88), Bonnie G. Smith expresses her concern that in

> deploring the suffering produced by the historic alignment of sex and reproduction, D'Emilio and Freedman interpret these two terms as binary opposites whose fusion has amounted to a tyranny over sexuality. Yet the idea that one must repress sexual connections to the reproductive to be healthy leads to troubling conclusions about the human condition.

Do you think you've wittingly or unwittingly implied in your book that we must repress the connections between sexuality and reproduction in order to be healthy?

D'EMILIO: I think she was reading a different book. You know, she also implies that we glory in capitalism as having liberated sexuality from reproduction! I thought we described something that is so self-evident that it would be hard for a reader to miss it: that 250-300 years ago there was a basic, indissoluble link between sexuality and reproduction; that the two categories were almost collapsed into each other—they weren't separate at all; and that two and a half centuries of massive social and economic change have led to the separation of those two categories.

FREEDMAN: As for "deploring the suffering of the alignment between sex and reproduction," I don't remember our saying anything that could be even remotely construed this way. We may allude to the frequent suffering of women in association with childbearing, but we do not "deplore" these "terrible Puritans" in any way.

D'EMILIO: Having said that, though, I *do* think it's wonderful that sex and reproduction are no longer the same thing. It is good that there can be sexual intimacy without it meaning that every 18 months, if you're a woman, you're going to have a baby until you reach menopause or die in childbirth. The separation of sexuality from reproduction has meant that both now figure as areas of choice in human life.

FREEDMAN: Having no choice in the matter—*that's* what's deplorable. But I think she's talking about something else, about some contemporary women who are having children now and who are struggling with issues of being sexual and reproductive. And that's an important thing for us to think about. I certainly have no problem with that. It *shouldn't* be an either/or choice. For example, I don't like the split between a gay male ideal of a sexually active subculture with no sense of reproductive responsibilities and a maternal ideal that women aren't supposed to be sexually active. I think that in some ways breaking down those boundaries is a wonderful idea. I think it's a positive development that there can be a different kind of overlapping of sex and reproduction, one in which women can have some degree of control over reproduction. But Professor Smith, who I understand is a feminist, seems to unwittingly hint that women are better off when they are married reproducers, that sex is somehow better for them when they have no reproductive control. I can't believe she means to say that, but that's the implication.

MASS: John, in your essay "Capitalism and Gay Identity" [in *Powers of desire: The politics of sexuality*, ed. by Snitow et al., 1983], you wrote:

> In divesting the household of its economic independence and fostering the separation of sexuality from procreation, capitalism has created conditions that allow some men and women to organize a personal life around their erotic/emotional attraction to their own sex. It has made possible the formation of urban communities of lesbians and gay men, and more recently, of a politics based on a sexual identity.

The observation that capitalism facilitates gay among other subcultural identities is rich and persuasive. The implication that capitalism has created and is entirely responsible for sexual identity seems more controversial. It's clear, for example, that there are many persons who identify themselves as homosexual, lesbian, or even gay in socialist countries, in many of which same-sex relations are morally and legally proscribed. Do you think most of these persons are simply responding to Western influences and oppression? Are there examples of contemporary, literate, nontotalitarian, noncapitalist societies in which persons engaging in same-sex intimacy do not think of themselves as bisexual, homosexual or lesbian?

D'EMILIO: I would never say that capitalism is entirely responsible for or has created certain kinds of sexual identity, such as gay life in Greenwich Village in the 1970s. But I do think that to understand why [lesbian and gay subcultural life] has come about in the West in the last 100 years, one has to understand the larger economic context that has created the conditions that then made what happened possible. There's nothing about capitalism that says there *will* be lesbians and gay men. If anything, capitalism has been very hostile to gay people. The nineteenth and twentieth centuries have been among the most anti-homosexual eras in Western history. But capitalism did open up the possibility for people to live outside of the family, to not have to belong to families as the condition for survival. It's in this sense that capitalist development and capitalist social relationships leave room for same-sex intimacy and same-sex eroticism.

It doesn't surprise me that one would have very strongly gay- or lesbian-identified persons in Eastern Europe or the Soviet Union because those socialist societies have grown out of a capitalist foundation. They're building upon what capitalism has already created. And in building upon capitalism, they too are anti-gay. But the material basis for gay life — namely, that you don't need to belong to a family in order to make a living — remains.

I do think it's interesting to contrast gayness as we know about it in Eastern Europe with gayness as we know about in Cuba. In Cuba, male homosexuality is based much more on a gender role reversal model. To a large extent, one finds gay men, who are essentially queens, and then there are their sexual partners, who think of themselves as "real" men, not as gay men.

FREEDMAN: We should acknowledge too that Western influence helped create a particular international gay subculture in pre-revolutionary Havana. I suspect the same was true of Shanghai, where there was extensive international commerce prior to the socialist revolution in China. One of the reasons the socialist revolutions were so anti-gay is that they associated homosexuality with Western economic and cultural penetration, and with corruption. Homosexuality, like prostitution, was seen as one of the sins of capitalism.

MASS: In East Germany, as I understand it, homosexuality is legal, but a homosexual subcultural identity is not felt by East German lesbians and gays to be so important as we regard it in the West. Perhaps this is a product of the kind of thinking that says that such and such many *citizens*, as opposed to Jews, gays, gypsies, etc., were mass-murdered at such-and-such a concentration camp.

D'EMILIO: I don't know that homosexual subcultural identity in East Germany is actually *felt* to be less important than we regard it in the West. I think it's less fully developed because state power in Eastern Europe is more extensive. Consider, for example, how a society which grants housing only to married heterosexual couples would, in effect, circumscribe a gay or lesbian subculture.

FREEDMAN: In Cuba, for example, there was a housing shortage, certain rooms were designated for courting couples to have sex. But access to these rooms is more difficult for gay or lesbian couples.

MASS: In Chapter 2 of *Intimate Matters*, "Family Life and The Regulation of Deviance," you emphasize that sexual identity is a relatively recent development. "Like other sinners," you observe, "women or men who were punished for unnatural sex acts did not acquire a lifetime identity as 'homosexuals,' and they could be reintegrated into the fold." Likewise, in Chapter 6, "Outside The Family," you discuss "same-sex intimacy" and make the controversial claim that "the modern terms *homosexuality* and *heterosexuality* do not apply to an era that had not yet articulated these distinctions. Only in the late nineteenth century did European and American medical centers apply these categories and stigmatize some same-sex relationships as a form of sexual perversion." And in Chapter 10, "Breaking With The Past," you state that "By the turn of the century, the spread of capitalist economy and the growth of huge cities were allowing diffuse homosexual desires to congeal into a personal sexual identity . . . Some men and women began to interpret their homosexual desires as a characteristic that distinguished them from the majority."

Doesn't your phraseology here imply not simply that personal sexual identity as homosexual or lesbian hadn't been articulated, but that we can be quite confident it really didn't exist prior to the late nineteenth century? In other words, the anonymous male patient from the early 1900s whom you quote on page 226 as feeling that "I am a woman in every detail except external appearances," would not have had such feelings, or would not have felt or identified with such feelings so deeply, if he were an early American colonist. And the same would be true of the men the vice investigators in Chicago found in 1911 (see pages 227-228) who "mostly affect the carriage, mannerisms, and speech of women [and] who are fond of many articles dear to the feminine heart." Have I misinterpreted you?

FREEDMAN: Yes, you have. The question we're asking is when, historically, was the term "homosexual" introduced to describe a life-long condition. This does not deny that individuals had erotic feelings and experiences before society began to conceptualize and label those feelings and experiences.

D'EMILIO: One of the things we get confused about, I think, is the idea that social construction can explain everything. When we talk about the formation of identities, we're talking about a social phenomenon, about social roles. We're talking about phenomena that are given recognition and articulation within specific societies. I have no doubt whatsoever that there were men in colonial America who felt extremely strong physical attraction to other men. But these people did not call themselves "homosexual," a word that was not known or used during that period, a word that has so much contemporary meaning. Instead, what they might have said to themselves is, "I'm really a woman" or "I'm one of God's sinners."

FREEDMAN: There was, in fact, a case we didn't use in the book of a seventeenth-century American who thought of himself as a woman, and who dressed as a woman, but who did not have same-sex relationships. So there are all kinds of individual experience and longing. But what we're saying is that in the late nineteenth century certain ones congeal around a definition that becomes our modern notion of what it means to be homosexual, which is different from older notions.

MASS: With regard to the preceding examples of "this inchoate subculture," you add that "the frequency of such observations points to the continuing salience of gender in shaping an individual's sense of sexual meaning, and to how the erotic remained attached to conceptions of gender." In a less sexist and sexophobic society, you're implying, cross-gender identifications would be a lot less salient in association with same-sex preference. Are there some examples of such societies or time frames of American history, wherein an individual's sense of sexual meaning is clearly much less attached to conceptions of gender? (Was this a real achievement of the sexual revolutions of our time, or are we still so far away from such a detachment that we might say it is still not much more than an ideal for the future?)

FREEDMAN: I don't agree that we're implying that in a nonsexist society there would be less gender identification. For example, native American culture may be much less "sexist" than modern American culture, but the *berdache* was a cross-gender institution.

D'EMILIO: But there are examples of this point. Today, for instance, most gay men and lesbians don't interpret their experience as a phenomenon of being of the opposite gender, even though they are attracted to someone of the same sex. So, gender identity today is less attached to sexual object choice. But a hundred years ago, many people whom we would call gay or lesbian were saying "I'm a man trapped in a woman's body" or "I'm a woman trapped in a man's body." In this sense, their sexual desires were subsumed to gender definitions. That's what we mean when we talk about the continuing salience of gender. When we look at the beginnings, a hundred years ago, of what led to a gay and lesbian subculture, we're not yet seeing a lesbian and gay subculture. We're seeing people who interpret their erotic desires in terms of gender definitions rather than sexual orientation. Today that has changed. I'm not sure that it's changed because we've become less sexist or less homophobic, but we are definitely in a process of detaching sexual desire from "maleness" and "femaleness."

MASS: Perhaps you can help me interpret my own situation. As a child in Macon, Georgia, in the late 1940s and early 1950s, I cross-dressed, was attracted to men (my father being the first object of this desire), and had a strong sense that I was "different" from most of the boys I grew up with, even though I managed to adapt to the extent that I wasn't traumatized for being a "sissy." (By contrast, I *was* traumatized for being a Jew.) Though I did have sex with some of my male and even some of my female friends, I still had this sense of difference from them. And indeed, most of them went on to standard heterosexual dating and marriages. Throughout my childhood and early adolescence, I knew nothing about "homos" or "queers," except that they were supposed to be as lowly and bad as "niggers," as blacks were called by my classmates, and almost as bad as "yankees" (the worst). Nor did I know any such persons, at least not for sure. At age 11, my family moved to Chicago. Chicago was the first of a series of large city environments that would play major roles in my coming to grips with my homosexuality.

Today, I believe that my sexual identity is rather like my skin color or my Jewish ethnicity. It's something that does not constitute a genuine "difference" from others. Rather, I think of it as a variant, like hazel eyes or left-handedness. In this sense, your conceptualization of gay identities and subcultures as *largely* the social constructions of sexual politics, as made up of persons who perceived/perceive themselves as "different" because of society's prejudices, is lucid and convincing. But the certainty that homosexual identity is nothing more than that, nothing more than a matter of diffuse homosexual desires being allowed by capitalism and large cities to congeal into that identity simply does not ring true with regard to my own experience and my own sense of a homosexual identity. Beneath and beyond my sense of being different during my childhood, a sense that I can now see was badly exacerbated by ignorance and prejudice, by homophobia and sexism, what I now call my homosexual identity still seems to me to have been present from earliest childhood and was already well along to fruition, if you will, long before I met anyone else like me and long before I was exposed to any real metropolis. Conversely, I believe that this sexual identity, while largely shaped by sexual politics, was of such power that it would exist and be recognizable in some form regardless of the vicissitudes of those politics.

Can you see some obvious flaw in the way I've conceptualized or characterized the circumstances of my own development?

FREEDMAN: First, I think it's very important to separate the individual from the social. When we talk about the social construction of identity, we're not talking about the social construction of *your* identity or *my* identity. We're talking about the construction of social categories in which individuals might place themselves. Throughout history, individuals may share what you describe as your childhood feelings, but they don't always name them "homosexual identity." In our historical era, there's a concept of homosexual identity that has been created for the historical reasons we've described. Once exposed to that concept, you can then use it to organize your individual experiences and give it a label that is shared with other people, which would help create a subculture. Do you see what I'm saying?

MASS: Yes, but I think we're still not getting to the underlying concern, which is at the heart of the essentialist-social constructionist controversy: Did the movement from individuals with diffuse feelings and desires to a subculture that involved a designated identity result in a transformation so major that the modern individuals— the "homosexuals"—should not share the same name, admittedly a relatively recent name, with their predecessors? Although women

in Asia during the Neanderthal period were very different from
women in New York City in 1988, we still call them women, even
though the Neanderthals may have had no word or a different word
for women, implying some very different cultural and subcultural
meanings.

D'EMILIO: I think there's a major issue here that needs grappling
with. It's an extremely important issue for the gay movement. It's
the question of "am I really gay?" or "do I have to be gay?" Early
gay liberation rejected a whole range of questions that have to do
with causation. We were never supposed to ask these questions because that's what the oppressor was asking: "Why are you gay?"
"How did you become gay?" "Can we change you?" But given
that the oppression persists, there's still this niggling doubt. Why
am I gay? I think the answer that the movement has come up with
since the early 1970s, after that brief moment when the radical
counterculture answer was that anybody and everybody could be
gay, is that you are gay because that is your sexual orientation.
That's a very circular answer, of course. But it implies that something has happened to you early on in life that has made you the way
you are. Early determinants have likewise made your brother heterosexual, and your brother is as heterosexual as you are gay. So,
when Jerry Falwell stands up on a pulpit and says, "You are sinners, Repent," we can say, "No, we're not sinners, this is our
sexual orientation, we're gay."

Then, social construction theorists come along and say, "No,
homosexual identity is a product of large social forces that create
the possibility of these diffuse desires to congeal into an identity
. . ." And you think, "if my identity was constructed, does that
mean that I can deconstruct it?" And does that in turn mean that
these social constructionists are saying the same thing Jerry Falwell
is saying—that you don't have to be gay, that being gay is really
socially constructed?" But, of course, the big difference is the
moral tone that you attach to it. Jerry Falwell is labeling good and
bad. Social constructionists are just describing value-free, morally
neutral, historical processes.

The other thing, though—and I think this is the strength of what
social constructionists are describing—is that these categories are
so convincing to us that in the 1970s and '80s, we speak about

sexual orientation as if it is real, in the way we have arms or legs or eye color. And I think "sexual orientation" is a social role that we cooperate in the perpetuation of. And the way we do it is that, as we become older and these categories are more explicitly presented to us, we take our complex emotional histories and our complex biographies and begin to select what we see as important. One of the essences of coming out stories, for example, is that all of us who come out begin to reinterpret our entire past lives so that the gay episodes are in boldface, and the others begin to recede in significance.

FREEDMAN: I think that's an interesting aspect of the lesbian choice issue: women come out politically, through feminism, and then make a choice to be with women. Some of these women reinterpret their lives. They say, "I always was a tomboy. Now I understand that from the beginning, I was really a lesbian." Maybe, in some cases, these women were lesbian from their earliest childhood. In others, however, the only reason for conceptualizing oneself as a lifelong lesbian is that, having had the opportunity to enter a lesbian world, they've learned this new category, "lesbian," as it has been defined in our time. Do you see what I'm saying?

MASS: Yes. You seem to be acknowledging, on the one hand, that a lesbian orientation from earliest childhood may distinguish some lesbians from others. On the other, however, you seem to be questioning whether a lesbian "orientation"—a marked preference, present from earliest childhood—has ever really existed. In her essay on "The 'New Gay' Lesbians" (*Journal of Homosexuality*, Winter, 1984), Lilian Faderman notes that "In the 19th and 20th centuries, lesbian identity has often been a response to a sexist society rather than the frustration of childhood sexual orientation." The "new gay women" Faderman describes are like the women you're characterizing who have discovered their lesbianism in the course of becoming feminists. Like you, Faderman doesn't clearly disclaim that there are lesbians who do feel that their sexual identities as lesbians is the result of a very primary sexual orientation, present from earliest childhood.

In your discussion of same-sex intimacy, you note that "Women themselves clearly discovered the erotic possibilities between loving friends." But again, are we really certain that *at least some* of the women who were making these "discoveries" of "erotic possibilities" — as adults, accidentally, and in the course of their "friendships" — hadn't been doing so on the basis of a more primary orientation that had determined the contours of their "friendship" in the first place?

FREEDMAN: I'm not saying some people didn't feel their feelings earlier than others, or before they had the opportunity to express their feelings in relationships. But "primary orientation" . . . what does that mean?

D'EMILIO: I think those nineteenth-century relationships probably encompassed a range of possibilities. There were women whom we, today, would call heterosexual. Because of the way men and women were socialized and lived, they were passionately attached to their women friends and would rather have spent time with them than with their husbands. Yet they weren't thinking about what we call sex, what today's lesbian couple might be doing at home on a Saturday night. Then there were others who, because of the way many middle class women were denied information about sex in the nineteenth century, may actually have discovered the erotic possibilities in the friendship or companionship that they had.

FREEDMAN: That's where that phrase "discovered the erotic possibilities between loving friends" comes from, in contrast to the theory that women are kept ignorant of sexual possibility until marriage — in contrast to the stereotype of Victorian women as asexual. They may have figured out the possibilities of erotic satisfactions that no one had ever taught them they could have. They had to figure it out for themselves.

D'EMILIO: And there were probably some who had always lusted after women. There may have been a real continuity between the games they played as five year old girls to their schoolgirl crushes at the age of 14 to their live-in relationships at the age of 30.

FREEDMAN: And there were some who had crushes at five who eventually married and never fulfilled those same-sex instincts because the opportunity never arose. There were all kinds of possibilities. What we're saying in this section is that nineteenth-century women discovered their eroticism in the course of passionate friendships.

MASS: In this sense, your discussion of Walt Whitman is extremely interesting. You note that "Whitman provides a good example of the filtering of middle-class romantic friendship across class lines." And later, that "Whitman's life embodied the tension between romantic and sexual love among same-sex friends in the nineteenth century." But you also note that Whitman considered the possibility that he was homosexual and that his "reluctance to be identified as a homosexual may have been due to the growing importance of the medical model of sexual disease." You conclude this section, "Same-Sex Intimacy," with the observation that "Both men and women would continue to engage in same-sex relations, but with greater self-consciousness about their sexual component."

As we touched on in the preceding question, there are studies that suggest that many "lesbians" choose same-sex relationships for political reasons. On the other hand, do you know of any studies—historical, sociological, or other—that suggest that the same is or has ever been true for many male homosexuals; that is, that male homosexuals "choose" to be homosexual? Do you think that Whitman was a man who, at some point in his early adulthood, simply "discovered the erotic possibilities between loving friends," or was he "a homosexual"—a man whose homoerotic preferences were present and dominant since earliest childhood?

D'EMILIO: This is a fascinating question. It's true that we do more often see statements from women claiming to have made a decision, a choice, about their sexual preference, than we do from men. I suspect there are two different things going on here. One is that, given the structures of sexism and male power in society, at certain times and in certain places it becomes a step outside of the oppression of women for them to choose same-sex relationships that are primary. On the other hand, I don't think women would be able to do this if human sexuality weren't, generally speaking, more malleable than we've realized, so that, as a way of escaping gender oppression, one is able to change the object of one's sexual desires. By contrast, it would represent a loss of power and an *acceptance* of oppression for a heterosexual man to look at his life and say, "I think I'll become gay." On the other hand, if you look at the life histories of many gay men, one finds that in fact there has been a lot of choice going on. Look at all these men who lived heterosexual lives before coming out. In saying they came out, of course, we've finessed the question. But in fact, a man who was married and who has three children and who was living in the suburbs and who, at age 37, decided to come out, has *chosen* to be gay. Why do we give more credence to this deeply hidden feeling that suddenly explodes outward than to the reality of his everyday life during those previous years? It seems very clear that lots of us do, in fact, choose to be gay.

FREEDMAN: In addition, for many women in the 1960s and 1970s, political lesbianism seemed a lot more respectable than sexual desire, given our society's conflicts about women's expression of sexuality. For some women, it is easier to talk about their feelings in terms of gender politics than in terms of lust. Men, as sexual creatures in American culture, can say "I lusted after men." By contrast, it's easier for women to say "I took a moral stand" than to say "I wanted her body." On both sides, the coming out narratives are constructed by certain conventions that are very highly gendered.

D'EMILIO: Suppose we say that no man chooses to be gay—i.e., that you *are* gay. If we agree that no man chooses to be gay, then we have to say that lots of men choose to be heterosexual. How else do we explain how these gay men were living until they became gay? They may not "choose" to be gay because they're "really" gay, but they did choose to be heterosexual for, say, seventeen years. I think that what's going on is that the primacy in the culture of sexual orientation as the way we men understand this allows us to completely distort our experience, our feelings, our emotions, everything about our lives; that at the moment we become gay or acknowledge our gayness, we deny that we ever loved Suzy or Mary or Jane. . . .

MASS: But most of the men you're talking about are men who in fact really didn't love Jane or Suzy or Mary . . .

FREEDMAN: How do you know?

MASS: Certainly there are exceptions, such as genuinely bisexual men, and many of these men have cared deeply about their wives and loved their children, but there is extensive documentation of the extreme unhappiness of so many of these men in their married lives.

FREEDMAN: You are repeating the story that our generation has learned to tell, has learned it's acceptable to tell. I think that you might find a lot of other men who, given the opportunity or another set of narrative conventions, might very well say "I loved Suzy, I enjoyed sex with her, I met Sam, I chose Sam." So not all of these men deny that they ever loved or lusted over their wives.

MASS: I don't argue that there are no such persons. In fact, it's now clear that there's a lot more bisexuality and sexual fluidity (to use anthropogist Gilbert Herdt's phraseology), than straight *or gay* cultures of the 1970s and early '80s ever came close to acknowledging. Even so, when interviewed in contemporary studies (such as the Kinsey II study, *Sexual Preference*), men who primarily identified themselves as gay felt that they were strongly, preferentially homosexual from their earliest childhood memories. In many instances, such persons got married, not out of erotic attraction or love, but for mixed reasons of self-hatred, of trying to overcome their homosexuality, of trying to do what was "moral," what was "right," and were admittedly *not* sexually attracted to the wives they were barely managing—often with their eyes squinted shut—to have sex with. Now I'm not saying that men can't be bisexual or even that these same gay men could never, under any cultural circumstances, be capable of greater sexual fluidity, of functioning bisexually without squinting their eyes shut. But I do think that a majority of the men who call themselves gay might well remain strongly, preferentially homosexual, even if the narrative conventions, as you put it, were different. *That's* what would seem to distinguish them over time and place.

D'EMILIO: As we've said, there are cultural reasons why it looks so different for men and women. But as Estelle observed, there's also much more similarity than our culture admits. There are women who feel they were born that way and women who say they made that decision for political reasons. There are men who are absolutely sure they were gay from the day they were conceived and other men who, as adults, one day decided that it no longer made sense to them to live the way they were living. The percentages of persons in one camp versus the other may change, depending on the culture, but the spectrum will remain similarly broad.

MASS: While you do survey the views of such influential sex researchers as Freud, Havelock Ellis and Alfred Kinsey with regard to sexuality and homosexuality, there's no updating of those views among more contemporary sex researchers, such as Masters and Johnson (who are mentioned once, but only with regard to their early work on human sexual responsiveness/sexual physiology), Bell, Weinberg and Hammersmith. The Masters and Johnson study, *Homosexuality in Perspective*, which caused such a commotion, and The Kinsey I and II studies of homosexuality, *Homosexualities and Sexual Preference*, are not discussed or even mentioned. On the other hand, there is discussion of the findings of the Blumstein and Schwartz study of American couples. Preceding this discussion, you state that "the historic invisibility of gay male and lesbian life makes it impossible to compare the erotic dimension of gay experience from one generation to another. Even in the 1970s there were few studies that moved beyond the impression of journalistic observations." First, what do you mean by "the erotic dimension of gay experience?" Second, would you categorize the Masters and Johnson study, *Homosexuality in Perspective* (1979), and the two Kinsey studies of homosexuality (*Homosexualities*, 1980, and *Sexual Preference*, 1981) as studies that had not really "moved beyond the impression of journalistic observations?" In sum, have you eschewed the findings of contemporary sex researchers with regard to homosexuality and if so why?

D'EMILIO: It's true that we don't discuss some of the studies you mentioned. In a book that is covering the entire scope of sexual history, we're obviously compressing and looking for highlights. Freud, Ellis, Kinsey and Masters and Johnson became household words. It wasn't just their findings that were significant, but the incorporation of those findings into society's consciousness. The Bell, Weinberg and Hammersmith studies may have been important, but they hardly created a ripple in American life in the larger sense, in contrast to the impact they may have had on the intellectual gay community or in sex research circles.

MASS: But the Masters and Johnson study, *Homosexuality in Perspective*, was big, front page news. They were even interviewed on Meet The Press. . . .

D'EMILIO: Yes. . . . but it came and it went very quickly. Our sense of its importance reflects how close we were to these issues rather than its real impact on public consciousness. If we detach our personal interest and look at the history of sexuality in America from World War II to the present, you would see Alfred Kinsey and you would see Masters and Johnson and the endless female orgasm, but you probably wouldn't see the Masters and Johnson study of homosexuality or their more recent one on AIDS. That's why these studies weren't discussed.

FREEDMAN: If this were a book about homosexuality . . .

D'EMILIO: . . . Or if this were a book about the scientific study of sex, we would certainly have covered these studies. Now the Blumstein and Schwartz study we felt was different from the others. Instead of trying to talk about what causes homosexuality or sexual orientation, of trying to come to a scientific understanding of homosexuality and homosexual life, these authors were simply comparing and contrasting the way people live. For our larger purposes, it was the one study that significantly compares the experience of gay, lesbian, heterosexual, married and cohabitating couples, all of whom were being asked the same questions. It looks at the same issues for all of these couples. So, it's not that the Blumstein and Schwartz study is better or more important study, but it is more easily usable as social history.

FREEDMAN: And that's really the focus of our book, behavior and social history. It's not an intellectual history of sexology.

D'EMILIO: We're also not saying that these other studies don't move beyond journalistic observations. In fact, they are among the few that do. But we're not significantly concerned with the twists and turns of scientific debate about etiology and causation and explanation. We're much more concerned with dominant definitions and social experience. There's very little that you can cull from the Masters and Johnson study about how gay men and lesbians were living in the 1970s, whereas the Blumstein and Schwartz survey, and to some extent the Kinsey studies, is a goldmine for this kind of information.

MASS: So all these studies of sexual orientation and preference, if they're not important enough to discuss or even mention individually, what larger trend do they fit into?

D'EMILIO: The larger trend they fit into is not the debate over causation. What's significant about them is that, suddenly, there are major scientific studies that are *not* arguing whether homosexuality is good or bad or right or wrong. All of them are accepting of homosexuality as a legitimate way to live, and they're trying to understand why some people are homosexual. If you went back to the 1960s and '50s, the studies of that era are all concerned with etiology. What they all share is that it is unfortunate that there is a causation for homosexuality because you don't want people to be that way. What's most significant about these more recent studies is the thing not stated, namely that they take the existence of gay people for granted. They're not trying to cure or change.

FREEDMAN: Yes. We've gone through a process of deproblematizing, from a period, in the 1950s, of this-is-a-problem-to-be-solved to a time, in the 1970s, of this-is-a-problem-to-be-understood, to the present thinking (at least of some) that this-is-not-a-problem-at-all.

MASS: As social constructionists, your statements about sexual identity place you in conflict with historians such as John Boswell or Walter Williams who feel they can not only speak about homosexuals in history and in disparate societies, but even call them gay as far back as the middle ages or earlier. As Boswell put it in his essay, "Revolutions, Universals, Sexual Categories" (*Salmagundi*, No. 58-59, Fall-Winter, 1982-83):

> . . . city-states in the ancient world did not, for the most part, discriminate on the basis of sexual orientation, and, as societies, appear to have been blind to the issue of sexual object choice, but it is not clear that individuals were unaware of distinctions in the matter.

In his critique, "Male Homosexuality in Western Culture: The Dilemma of Identity and Subculture in Historical Research" (*Journal of Homosexuality*, Vol. 10, Winter 1984), Gregory Sprague likewise concludes:

> By focusing on macroforces, historians of sexuality may miss important microdetails which could illuminate the complex nature of homosexual identities in the past. It is true that past configurations of homosexual behavior are embedded in social and economic contexts. However, historical inaccuracies can result from historians deducing the formation of the homosexual identity from the larger social context.

Even Martin Duberman, in his otherwise extremely favorable review of *Intimate Matters* for *The Nation* (5/14/88), implies skepticism when he observes that:

> Nonetheless, [D'Emilio and Freedman] resort a bit too often to listing economic changes as if those had determined—rather than, sometimes, had merely accompanied—the reshaping of American values.

Is it possible that you've missed at least some important "microdetails which could illuminate the complex nature of homosexual identities in the past?" And if so and if you realized this when you were writing *Intimate Matters*, how could you then state without qualification, as you've done in *Intimate Matters*, that personal (homo)sexual identity didn't exist in America prior to the mid to late nineteenth century, that "the modern terms 'homosexuality' and 'heterosexuality' do not apply to an era that had not yet articulated these distinctions?"

FREEDMAN: This goes back to what we've said earlier. Again, we're not denying that feelings that may have been named something else or organized differently, reflecting different opportunities, existed prior to the use of this terminology. We're simply saying that those feelings weren't connected to this terminology.

As for the microhistory question, I think we do a lot of microhistory of homosexuality. We use social-historical sources, from sodomy cases in the Colonial period to nineteenth-century letters and diaries. Our interpretation comes from these sources, as well as in some that didn't get into the book. Take the example of Walt Whitman we discussed earlier. It's clear that in the early period of his life, when he's writing quite openly about his feelings about men, he's doing so *before* the term "homosexuality" had entered our vocabulary. It's only in a later period, when this term was being used in a negative way, that he pulls back from it. You don't have him struggling over a homosexual identity earlier at all, but he has to struggle with it when someone asks him, "Are you a 'homosexual?'" In the section on Whitman, we stick very closely to Whitman's words and experience. We're not just making this concept up and plugging Whitman into it.

But the Whitman example does demonstrate the point John was trying to make about capitalism and gay identity. Here's a man who can live apart from his family, earn wages and meet other wage-earning men who are living apart from their families in the anonymity of the city. The next thing we know, someone is naming what they're doing, giving it an identity. They begin to form a subculture. Then you have to choose. Am I that or am I not? You didn't have to choose before. Economic and social change has created possibilities for behavior, and then behavior is labeled in certain ways, creating a stronger identity, a new identity.

D'EMILIO: I agree, and I also think social constructionists and essentialists are interpreting the same evidence differently. Social constructionists are often accused of overtheorizing, but part of the reason this theory is persuasive is that it helps explain the accumulation of microdetail. Now it's always possible that more detail will get discovered that ceases to be illuminated by this perspective, and then you begin to modify your theory. But we argue that identities get created because of the evidence we've uncovered, evidence from the seventeenth, eighteenth, nineteenth and twentieth centuries.

MASS: But what about Boswell's point, that the absence of evidence isn't a real proof that these distinctions of identity didn't exist?

D'EMILIO: Let's grant that historians will never have evidence for everything that may have occurred in the past. But to say, "I have such and such a position, and just because I don't have evidence from a certain period doesn't mean that my position is wrong," well, how can anyone say that position is sounder than the one that *is* consistent with the evidence we *do* have?

Let me give you another example of how I think we're using microdetail to sustain our interpretation. There's a wonderful seventeenth century case from Connecticut, one of the richest Colonial cases we have, that Jonathan [Ned Katz] talks about in his gay/lesbian *Almanac* and that Alan Bray is working on more extensively. It's a sodomy case. In the course of the trial, it's revealed that the accused has been engaging in sodomitical practices for about 20 years. You could look at that evidence and say, aha!, we've found a colonial homosexual; for 20 years he was running after men." But you could also look at it and say, hmmm, "isn't it interesting that this case, which seems to be so confirming of a homosexual identity, involves a man who was married, who had relationships with men who were not his social equals, and who was not involved in any ongoing, long-term relationships?" This was homosexual behavior, but it looks far different than what we associate with gay life in the twentieth century.

MASS: It does? I guess I'm afflicted with a kind of reflex essentialism . . . (everyone laughs) . . . because I still can't help thinking about universals over time. Let me give you an example. Take Gilbert Herdt's study of Melanesian homosexuality. [Herdt is the author of *Guardians of the Flutes: Idioms of Masculinity* and *Rituals of Manhood: Male Initiation in New Guinea and Ritualized Homosexuality in Melanesia.*] What I can't help wondering is whether, beneath and beyond the ritualized homosexuality that all the men in so many Melanesian tribes engaged in, there might not still have been an identifiable subset that appreciated what they were doing (who knows, maybe even who initiated some of these tribal rituals in the first place) very differently from the others. Was there still a distinguishable subset of persons we'd recognize, by their cross-gender feelings if not behaviors, as homosexual, even if all the men were engaging in some kind of homosexual behavior? Now, is this just me projecting my own value system onto these societies?

FREEDMAN: Well, let me propose that another way of wondering is whether, in a society where homosexual behavior is so ritualized, there would be any need for other homosexual feelings. Maybe you only have such feelings in societies where homosexuality is taboo.

D'EMILIO: What you're wondering is definitely not unique. Most of us probably share this. But I do think we are projecting. And this poses questions we haven't even begun to explore yet. Namely, why are we so fascinated by this question? What is it about the social construction of sexual identity in the twentieth century that makes us so obsessed with the issue, and that makes it seem so encompassing as a definition and structure of sexual experience that we cannot believe it was different in another time and place? I think what we're seeing is a number of intellectuals — historians and sociologists and anthropologists — developing and elaborating social construction theory around the issue of homosexuality, and that theory seems to fit the historical evidence. Yet the world in which these social constructionists live can't acknowledge that this might be true because sexual identity is so powerful as an organizing principle. The reaction is that this must only be a theory, it can't be real.

MASS: In social constructionist analyses, there's little or no discussion of limerence or of a falling-in-love stage of pair-bonding as an important aspect of sexual identity. [In the Kinsey II study, *Sexual Preference*, feelings of limerence for partners of the same sex, in the absence of limerence for partners of the opposite sex, were seen as a major determinant of adult homosexual preference.]

FREEDMAN: Most cultures we've learned about have some form of pair-bonding. But love in conjunction with pair-bonding is historically and culturally specific. And "falling in love" as a phenomenon that leads to pair-bonding is even more culturally and historically specific.

D'EMILIO: One might also argue that the point in Western history when you first begin to observe the propagation of the romantic notion of falling in love comes precisely at the moment when significant free choice in marriage for certain groups in the population begins. It's almost as if falling in love gets constructed and structured at the point at which there is nothing else creating these heterosexual pairs. Family, survival and property, the former determinants, are no longer pushing these two people together.

FREEDMAN: Which isn't to say that love feelings or falling in love feelings might not have been there in some cases and to some degree, but it becomes elevated to *the* reason, as opposed to some minor or occasional motif. And as for microdetail, for evidence, we found in preparing our book that a new language of affection in courtship emerges in the late eighteenth century. It's not there before. Affection after marriage? Yes, earlier. Affection leading to marriage and looking for one's soul-mate? Later.

D'EMILIO: And it's also class-specific. At a point at which large segments of the middle class in the nineteenth century adopt this elaborate language of mutual attraction and passionate feeling, there's also evidence from immigrant groups that the way in which they looked upon marriage had to do with such issues as providership. There was little or no expectation of falling in love.

MASS: But regardless of their expectations, did they in fact fall in

love, involuntarily, perhaps, or in conflict with their needs and expectations of what marriage should be?

FREEDMAN: We're not saying that nobody fell in love involuntarily, but their lives may have been structured in such a way that it
was the last thing on their minds. So, yes, sometimes it happened,
but love may not have been the primary motivation at a particular
time. We're not saying these feelings aren't ever there, but we ask
which feelings become dominant, in association with sex. It depends on what opportunities people have, and these change over
time.

MASS: Let me ask you to compare the use of the terms "homosexual" and "black." Do you believe it's similarly inappropriate to
use the word *black* to talk about "black people throughout history"
or "black history" or even "black American history"? Should
black people be called black only with the advent of the civil rights
movement in America or other event(s) of the modern period (e.g.,
only since we've begun to use this term, which replaced the use of
"negro")? Please compare your understanding of the use of term
homosexual with that of such terms as *black, Jewish* or any other
designation of minority personage that you think will clarify your
position.

FREEDMAN: I think it's legitimate for someone to say, "I study
black history." Then they can turn to some documents from the
seventeenth century, when the term was "African." And then they
can turn to documents from the nineteenth century, when the term
was "negro." In those situations, they must use historically specific terms, even if they're doing "black history." The designation
of black history is acceptable because that's the term we're using
today. The use of the term *homosexuality* is similar. Even though
they didn't use this word in the seventeenth century, we can talk
about the history of homosexuality because that's the term we're
using today—*if* we're clear all along the way not to misuse this
word, as if it were being used at that time.

MASS: But your phraseology in *Intimate Matters* about the use of
the term *homosexual* seems inconsistent with what you've just said.
In your book, you say that "the terms 'homosexual' and 'heterosexual' do not apply to an era that had not yet articulated these distinctions." That seems different from merely noting that these terms

weren't used prior to a certain period. Am I belaboring a minor semantic point?

FREEDMAN: I think so. Say we had someone who was arrested for sodomy in the 1830s, before the term *homosexual.* We can't say this person was a homosexual because there was no such category. That's one aspect of what we're saying. But there's another perspective. If you look at same-sex behavior from that period, you see some seeds of what later become what we now call homosexual behavior. But we must also ask if we aren't seeing things that were specific to that time that aren't there later. We're simply being historically specific. We're not making a universal statement: Aha! Arrested for sodomy in the 1830s. A homosexual lifestyle! Those two things are very different. They're *not* the same thing.

Maybe I'm inconsistent. I certainly do use the terms *gay* and *homosexual* to talk about same-sex intimacy when I teach and in general conversation, but in my writing, I try to be more specific.

So I think we should reemphasize here that we're not denying that people have feelings and instincts and even inchoate identities during periods before there is a label.

D'EMILIO: There are ways in which the terms *Jewish* and *black* and *gay* have a lot in common. *Black* is much more equivalent to *gay* in that it's a word that comes into use in the 1960s. At a certain point in time, the people who were so labeled say, This is how we choose to be called. In the absence of racism in this country, the term *black* would be used very differently than it's used now. It might be used only for people whose ancestry was fully African. Otherwise, we might have many terms to describe the complexities of racial ancestry. Because of oppression, different terms, such as *negro* and *colored*, get used during different time periods. The term *Jew* exists because this group of people with this set of beliefs and this cultural heritage have a consciousness of their heritage and identity, which they also have as a result of oppression. In the absence of the oppression, one wonders how strong the cultural identity would be. If one could really imagine a world without anti-Semitism, would we be so clear about who is a Jew and who is not? The terms homosexual and gay are certainly similar in reflecting not only a way of living, but oppression. In the absence of that oppression, we might stop talking about such things. In a more egalitarian society, you'd notice whom a person was involved with, but it wouldn't be remarkable that a person was gay.

MASS: The other aspect of this, though, is that Jews have been called Jews throughout history, even if they've also been called Hebrews, Israelites and other things.

D'EMILIO: If one looks at Jewish history over the last 2700 years or longer, it's a complex identity and one that has been shaped in part by oppression. In the absence of anti-Semitism, who knows how strong our conceptions of Jewishness would be?

FREEDMAN: This is really applicable to the critique of essentialism and biological categories. Skin color, you might think, is obviously biological. You can actually see the differences. But then you realize that the idea of race is socially constructed. Think of all the different *shades* of color of people! In fact, there really are no biological or genetic differences among the various "races." These so-called races are *our* lines of demarcation, our social constructs.

D'EMILIO: In this country there are people of Italian ancestry whose skin color is darker than that of many people who are called black. So when we talk in this country about races, we aren't talking about real biological categories.

MASS: I couldn't agree more with what you've said about how profoundly culture has shaped our concepts of difference and about how enormous are the gray areas of most—of all—of our current subdivisions, subcultures and other categories of persons and behavior. I also agree that in the absence of ignorance and prejudice, the question of a person's skin color or sexual preference would have no more interest or significance or power than the question of a person's eye color. The same would be true about most of the so-called differences between "men" and "women." But "men" and "women" have existed, identifiably, throughout history and across cultures, despite profound cultural differences of personal identity and social role. In our discussion, however, we've decided that "homosexuals," like "dark-skinned" or "black" people, and "Jews," really haven't existed except during varying periods when ignorance, prejudice and politics tried to distinguish them with labels and categories. Is this correct?

D'EMILIO: No. The discussion is reminding me that analogies often end up generating more confusion than light. African, African-

Americans and Jews have a clear historical identity of long duration. Racism and anti-Semitism affect how and who a society identifies as "black" or "Jewish," but the identity is not based on prejudice alone.

"Gay" and "homosexual" are also not based on prejudice alone. But gay people, or homosexuals, in Western societies are not identifiable throughout Western history. For most of this history, erotic activity between men or between women did not sharply mark off a distinct social group. Changing social and economic conditions, interacting with inherited cultural prejudices about sexual behavior, have led us to a point in the modern era where a new social group has come into existence. Were the prejudice and the oppression to fade away, who knows whether gay would remain as an indentifiable category. It might, but then again it might not.

MASS: In *Intimate Matters* you don't draw parallels between the social purity movement of the late nineteenth century and the Women Against Pornography movement of recent years. It seems the same decision not to draw parallels is likewise true of your discussion of the AIDS crisis. As Larry Goldsmith notes in his review of *Intimate Matters* (*Gay Community News*, 7/10-16, 1988), "It is perhaps unfair to fault historians for an inadequate assessment of events still taking place, but it is puzzling that D'Emilio and Freedman's brief section on "The AIDS Crisis" fails to note the obvious parallels to events of the Social Hygiene Movement."

Actually, you do compare the greater, aggregate "contemporary political crisis" with experiences of the past, but these comparisons tend to be very broad, sparse and terse – e.g., that the hysteria surrounding the AIDS crisis is of the same substance as that which attended nineteenth century controversies over female purity, prostitution and slavery. Why didn't you discuss these parallels – i.e., between the social purity and anti-porn movements, and between the social hygiene movement and the AIDS crisis – in greater detail?

D'EMILIO: I have a strategy when I write. I don't want to be polemical. I want to present the evidence in a way that is so compelling and so clear that the reader does not feel that she is being forced to agree with me. I want the readers to be able to come to thoughtful, intelligent conclusions of their own. I prefer it when they come to *my* conclusions, of course! But I think that one of the reasons why readers find the parallels between the social hygiene movement and the AIDS crisis so obvious is that we've made them obvious. Rather than have an extended discussion along the lines of just-as-they-did-this-the-others-did-that, etc., which would infuse it with a lot of righteousness and moral fervor, I structured the presentation on AIDS and the presentation on the social hygiene movement so that it is easy to come to the conclusion that there are obvious parallels between these two developments.

MASS: You observe in your Introduction that "we cannot fully escape the limits of the field [the history of sexuality] which has tended to tell us more about women (one of the few areas of history where this is true). . . ." Why has the history of sexuality tended to tell us more about women?

FREEDMAN: A lot of the history that has been written about men's lives has to do with politics and public life. When you get to the history of the family, of childbearing, intimacy, the home, the personal side, you're looking more at the history of women. In addition, historians of women have begun mining material about the history of sexuality. By contrast, male historians have been more interested, generally speaking, in studying men in public positions of power. The feminist insight that the personal is political has only slowly filtered to male historians who have come to realize that sexuality is about politics too. We had to bend over backwards to learn as much as we could about the history of male sexuality, which remains a wide open field for research.

MASS: The conclusion of *Intimate Matters* is stunning. After reviewing the contemporary events that demonstrate "the power of sex as a symbol capable of arousing deep, irrational fears," "the persistence of sexuality as a vehicle for social control," "the power over sex [as] the power to affect the life and death of Americans," you conclude that "as in the past, sex will remain a source of both deep personal meaning and heated political controversy." Are you saying that the bottom line for real change is that sex needs to have much less "deep personal meaning" and if so, what, very broadly speaking, are some of the principal strategies by which this might be engendered (e.g., education, socialism, etc.)? Can you cite other systems and/or societies which you think have made significant progress in this direction (e.g., Holland, Sweden, the Soviet Union, etc.)?

FREEDMAN: I know I didn't think of the statement that sex will remain a source of deep personal meaning as a criticism, at least not consciously. At the time it was written, I think that we meant it quite literally.

D'EMILIO: Right. I don't think we were originally, consciously intending this statement to be a criticism, but I think you may have seen something we didn't. I think it's logical to ask, does the only hope for real change lie in a situation in which sex comes to have much less deep personal meaning? Because as long as it has some kind of deep personal meaning, whatever the details, it may very well continue to engender heated political controversies.

FREEDMAN: But I think we're also saying that as long as sex continues to be a mechanism for perpetuating social inequality, which is one of the main themes of *Intimate Matters*, it will remain heated and political and controversial, and therefore it *needs* to have deep personal meaning, because it does socially structure our lives — not in some essentialist way, biologically, or even in deep psychoanalytic ways (that it will always be deep and personal because of some primary Oedipal struggle or something like that), but because, historically and socially, it is one of the ways in which inequality is perpetuated. Of course, we can also speak in a Utopian way about a more egalitarian world in which sexuality would not be the means to perpetuate inequality, in which case sex *could* have less personal meaning and be less heated politically.

D'EMILIO: But would we ever get to a more Utopian, egalitarian state, if our political strategies are premised on the fact that sex is "deeply meaningful" in some inherent way?

FREEDMAN: We're certainly not saying that sex has some *inherently* deep, personal meaning. Rather, in the world we live in today, we've come to this point.

D'EMILIO: Maybe we ought to be developing strategies in which we're trying to *defuse* the significance of sexuality.

MASS: Yes, what I read into what you're saying is that perhaps we should be developing strategies of education that emphasize that most sex differences are no more deeply important than, say, hair color.

FREEDMAN: Our book, I believe and hope, is part of this strategy of education. Ideally, it will make people more conscious of how meaningful sex has become, personally and politically. The more you make people conscious of these issues, of what has been unconscious, the more you're able to help them give an appropriate place to sex in the greater context of their lives and of the socioeconomic world they live in.

D'EMILIO: I'm trying to think of another social category of identity that, like sex, once had deep personal meaning and once was a source of heated political controversy and now is less so. . . . Religion in Western society is one such an example. I think it's no accident that the extent to which religion is really powerful and significant today has to do with its associations with sex, whether it be abortion or homosexuality or adultery or whatever. In fact, you can actually substitute the word *religion* for the word *sex* in our statement so that it would read: As in the past, religion will remain a source of both deep personal meaning and heated political controversy. The seventeenth century is the time when one might have encountered a statement like that in Europe. Two hundred years later, it held less significance *and* engendered less controversy.

FREEDMAN: Of course, religion continues to be a source of deep personal meaning for many individuals as well as a source of heated political controversy. But the impact of religion, I think, is felt by smaller and smaller proportions of the world's population.

D'EMILIO: As for your question about other societies, I think it would be interesting to study sexuality in the Netherlands, Denmark and Sweden because it does seem to me that they're doing something different. They're all capitalist countries, although they have the most highly elaborated social welfare systems. All of them passed their primes as powerful nations at least 200 years ago . . . I wonder what it is that has allowed them to develop such sophisticated and tolerant attitudes toward sex.

FREEDMAN: Well, there's your next project: a comparative study of the history of sexuality in different societies.

Sexual Categories, Sexual Universals

A Conversation with John Boswell

John Boswell is professor of History at Yale University. He is the author of *Christianity, Social Tolerance and Homosexuality*, which won the 1981 American Book Award for History. His most recent book is *The Kindness of Strangers*.

The following interview took place in Professor Boswell's office at Yale on April 28, 1989.

MASS: A recurrent fallacy of social constructionist arguments about homosexuality, it seems to me, is the idea that because some patterns of same-sex intimacy in history were clearly shaped by social class and custom (just as they are today), we can be certain that less circumstantial patterns of same-sex preference have not existed over time. For example, after pointing out that "the dangers of taking our sexual categories for granted are well illustrated by the work of Boswell," David M. Halperin's asks: "Does the classical Greek adult, married male who periodically enjoys fucking a handsome youth share *the same sexuality* with the native American adult male who from childhood has taken on many aspects of a woman and is regularly fucked by the adult male to whom he has been married in a public and socially sanctioned ceremony?" (from [Questions and Answers about Social Constructionism] by David M. Halperin, for the *Harvard Gay and Lesbian Alumni Newsletter*, fall 1988, and reprinted in *100 Years of Homosexuality* by Halperin).

The answer to this question, of course, is no. The kind of circumstantial, socially facilitated or "constructed" bisexuality Halperin is talking about with regard to the Greeks is *grossly* comparable to the kind of circumstantial, socially facilitated or "constructed" bisexuality we see today in prisons. Yet no one I know of, neither within the gay movement nor from without, is saying that bisexually active, otherwise exclusively heterosexual male prisoners are homosexuals or gay men. Even most of the gay movement's growing numbers of constructionists aren't claiming that because these circumstantially bisexual male prisoners exist, homosexuals and gay men don't.

According to Halperin, John Boswell is a real exception. Is Halperin right? Are you the only person left in the world who is still saying that the Greek adult who periodically enjoys fucking a handsome youth, etc. is, like today's circumstantially bisexual male prisoner or "trade," *the exact same* homosexual as the American-Indian berdache or as today's gay man?

BOSWELL: People who are circumstantially bisexual or even homosexual are not the people I'm talking about when I use the word gay. I'm a little surprised that Halperin and other constructionists misunderstand me on this, because I think my usage of this word is perfectly clear. What I mean by gay is a person who *prefers* his own gender for erotic reasons. That's very different from being *constrained* to engage in sex with persons of either gender. There are people who are constrained in all sorts of ways. Some are constrained not to have any sex. That doesn't mean they're not sexual. Some are constrained because only one sex is available. There are people who are constrained, as in ancient Athens, by a constellation of social factors, such as relatively less access to women of one's own social class and the expectation that boys are a suitable sexual outlet for men. There are all kinds of ways institutions, social patterns and other circumstances constrain people. Most people are malleable enough to find sexual outlet in constrained circumstances. But that's very different from what I'm talking about when I use the word gay. Gay means to me that without constraint, with free and open choice, you *prefer* your own gender. And I *think* (I'm not certain) that there is a variable proportion of people in all the societies I've studied who, regardless of constraints, prefer their own gender.

MASS: In your essay for *Salmagundi*, which has been updated for publication in the forthcoming anthology, *The New Social History of Homosexuality* (edited by Duberman, Chauncey and Vicinus), you discuss ancient views of sexuality:

... city states of the ancient world did not, for the most part, discriminate on the basis of sexual orientation, and, as societies, appear to have been blind to the issue of sexual object choice, but it is not clear that individuals were unaware of distinctions in the matter.

[Ed. note: This anthology was retitled *Hidden From History: Reclaiming The Gay and Lesbian Past* and published by N.A.L. in the fall of 1989.]

When I interviewed John D'Emilio and Estelle Freedman, D'Emilio commented on your observation as follows:

Let's grant that historians will never have evidence for everything that may have occurred in the past. But to say, 'I have such and such a position, and just because I don't have evidence from a certain period doesn't mean that my position is wrong, well, how can anyone say that position is sounder than one that *is* consistent with the evidence we *do* have?

Now, in the introduction to your new book, *The Kindness of Strangers*, one of your legendary footnotes addresses the use of "boy" and "girl" as standard designations of the beloved in ancient romantic literature. In this footnote, you explain that it would be fallacious to assume that just because designated polarities of youth and age were commonly depicted in the homoerotic art of the ancient Greeks, this was the exclusive form homoeroticism took in that society. It would be just as fallacious, you state, for future historians to take "expressions like 'my old man' or 'hot mama' to indicate widespread intergenerational incest among the American population of the twentieth century."

The fallacy in your argument, D'Emilio's statement implies, is its assumption that we can be confident that Greek art, if we had a much greater sampling of it, would be *certain* to reflect a much wider spectrum of homoerotic pairings and acts in the same way that a broad sampling of today's pop music would reveal a wider diversity of erotic possibilities than is suggested by such phrases as "my old lady." (On the other hand, such a survey of today's pop music would reveal little or nothing of the diversity of homoerotic pairings and acts.) Is D'Emilio right? Is it more presumptuous than reasonable to assume that there *was* a broader spectrum?

BOSWELL: The real question here is the nature of the evidence and what it tells us. It seems to me that a lot of what the constructionists and I might argue about is what kind of information can be gleaned altogether. An example I often use is the intercrural (or interfemoral) intercourse ["thigh-fucking"] you see in ancient Greek vase painting. Some people have inferred from this that the Greeks did not in fact engage in anal intercourse. This seems to me completely wrong. There's an enormous wealth of terminology in Greek for anal intercourse. This terminology clearly designates an act that was familiar and common among Greeks. So what is the meaning of the vases? Are they directed to a certain social class that doesn't engage in anal intercourse? Are they a peculiarity of some artistic convention? The problem here is that often language and art and other cultural phenomena are stylized and conventionalized. The historian cannot simply take them at face value.

What I point out to people when we talk about the vases is that if you looked at American homosexual erotic pornography and videos, you'd see that in virtually all cases, when one man is fucking another—or for that matter in heterosexual pornography when a man is fucking a woman—he pulls out before he comes. Now what do we make of that? 2000 years from now, will historians assume that that's the way people made love? Will they think that it had something to do with safe sex or avoiding pregnancy? But it isn't that at all. It's an artistic convention. People want to see the man coming and that's why he always pulls out in pornography. It has nothing to do with real sexuality.

My argument is that in all cultures and languages there are two separate things. One is real, experiential sexuality. The other is the way the culture talks about and records that experience. In our culture, for instance, there's a generalized convention that men are interested in young girls. In fact, if you look at statistics, American men aren't particularly likely to marry or go out with women who are much younger (as opposed to slightly younger) than they are. Likewise, in ancient Greece, it was generally assumed that setting up a relationship would require an older person with money and a younger person with beauty. That's because households in Greece involved a male who had to be able to support a wife. In these marriages, by and large, there was often a great disparity in age. Not always and everywhere, but in many periods. This became the conventionalized way of viewing this kind of relationship and it affects the way people view erotic relationships of other sorts as well. The general expectation is that an older man will have enough money to court a younger man who has beauty to offer. But the fact that these things are conventionalized in this way — people pulling out in movies, intercrural intercourse, older people with younger people — the fact that the cultures produce these conventions doesn't mean that historians should take them at face value. I'm just astonished at such arguments. It's like believing everything the government says in its edicts. Or imagining that in a court case there might not be things going on that aren't recorded, like bribes or plea-bargaining. To take this evidence at face value is just bad historical method.

MASS: OK, but what about the problem of not having at least some affirmative evidence of a broader spectrum?

BOSWELL: We do. We have lots of evidence. The words *philandros* and *philomeirax* (roughly, "a man who loves men," and "a man who loves male teenagers") occur in Greek sources along with *paiderastes* ("boy lover," though probably not taken literally by native speakers, as noted previously). The Latin word *exoletus*, which occurs widely in imperial literature, specifically refers to an adult male prostitute. Who do the constructionists imagine patronized such prostitutes — young boys? Martial, Juvenal, Catullus, Petronius and nearly all Roman *littérateurs* who allude to homosexuality specifically mention or imply relationships between adult males as well as age-differentiated couplings. Artemidorus Daldianus devotes a long discussion to the relative desirability of different combinations of age and wealth in male-male couples, making quite plain that all occur, though some seem more desirable to him than others. Constructionists are simply ignoring such counterevidence and pretending that the stereotype of older man/younger boy is the whole reality of ancient sexuality instead of a cultural convention. I find it particularly puzzling that the constructionists, who are usually quite adept at deflating and deconstructing the conventions and myths of more recent societies, instead simply taking their myths and stereotypes as accurate historical information.

MASS: But the Greek vases don't depict older men with younger women ("girls") to the extent that they depict older men with younger men ("boys"). Is this correct?

BOSWELL: Greek vases nearly always stylize some difference between partners, whether they are heterosexual or homosexual. Females, for example, are nearly always lighter in color than males on the same vase. This is not meant to suggest that they're of a different race. It's simply that pale skin was idealized as an erotic aspect of women. Doubtless some Greek men (especially if they worked indoors) had skin as fair as most women, but I would hardly expect vases to reflect this. Most people are lighter in coloring as children than they are when fully grown, and one could argue that these are therefore "girls," and that heterosexual relations among the Greeks were pederastic. As I've mentioned, Greeks did expect older men to court somewhat younger women, but that is not the meaning of this convention. It is simply an erotic polarity: beautiful, white-skinned women with darker men.

"Boys" are generally distinguished from "men" on vases by size (i.e., somewhat smaller than the partner), by position or gesture, by clothing, by long hair, or by lighter color. Nothing specifically indicates how old they are, and the meaning of long hair or smaller stature or lighter color is probably related both to the cultural convention of an older, established male courting a younger, beautiful person (of either gender), or the result of artistic efforts at depicting erotic complementarity. In most modern homoerotic art there are corresponding polarities — dark-haired men with blonds, large men with small men, hairy men with smooth men, older with younger, etc. Rarely does one see — in art — partners very similar to each other. But it would be fatuous to take these erotically charged artistic conventions as descriptions of sexual reality. Like pale-skinned women, or the class differences among lovers of both sexes so common in Victorian erotic literature, or dozens of other titillating sexual complementarities from other times and places, they must be understood as part of a cultural erotic discourse, not as Kinsey figures about sexual practice. Most American gay couples (even if they themselves view and enjoy such art) would not satisfy

artistic needs in this regard: they are not a cop and a willing prisoner, or a burly muscleman and a sweet little boy, or a dark,
bearded biker and a blond surfer, although they may play such
roles, or others to suggest them. There is no reason to suppose that
Greek art was a mirror of reality rather than a titillating exaggera-
tion, like its modern counterparts. Indeed, I think it would be fair to
say that erotic art works best when it is *not* quite realistic, but meets
and stimulates certain fantasies that are not fulfilled in everyday
life.

MASS: We talk about black history, Jewish history and the history
of women, even though each of these terms may encompass many
persons and circumstances and events that are not clearly "black"
or "Jewish" or "female." Black history includes so many shades
of brown and cafe-au-lait. How much of Caribbean history, of Cu-
ban history, is also black history? And what about all the half- and
quarter- and eighth-Jews in history? Clearly, the gray areas involved in such categories are enormous and *ultimately* overriding,
yet we continue to speak generally and appositely about black history and Jewish history and women in history. Is this any more or
less than what you're doing when you speak of gay and lesbian
people in history or gay history?

BOSWELL: I've just finished an article for the *Yale Journal of Law
and Humanities* in which I compare the history of Jews in the West
with the history of gay people in the West. That comparison is
implicit in a lot of my work, but here I made it very explicit in a
long, extended comparison. One of the things that came across very
clearly to me is how similar the ambiguities are in both cases. There
are a lot of instances where it's not clear how we should view a
particular person. For example, the problem of the *conversos* in
Spain after 1492, when huge numbers of Jews had been forced to
become Christians. One doubts their sincerity for obvious reasons — they were given the choice of death or Christianity. What do
we call them? Do we call them Jews? Do we call them Christians?
Do we call them *Marranos*, a term of derogation [trans: "filthy
creature"]? It's not absolutely clear what we should call them, but
that doesn't mean they aren't a part of Jewish history. "Gray" is
apposite to the study of both "black" and "white," and the fact
that there is much gray does not mean there is no black or white.

Certainly there is gay history. Even if I were a constructionist, I would think there could be gay history because there could be the history of what is interesting to modern gay people; that is, of people with whom they have affinities in the past, even if they aren't "gay" people in some specific modern sense. But I'm not a constructionist, and I think that there were people with sensibilities much like those of modern gay people in almost every pre-modern society. I also think there would have been people in ambiguous categories—people who for circumstantial reasons engaged in same-sex eroticism, people who denied their sexuality or never came to grips with it. I'm sure there are a lot of gray areas, but as you point out in your question, there are gray areas in every kind of history.

It interests me that no one has claimed that there can't be family history. In fact, many of the people who are most constructionist about sexuality are ardent advocates of family history, and yet the family has changed much more over time than ordinary forms of eroticism between two people. What a family was in Augustan Rome and what a family was in the twelfth century in Europe and what a family is now are entirely different, insofar as I can see. Indeed, the basic meaning of the word changes from Latin (*familia*, which means "house-hold" and includes unrelated persons, such as clients, servants, slaves) to English ("family" refers specifically to related persons unless it is used metaphorically). Yet nobody says there can't be "family" history. Everyone recognizes that the family wouldn't be *exactly* the same in a previous age. What social phenomenon is exactly the same in a previous age? Marriage is different, government is different, banking is different, the Church is different.

MASS: Is it true that constructionists don't argue with a history of the family?

BOSWELL: I don't know of any who argue that because the family wasn't always the same, there was therefore no history of the family, or that because Romans conceptualized family in a way quite different from the way a modern Manhattanite would, Romans aren't part of "families." But that's really what they're saying about gay people, isn't it? Because gay people weren't always the same, there's no history of gay people? At one level that's obviously true, because nothing is the same from one minute to the next. But at the level they mean it — that it isn't recognizable, that it couldn't come under the same rubric — it's much more true of the family than it is of gay people. One of the things that's always puzzled me about constructionism is why there's such a focus on this one thing, as if it were the sole social entity to undergo diachronic transformation.

MASS: One reason, I think, is because there's never been any unassailable proof that sexual preference has any kind or degree of biological basis. Not even the most rigid constructionist will claim that biology has *never* had anything to do with being female, even if the roles women have assumed in the past have been, often or generally, profoundly manipulated by culture, but that claim is being made about sexual preference. So in the paradigms of constructionism, the phenomenon of sexual preference and more specifically of modern gay culture would seem to be a kind of pinnacle example of just how extremely manipulative, how determinant, culture can be. On the other hand, is it really such a focus? I mean, aren't there parallel constructionist views of the histories of many other aspects of gender, sexuality and intimate human relations?

BOSWELL: One equivalent in family studies is the theory of people like Philippe Ariès or Lawrence Stone that parental sentiment is a modern social construction and that in earlier societies people didn't have natural sentiment for their children, or even lacked a concept of "childhood," because children died at such and such a rate or were reared by servants. But few current historians of the pre-modern family believe that anymore. Most medievalists think Ariès's idea was so silly that it's not even worth arguing against anymore, although it enjoyed quite a vogue for a decade or so. I wouldn't be surprised if some of the social constructionists still buy it, but I challenge them to find a medievalist who would defend it. Of course, society affects how one expresses feelings for one's children. And of course there are individuals who were bad parents and callous, but in fact all of premodern literature is filled with references to intense parental devotion to children, strikingly like modern parental devotion to children. It's astounding to me that historians could ever have gotten away with making such arguments, since all three of the major Western religious traditions use paternal love as the primary, intuitive model for describing divine love.

MASS: In a 1989 Postscript to your *Salmagundi* essay in the new Duberman/Chauncey/Vicinus anthology, you answer the preceding question at some length. First you point out that the so-called essentialist-social constructionist debate isn't a real debate because "no one involved in it actually identifies herself or himself as an 'essentialist,' although constructionists . . . sometimes so label other writers." Then you redefine "gay persons" more simply as "those whose erotic interest is predominantly directed toward their own gender (i.e., regardless of how conscious they are of this as a distinguishing characteristic)." In this sense—the sense in which you believe the word "gay" is used by most American speakers—you say that you "would still argue that there have been 'gay persons' in most Western societies." But you add that "it is not clear to me that this is an 'essentialist' position." You conclude that "even if societies formulate or create 'sexualities' that are highly particular in some ways, it might happen that different societies would construct similar ones, as they often construct political or class structures similar enough to be subsumed under the same rubric (democracy, oligarchy, proletariat, aristocracy, etc.—all of which are both particular and general)."

First, what about non-Western societies? Are you saying that you would not argue that there have been "gay persons" in most non-Western societies?

Second, I'm not sure I understand the analogy to political structures. Are you saying that "gay persons" can include facultatively bisexual, otherwise heterosexual male prisoners as well as "Castro Street clones" in the same way that "political or class structures" can include democracies as well as aristocracies? Or would you substitute "homosexually active persons" in this analogy for "gay persons?"

Third, why do you keep saying that you are not an essentialist? Or are you saying something slightly different—that your essentialism may include or accommodate constructionist viewpoints even as constructionists insist that what *they* consider to be essentialism must categorically preclude any and all constructionist viewpoints.

BOSWELL: First, I believe that there have been gay persons in most non-Western societies, but I'm not an expert on very many of them, and limit my written statements to what I have studied. The ones I do know—for instance, Islamic society in the Middle East—have gay persons, it's clear to me, and have had gay persons in the past. There's language that reflects this and lots of evidence in literature. In the *Arabian Nights*, for example, a wise woman notices a man looking at a beautiful young man, and says to him, not something circumstantial like "I see you fancy my brother," but "I see you are one *of those men* who prefer males to females." She clearly has a category in her mind and clearly expects that the audience is going to understand it. Much Islamic literature attempts to explain why there are basically three categories of sexuality—preferring one's own gender, preferring the opposite gender, and liking both. All three are quite familiar in the Muslim world. A difference between this society and our own—one which causes some confusion—in it (as in classical Athens and in certain other societies) some forms of homosexuality are institutionalized. So a higher percentage of men would use homosexual activity just as a sexual outlet. That's the kind of circumstantial homosexuality we were talking about before. It's rather like masturbation. There are lots of people who masturbate, even a lot, but who would actually prefer some other kind of interpersonal relationship. In the Muslim world, a lot of men will have relations with boys, even though, if they had a free choice, they would prefer women. But that in no way contradicts the fact that there are also men in the society who *prefer* men, as is made clear in Arabic literature in a great many ways: for example, there is a whole genre of debates about which is better, to be gay or straight.

To answer your second question: no, I'm not including everyone who engages in homosexual behavior under the rubric "gay"—only those who *prefer* sexual interaction with their own gender (not, for example, prisoners who have no other choice, or children or slaves forced into it). Suppose we accept, for the sake of argument, Greenberg's theories about certain patterns of homosexual behavior being inspired by childhood relations with parents, others being established as the result of adolescent interaction with older males (or females), still others as instilled by same-gender bonding patterns in the army or harem. If each of these produces persons who, all their subsequent lives, prefer erotic interaction with their own gender, they could all be called "gay" in my sense, and in the sense I believe most American speakers would use the term. I don't think the word presupposes anything about etiology or phenomenology beyond eroticism and gender. So, although one could establish categories that would not group Athenian men who preferred sex with other men — of whatever sort and for whatever reason — in the same category as modern American males who prefer sex with other men — of whatever sort and for whatever reason — I don't believe "gay" is that specific. Like "democracy," it is broad and diachronic, but still useful to most speakers and writers.

Now, the third question. Why do I keep saying that I'm not an essentialist? Well, it's not that I'm afraid to be labeled something unpopular or much criticized. The problem is that this is such a murky area, and people misunderstand each other so much, and it seems to me that the common understanding of essentialist is a kind of stereotype presented by constructionists as a target rather than a position ever outlined by anyone who actually believes it. I don't subscribe to some of the ideas that are often called essentialist. For instance, I'm an agnostic about what sexuality is. I disagree very strongly with constructionist positions that assume we know that sexuality is constructed anew, as it were, or independently in every different society. I'm sure we don't know that, and in many ways it seems to me that the similarities among different societies in regard to sexuality outweigh the differences. But *I don't know what sexual orientation is or isn't and neither does anyone else.* We don't know how much of it might be genetic, how much physiological, how much learned. My *guess* is that almost everybody's sexuality is a combination of hard- and software, as it were, of things that they inherited and things that they learned. And I would *guess* for that reason that no two human beings will have the exact same sexual feelings or experience, but that the *ranges* of those feelings and experiences among nearly all peoples can be characterized under headings that are diachronic. If the position I've just outlined is an essentialist position, then I'm an essentialist, but essentialist isn't a term that most people like me feel committed to. I'm not interested in rallying under a banner. I'm really only committed to understanding the matter better. I don't know where sexuality comes from. I keep up with the scientific literature, and I can tell you that the scientists don't know, either. Clearly, nobody knows, but constructionists seem to have a much greater confidence than I that their hunch is the correct one.

MASS: In this Postscript you state the following:

> although it is probably still accurate to say that "most" constructionists are historians of the nineteenth and twentieth centuries, a number of classicists have now added their perspective to constructionist theory. This has broadened and deepened the discussion, although, strikingly, few if any historians of periods between Periclean Athens and the late nineteenth century articulate constructionist views.

Have you seen the new anthology *The Pursuit of Sodomy: Male Homosexuality in Renaissance and Enlightenment Europe* by Kent Gerard and Gert Hekma? Doesn't this new study demonstrate that constructionist views are increasingly applicable to all of history?

BOSWELL: I have seen *The Pursuit of Sodomy* and I do think it shows that constructionist views can be applied to other periods of history. But it still strikes me that constructionist historians converge in schools — e.g., the school of classical constructionists and the school of modern constructionists. There haven't been schools in between, though some material is now emerging. Saslow's *Ganymede in the Renaissance* and Alan Bray's *Homosexuality in Renaissance England* carefully avoid taking sides on this issue and include material that could be interpreted in either direction. The constructionist schools remain clumped at either end of Western history, but I would agree that constructionism is a methodology that can be applied to any period.

MASS: In the introduction to *The Pursuit of Sodomy: Male Homosexuality in Renaissance and Enlightenment Europe*, co-editors Kent Gerard and Gert Hekma state the following: "Male homosexuality has a history, but this history consists principally of sodomites and buggers, pederasts and catamites, berdaches and 'contrary lovers' rather than homosexuals or gays in the modern sense."

First, why aren't "buggers," "sodomites," etc. in quotes in this statement, the way "contrary lovers" is?

The fallacy here, it seems to me, is in the assumption that because "sodomites" and "buggers" didn't have such neutral or self-selected terms for themselves as homosexual or gay, they were therefore definitionally different people. On the other hand, isn't the labeling of European homosexuals as "sodomites" the equivalent of labeling male homosexuals in America during the 1950s and '60s as "faggots" and/or "queers" and/or "perverts," etc.? If so, does this mean that a study of male homosexuality in America during the 1950s and 60s would be more appropriately entitled *Brown Noses, Degenerates, Faggots, Fairies, Fems, Froufrous, Fruits, Fudge-packers, Gays, Homos, Homosexuals, Inverts, Pansies, Patsies, Pederasts, Perverts, Psychopathic Personalities, Queens, Queers, Screamers, Sissies, Sodomites, Swishes, Transvestites, Transsexuals, Twinkies* and *Wimps*, than one that read *Gay Men in America from 1950 to 1970*?

BOSWELL: That sentence from their introduction strikes me as an extreme conceptual misprision. A bigot who calls me a "queer" and a friend who refers to me as "gay" are saying largely the same thing in different terms and for different reasons. Both are pointing out something distinctive about my sexuality, and neither really means more than that I prefer males—which makes one speaker hostile and derogatory but is accepted calmly by the other. Neither is commenting on the age of my partners, my political beliefs or commitments, or how I came to be this way.

There people of color not people of color when they were called "niggers," or "negroes," or "blacks?" Weren't they the same group? Perceptions of them changed, and these changes affected them and the world around them, and speech is a good indicator of these shifts, but none of this means that the people themselves were different, any more than a man's sexual feelings are changed when he moves to another country and uses a different language to describe them.

There are "closeted" men and women today who would deny that the terms "gay" or "homosexual" apply to them, for political, economic, family, religious, social or psychological reasons, even though an observer of their private sexual acts would call them "gay." Should they be included in a history of "gay people" in the twentieth century, even though they obviously do not have the same view of the matter as people who march in Gay Pride parades? I can see placing them in a particular category of "gay person," but not excluding them.

Should we say that in Spain in 1496 because there were *officially* no longer any Jews there were *really* no Jews? Just because they were now called *conversos* or *marranos*, terms which do not mean "Jew?" Of course not: historians realize that terms do not create or unmake living people. The way to determine whether there were Jews in Spain in 1496 is not to see whether Jews *are mentioned as such* in the documentation of the period, but to see whether the evidence *in toto* gives one reason to believe that persons who match a historical definition of "Jew" lived then and there (and they did, though they had to disguise themselves).

Moreover, some of the terms you cite are very, very close to their modern equivalents. As far as I can see, berdache is an exclusively gay category, as is catamite. Why should they not figure in a history of gays in the modern sense? Catamite refers to a man who is sexually passive only with other men. How is that different from a gay man today who is sexually passive?

MASS: I'm not sure I understand either. The implication here is that if someone asked you and me who we are, we'd say "we're gay men." By contrast, the editors and authors of *The Pursuit of Sodomy* are proposing that if you asked preferentially homosexual men from late Renaissance or Enlightenment Europe who they were, they might say or at least think, "We're buggers" or "we're sodomites" or "catamites" because (presumably) they had no other vocabulary or context for thinking about themselves. Conversely, we'd call them buggers and sodomites because the only information we have about them thus far comes from legal documents wherein they are so labeled.

BOSWELL: Now, wait a minute. Let me get this straight. If I ask someone in Spain if he's gay and he says "Yo soy entendido," or if I ask someone in France if he's gay and he says "Je suis pédé," does that mean he's not gay? Just because it's a different word?

MASS: No, not quite. I think most constructionists would emphasize that there's a more substantial difference, based not just on the use of different terminology, but on the basis of the contemporary understanding of what that terminology means. Today's Spanish gay man may still be persecuted in some Spanish-speaking coun-

tries as a "maricon," but he probably also has at least some access
to contemporary international knowledge about homosexuality and
to contemporary gay culture. That's different from the "bugger" or
"sodomite" in Enlightenment Europe who has no such access to
any such knowledge, isn't it?

BOSWELL: I have been friends with many gay Frenchmen during
my adult life, ranging from Michel Foucault to persons with no
formal education. Most of them, before the late '70s, used pédé to
describe themselves and other people we would now call gay. Pédé,
as you probably know, is a contraction of pédéraste, the French
equivalent of "pederast." Now, all of those same people (if, alas,
they are still living) would say they are *gai*. Do you suppose that
they were mostly pederasts before, and when they started using the
word *gai* they rearranged their sexual interests to focus on adults?
Of course not: not a single one of them was interested in children
then, and their sexual identities have only become more open in the
'80s, not the least bit different in terms of the age of the partners
they prefer.

Actually, this aspect of constructionist theory strikes me as gross
intellectual condescension, as if only white male and female writers
in modern industrial societies could perceive categories of sexuality
clearly: everyone else in other societies is limited by their primitive
culture and backward language.

Gay-straight distinctions exist in many parts of the world where
the kind of modern understanding of homosexuality and international gay culture we're talking about haven't penetrated at all. Of
course, different cultures, past and present, use different words to
describe the same experience. Or they might subdivide the experience differently. For example, in many parts of the world today,
people don't identify themselves as "gay" as a category that includes both "active" and "passive." For them the crucial thing
isn't gay versus not gay but active versus passive. Or modern notions become fused with older ones. In Egypt there are three categories. There's a term [*fa'il*] for the active gay man (it would be super-
fluous from an Egyptian point of view to use this term of a male in a
heterosexual context), one for the passive gay man [*maf'ul*] and
there's "gay," a term that the Egyptians now use to describe somebody who has his own apartment and does either one. But all three

terms mean "gay." All three are intended to describe men whose sexuality is directed towards other men. The fact that they have finer divisions than we do doesn't mean they have no concept of gay. It means they have a more highly developed *language*. French doesn't have a word for shallow, but that doesn't mean that the French don't understand what shallow means. We don't tend to break gay experience down into the same subcategories, but that's not because we don't have any understanding of them. That's what "Greek active" and "French passive" mean!

MASS: I think many constructionists wouldn't disagree with the distinctions you're making, but I think they'd emphasize what they believe to be a more important point about sexual identity—that an *identity* based on same-sex orientation or preference, like personal identities that are based on gender and ethnicity, is a Western phenomenon of modern times.

BOSWELL: A fundamental part of the problem here is in the assumption of a uniform, modern gay identity, which is a complete error. It assumes that everyone who is gay is a Village or Castro Street clone and shares the same lifestyle and is politically conscious, etc. But there are married gay men in Topeka, Kansas, for whom this one erotic aspect of their internal being defines little else about their mode of life. Even so, if we asked them, are you gay, do you really prefer your own gender, they'd say yes. What most English speakers mean by gay is simply preferring one gender over the other. That's all. There are many, many gay persons who don't live what some people might call a gay lifestyle: not only the married and closeted, but children with no sexual experience (yet), nuns and priests, the disabled, the very elderly.

MASS: So we're acknowledging that many persons who might identify themselves as gay may not have a very strong gay identity. And as for the married gay man in Topeka, as De Cecco, D'Emilio and Freedman have suggested, the proclaimed unhappiness of many gay men in their marriages might be a lot less under more tolerant social circumstances.

BOSWELL: I think that may well be true. In previous societies where people didn't associate love and marriage, it was quite comfortable for gay men to have a wife and children and male lovers on the side, just as many men might (then or now) have a wife and children and female lovers on the side. And the significance of the words gay and straight and bisexual, it seems to me, has to do simply with which gender is preferred for the lover. But the major point about these terms is that there are so many variations. There are Mexican and other Hispanic and Islamic men who only have sex with men and who only want to have sex with men but who say they're not "gay" because they don't get fucked. Now, if constructionists want to think up another word to characterize this particular subcategory of gay sex, that's fine. I have no argument with that. But I would argue that the way most English speakers use the word "gay" would include that subcategory of experience. On the other hand, I've known people who don't care what gender their partner is. They just want to fuck somebody who's small and blond, or tall and dark, or whatever.

MASS: This last point is important. You're saying one can use the word "gay" to refer to persons who prefer (who are more sexually aroused by) persons of their own gender. At the same time, you're acknowledging that there are persons who don't care what "gender" their partners are.

Your Postscript ends with the following statement:

> Most constructionist arguments assume that essentialist positions necessarily entail a further supposition: that society does not create erotic feelings, but only acts on them. Some other force — genes, psychological forces, etc. — creates "sexuality," which is essentially independent of culture. This was not a working hypothesis of *Christianity, Social Tolerance and Homosexuality.* I was and remain agnostic about the origins and etiology of human sexuality.

At the time of writing *Christianity, Social Tolerance and Homosexuality,* didn't you — like your colleagues Jim Weinrich and Richard Pillard, like most sex researchers and many psychiatrists, and like me — believe that being gay *was* probably mostly or significantly a matter of genes? Are you implying that you didn't share that belief when you wrote your book?

BOSWELL: No. In my everday responses to issues of sexuality, I think I assume that sexuality is fixed from a fairly early age, but I don't know what fixes it. I personally think it's likely that it has something to do with one's "hard-wiring," which obviously is determined by a constellation of genetic factors, but I really am honestly agnostic about this, and I was when I wrote *Christianity, Social Tolerance and Homosexuality*. I think what struck (or bothered) some people is that I'm quite willing to *entertain* the notion that sexual orientation is entirely determined by genes. This seems an extreme and heretical position to some people, but to me it is only one of the obvious possibilities. It's also possible in my view that it is entirely learned behavior. But even if it is entirely learned, that doesn't mean that there wouldn't be certain transhistorical forms of it that appear regularly. Just as speaking is learned behavior, but there are no cultures known to me in which people don't speak. The range of possibilities is great. I honestly don't know what causes sexuality and I didn't know then.

MASS: In your critique of David F. Greenberg's book, *The Construction of Homosexuality*, for *The Atlantic* (2/89), you note that eroticism and sexuality are stunningly absent from the author's analysis "except as they relate to guilt or heterosexual marriage patterns." "Would it not be more economical," you ask, "to hypothesize that a percentage of human beings in all societies prefer their own gender sexually, that they are sometimes able to institutionalize this preference, and that the majority of human beings are sufficiently flexible to be able to derive sexual satisfaction from either gender under institutional pressure, whether or not that gender is their first choice?"

I think constructionists would argue that the business of first and second choice is much more socially determined than we've realized. For example, when I asked them to comment on the recent concept of limerence — the state of falling in love or being in love, which has been used by "essentialist" psychologists and sexologists as a major, distinguishing characteristic of sexual orientation (if you fall in love with someone of your own gender, that's what makes you gay or lesbian) — D'Emilio and Freedman expressed skepticism that limerence, as opposed to pair-bonding, was a universal that can be identified over time. As Freedman put it, "Most cultures we've learned about have some form of pair-bonding. But love in conjunction with pair-bonding is historically and culturally specific. And 'falling in love' as a phenomenon that leads to pair-bonding is even more culturally specific."

Now, doesn't your statement in the Greenberg review presume something we don't know or haven't proven — namely that sexual preference for one gender more than another has existed universally?

BOSWELL: I certainly do not know whether preference for one gender has existed *universally* — in every culture. There's much argument among anthropologists about whether there are cultures in which there is no violence or no greed or no child abuse or no something or other. However that question is resolved, it doesn't mean that sexuality is entirely constructed anew in every society. If it could be shown that there were some societies in which there is no known homosexuality — and I'm not aware that there have been any such societies (I certainly don't believe anthropological reports prior to the 1980s because people had a lot of reason not to see or be told things of which they would disapprove) — that might then just be an exceptional society. It wouldn't demonstrate that by and large human societies don't include people who prefer their own gender. But I wouldn't say that I know that homosexuality has existed "universally." I don't have that knowledge.

The point about falling in love being socially constructed is very interesting. The literature of falling in love in all Western societies — and I know this literature very well, from Greek times to the present — is so similar that not only would a historian be struck that it is basically the same phenomenon being described over time, but in fact *poets* are struck that it's the same phenomenon and they constantly repeat the love literature of previous ages and apply it to their own experience. It's true that the connection between falling in love and marriage changes from one society to another, but it's not true that it's one way or another. For a long time, the modern world assumed that people in premodern societies married for romantic reasons. Now we know that they married *more often* for economic reasons and didn't necessarily expect love to sustain their relationships. But that's very different from claiming that people in the ancient world *didn't fall in love* or *never* married for love. In most premodern Western societies, many people were involved in arranged marriages, but *some* people married for love and everyone thought that there was *a relationship* between love and marriage. Sometimes the relationship was that love was not to be expected from marriage, but the very fact that this was expressed is evidence of the contrary expectation among *some* contemporaries. Sometimes spouses hoped for a kind of fraternal love in marriage; sometimes they hoped for erotic excitement; sometimes they expected that erotic interest would wane over time. But falling in love itself is a constant, either within or outside marriage. I don't know of any Western society where people didn't write about falling in love.

MASS: In the Greenberg review, you note that "again and again Greenberg dismisses the possibility that there were 'modern homosexuals' in premodern cultures by pointing out that persons who appear from the records to have preferred their own sex were nonetheless married or that their interests were not 'exclusive' — as if Oscar Wilde had not been married and a father, and as if all surveys did not indicate that a majority of American gay men have had heterosexual experiences." You and I know that Oscar Wilde was a gay man in a way that David Halperin's bisexual aristocrat prototype was not. But *why*?

BOSWELL: About the bisexual aristocratic prototype you mentioned earlier (the man who is not really or deeply committed to a particular sexuality), we can tell, I think, that a particular sexuality, one that is, for example, numerically a minority sexuality, doesn't affect his life or his sensibility in the way that it did Oscar Wilde. In talking about such things as "feasting with panthers," Oscar Wilde is saying something to us. He's saying this is risky, the majority of people don't understand it, but it's so wonderful, such a fundamental part of my life, that I have to do it anyway. And we immediately identify with that. But I would argue that we don't need to have a feeling of empathy with people in order to be able to recognize them as gay. There are, in fact, plenty of contemporaries of mine who have very different sensibilities but who are gay; people who are, say, cold mathematicians, who never express their erotic or romantic feeling anywhere near the way I do. I know a lot of gay men who seem never to be deeply in love in the way I am, who enjoy much more casual and frivolous relationships, but they are certainly as "gay" as I am. There's a great range of human eroticism, but that doesn't mean we can't organize it in terms of genders. Those whose eroticism is primarily directed toward their own gender I'd call "gay." As for the bisexual aristocrat, I don't think we can say that his eroticism is chiefly directed toward his own gender, and I wouldn't call him "gay."

MASS: A number of critics in the gay community have expressed wariness about the fact that you are a practicing Catholic. In seeking tolerance, if not full acceptance, from an institution that denounces and rejects homosexuality and homosexuals, are gay Catholics qualitatively different from gay Jews who seek tolerance and acceptance from conservative Jewish institutions, such as the state of Israel (which, however, recently abolished laws that criminalized homosexuality involving consenting adults)?

BOSWELL: This is such a funny issue. It strikes me as odd that many gay people assume that all Catholics are a certain undesirable thing when precisely what we are asking from society is that people stop regarding all gay people as a certain undesirable thing. I mean, the difference between the nuns who signed the famous *New York Times* [pro-choice] abortion statement and Cardinal Ratzinger is certainly as great as the difference between a gay man's abuse of a child and a consensual, loving relationship between two adult males. There are a great many non-Catholics whose attitudes towards gay people are closer to Ratzinger's than are those of the many Catholics whose feelings on the issue are accepting and tolerant. Part of the problem here is a kind of odd stereotyping of Catholics.

On the other hand, let me say quite clearly that I do what I can to change the attitudes of the institutional church in the same way that I do what I can to change the attitudes of Yale or the United States or any organization with which I find myself in close contact. I often get the feeling that what people are saying covertly is that Boswell is afraid to admit that the Bible condemns homosexuality or something like that because, in fact, he's Catholic and has to come to terms with the church. But that's silly. I've done as much as anyone to show how the church has been oppressive, wrong, unjust, mistaken. I regard the church as a human institution that makes terrible, gross errors. I know those errors as well as anyone and I'm quite willing to speak up about them. It should be obvious that I'm willing to be honest no matter what it costs me.

MASS: I think what troubles some observers and critics is something else. It's one thing to be ethnically Jewish. Because of the phenomenon of anti-Semitism, you're Jewish, if that's what you were born, whether you like it or not. I, for example, am that kind of Jew. When I was growing up in the rural South, I wanted to be Christian, not to be Jewish, the same way I so wanted to be straight during my teenage years and early adulthood. Today, I accept that I'm Jewish, am even proud of that fact, in much the same way I've accepted that I'm gay and have a lot of gay pride. But I don't relate to Jewish orthodoxy, which is homophobic, racist and sexist. Likewise, one might wonder why you would want to declare your allegiance to a creed that is not so distinctively a matter of lineage (though Catholics have periodically been persecuted as a minority).

BOSWELL: In the first place, I wonder where you (or the critics to whom you refer) imagine that I have "declared my allegiance to a creed." Do people follow me to mass on Sunday? I've certainly never published any credal statement of this sort. And isn't second-guessing a person's ideology from personal characteristics rather out of date? I would have thought that the days when Protestants would not trust "Catholic historians" or Jewish or feminist or Marxist historians were discounted because of their ethnic heritage, gender or political beliefs were long past. Would we consider it proper for heterosexual critics to write that I can not be trusted on the subject of homosexuality because they *have heard* that I'm gay, or assume I am because I write about this subject? In fact, even the most hostile heterosexual critics were too responsible to do so, but many gay critics seem to have gotten away with arguing that I can't be trusted on Christian history because they *have heard* or infer that I'm Catholic. (I might point out in this context that no one seems to have assumed on the basis of my first book about the Muslim minority in Spain that I am a Muslim.) And, as I mentioned before, the idea that all Catholics are alike, adhering mindlessly to some monolithic ideology, is a vulgar prejudice, probably left over from anti-Irish and anti-Italian sentiment in this country. Even if I agreed with the Vatican on every point, I would have no difficulty publishing empirical data embarrassing to such positions. I do not expect truths to be simple or easy, and I relish controversy and multiplicity of viewpoint.

Some people might say, well you can't help your ethnic heritage or being gay, so you might as well be honest about them, whereas you can choose which ideologies you support and you are responsible if you lend assistance to oppressive ones. This would actually be a curious argument from a constructionist, since both ethnicity and sexuality would be, in their view, to some extent constructed by individual experience rather than simply passively inherited. But leaving that aside, I understand that remaining a Catholic in the face of some Vatican pronouncements seems almost like remaining a member of the Nazi party after its intentions in regard to the Jews became evident.

Let me begin by saying that I don't think either Judaism or Catholicism deserves to be compared to the Nazis. I think they would be better compared to, say, the American government or Yale. There are ways in which one might decry Yale, being a traditionally elite white, male, patriarchal, elitist institution. And those things are true. I can see those things and I acknowledge them. But if one imagines that on the scale of human institutions Yale is therefore bad, then one has a strange historical view of what makes something good or bad. "Bad" institutions abound — totalitarian governments, Nazism, all kinds of fascism. Yale is not a bad institution. In fact, it is dedicated to goals I admire. So my inclination is not to reject it altogether but to try to change it, to make it better. And in fact I think it has become better in the last few years, partly because I've argued with people at Yale about the need for better attitudes on issues of gender and sexuality and race.

I might make the same analogy with the United States. Somebody might well say, how can you call yourself an American in view of what happened in Viet Nam? You could go to Holland or Canada. Yes, one could, and I respect the people who do, just as I respect those who have decided to leave the Catholic church. I also respect those who say, well, I'm an American and I'm going to try to make America better. That's the way I feel about being Catholic. Yes, there are very bad things about Catholic teaching, but it's not *all* Catholic teaching or *all* Catholics any more than it was *all* Americans who believed in and supported the Viet Nam war. The President directed the Viet Nam war; I did not even support it. The Pope says stupid, harmful things about contraception and gay people. That doesn't mean that every last Catholic feels that way, or even that a future pope won't adopt a better stance, just as the U.S. finally withdrew from Viet Nam.

MASS: Is John McNeill [who was dismissed from the Jesuits] still a practicing Catholic?

BOSWELL: Yes, I believe so. I must say that it amuses me when people assume that "practicing Catholic" means something like the square root of four, that it's absolutely specific everywhere. Italian Catholics, by and large, don't believe the finer points of the theology of the church. They're Catholic ethnically, the way many people are Jewish. They don't go to mass. They have their children baptised and they get married in the church, but if you ask them if they practice contraception, they all say, "Of course." If you point out to them that the Pope says it's wrong, they'll say, "So, the Pope says it's wrong." Whereas an American Catholic agonizes over this. Being Catholic is different all over the world. Is John McNeill a practicing Catholic? Well, according to whose definition? According to the Pope's, he's not. According to mine, he is. Am I a practicing Catholic according to the Pope's definition? No. I live with another man and have for the past nineteen years. Am I a practicing Catholic according to my definition? Yes. I go to mass every week. I believe probably as much of the Church's official teaching as the Pope does, to the extent that either of us understands it, but we interpret it very differently.

MASS: In his essay on *Christianity, Social Tolerance and Homosexuality*, Martin Duberman punctuated his very substantial praise of your study (which he characterized as "revolutionary" and "one of the most profound, explosive works of scholarship to appear within recent memory") with several critical observations, among which was the following:

> In reading Boswell, I now and then got the unnerving feeling that at the top of his own set of priorities is the wish to hold gay Christians to their religious allegiance—that he is more eager to defend the viability of church affiliation for gays than to bolster an emerging gay subculture whose left wing is decidedly—in my view, rightly—anticlerical. I don't know how else to account for Boswell's curious statement that "It is un-

likely that at any other time in Western history have gay people been the victims of more widespread and vehement intolerance than during the first half of the twentieth century.'' He may be correct in claiming that "the excesses of the Inquisition are often exaggerated," but after all, the death penalty for homosexuality (a rather extreme form of intolerance) had become legal proscription in most of Europe by 1300 A.D. (from *The New Republic*, 10/18/80)

In defending the viability of church affiliation for gays, are you thereby undermining an emerging gay subculture? Must one or should one necessarily preclude the other?
BOSWELL: The simple answer to this is that if by being affiliated in some way with an ideology that has sometimes been oppressive of gay people one is somehow precluding the emergence of a gay subculture, then no one can support *any* modern ideology, from psychoanalysis to democracy. Are Marxists precluding the emergence of a gay subculture because some Marxist regimes have been very oppressive of gay people? (In fact, a majority are still oppressive of gay people.) Gay people are more oppressed in most Marxist regimes than they are in most Catholic countries. But I certainly wouldn't say to a Marxist, you can't be a Marxist because that's somehow anti-gay. That's silly. All ideologies can be turned by bigots against gay people or Jews or blacks and most can be turned by liberal people to benefit Jews or gays or blacks.

Christianity has been an ameliorating influence in many areas of the world, as has Judaism. One could point out about Judaism that it has had regrettable attitudes towards women. That's true. But imagine a society in which husbands can just divorce their wives without any obligation to them, in which female children are regularly killed, in which men rape their servants with impunity. In such a society, the very strict family ethical culture of Judaism would improve the position of women enormously. That it doesn't improve the position of women as much as we moderns would like is part of the reason I would respect people for abandoning Judaism. But I think *they* ought to respect people who stay with it and try to make it better. It's an ancient force that has been very beneficial to a great many people and been very conducive to loving parent-child relations, and that seems to me a good thing. So while I respect people who feel that they can do more good outside it, I also respect the people who think, "This has been very valuable to many humans. Let's see if we can't make it better." And I'd say that about Marxism and any other ideology that has ever been used for ill, and most have.

MASS: Perhaps there are parallels here to some of the criticism Martin Duberman has encountered with regard to his monumental biography of Paul Robeson. In his time and ever since, Robeson has been categorically denounced for not speaking out against Stalin and the Soviets. Some of these critics are, arguably, justifiably disappointed that specific evils of Stalinism were not more outspokenly addressed. Others, however, are upset that the entirety of Marxism, of communism, was not altogether denounced and rejected.

In his review of *Christianity, Social Tolerance and Homosexuality*, Duberman states the following:

> I'll leave chief responsibility for evaluating Boswell's central avowal that "much of the present volume is specifically intended to rebut the common idea that religious belief—Christian or not—has been the *cause* of intolerance in regard to gay people," to those gay Christians who have insisted on the compatibility of their sexual orientation and their devotion to institutional religion and who have been working through such organizations as DIGNITY (gay Catholics) and INTEGRITY (gay Episcopaleans) to "maintain a dialogue with the Mother Church."

You are one such gay Christian. Have the events of the decade since your book was published strengthened or weakened your own evaluation of your book's central avowal about the relationship between religion and intolerance in regard to gay people?

BOSWELL: At the time I published that book, nearly a decade ago, I thought that the Christian world was generally moving in a more tolerant direction. Since then, some of the Christian communities, like the Episcopalians, do seem to me to have become more tolerant and open. As everyone knows, Catholicism is going through a period of hostility from the top. The Vatican issues hostile statements, such as the Ratzinger letter, which must have been aimed mostly at John McNeill and at me and at American Catholics: it was issued in English and obviously directed toward America. But I don't think that reflects the general attitude of Roman Catholics. In fact, I think the general attitude of Roman Catholics has become much more liberal. In dealing with gay couples and AIDS, for example, most priests have become much more tolerant and understanding and sensitive than they were ten or twenty years ago. That's exactly why the Vatican is so upset about what's going on in America. They think the American church has become soft on gay people. Accepting that terminology for the sake of argument, I agree with them. It is soft on gay people and I think that's nice. There are still some bigots in the hierarchy, of course, but I do think that by and large the Catholic hierarchy has become much more tolerant in the last eight years. The Vatican has had to force almost every American bishop to expel Dignity from his diocese. I don't feel that this vindicates *me*. I think it has to do with social forces. America in general is much more tolerant now, even though there are backslidings of various sorts. I deplore those and don't mean to trivialize them. But I think the fabric of American society is more tolerant.

MASS: At your talk on male and female roles in history at The Jung Foundation in New York in March, you alluded to research you've been doing on the history of gay marriages among the clergy. What can you tell us about this research? Will it be the subject of a book?

BOSWELL: Yes, I can tell you that it will be the subject of a book, which will be out in a year or two. The marriages were not just among the clergy, but among Christians, both male and female, lay and clerical. And in fact, it was mostly lay people. It was problematic for the clergy to be married, either heterosexually or homosexually. That's as much as I want to say about this material at this point, because without presenting all the documentation that goes with it, I'm afraid it will end up like announcements of cold fusion. All kinds of people will be arguing about it before they've even seen the evidence. So I'm working as hard as I can, when I'm not being interviewed (laughter), to get this material together. But this material, on a Catholic marriage ceremony performed by priests for two men or two women, is astonishing.

MASS: Incidentally, how did your lecture for The Jung Foundation come about? Are you a Jungian?

BOSWELL: No, I am not a Jungian. I was asked by a close friend who is a Jungian analyst to talk to the Jungians because he thought my point of view would be interesting to them.

MASS: Caryn James, who usually reviews movies, wrote an ignorant and petty review of *The Kindness of Strangers* for *The New York Times*. But did she have a decipherable point about the title conjuring up images of Blanche Du Bois when there was no conceivable relationship, at least not for the vast majority of nongay readers, between your book and the central character of Tennessee Williams play, *A Streetcar Named Desire*?

BOSWELL: It was a nasty review. Of course there's a relationship! First of all, how could I not have thought about it? But she seems to assume that all English readers have the mindset of New York literati. The majority of English speakers throughout the world have never read Tennessee Williams, but would understand the phrase "the kindness of strangers." To imagine that everybody in the world is struggling with Blanche Du Bois is very odd and parochial. *I*, of course, thought of Blanche Du Bois. That may be part of the reason that phrase occurred to me as the best English equivalent. It's not that there's no relationship. There's in fact a lot of relationship. Blanche is taken away by the kindness of strangers when her own family lets her down. That's a lot like the abandoned children. But a richer, more interesting association, I think, is that the "kindness" of strangers isn't really so kind. It's hardly an unmitigated good. She's being taken away to an institution, as were the abandoned children in my book. On the one hand, it's better than being abused by the family. On the other, however, it's not a happy ending. So, yes, of course I thought about it, and I felt that this association was a rich one. But it's incredibly ignorant of her to imagine that Tennessee Williams coined this phrase. He didn't. It's a very ancient phrase, and occurs in English long before Williams.

MASS: Do you think Williams was aware of it as an older phrase?

BOSWELL: He may have just heard it and written it down. I don't know if he was consciously playing on an earlier occurrence of it or not.

MASS: Were you personally offended by George Steiner's suggestion that your interest in the abandonment of children in history as "prurient?" (I certainly was.) It's the same accusation, incidentally, that is being leveled against Martin Duberman for his careful documentation of what is known about Paul Robeson's love life. Are these critics projecting their own erotophobia onto you?

BOSWELL: Yes, I thought the last two paragraphs of his review were deeply offensive. I thought it was more than erotophobia. I thought it was homophobia. The suggestion that a gay man writing about children is voyeuristic is, at best, an ignorant assumption that gay men don't have children and don't have a reason to care about them, and are therefore on the outside looking in at something, the way a voyeur would be: somebody not involved, just viewing. At worst, it's the ancient bugbear of homophobes that all gay men have some erotic interest in children, and that I am somehow sexually stimulated by writing or thinking about children and abuse. I thought it was extremely ugly and wholly unwarranted.

MASS: Were you adopted?

BOSWELL: No. *The Kindness of Strangers* is dedicated to my own natal family and to a group of people who I say "adopted me even though I was not abandoned." Those people are Jerry's (my other half's) family, to whom I'm now as close as I am to my own family.

MASS: Do you think being an adopted person constitutes an identity that is in some ways comparable to a gay identity?

BOSWELL: I think it might, but it would depend on the circumstances. I remember hearing a very charming story when I was a young man about a teacher who had two brothers in her class who were only about four months apart in age. She was confused by this, so she called one of them up to her desk and asked him how it was that his brother was only four months younger than he, and he said, "Because one of us is adopted, but I can't remember which one." I remember thinking that this was a very nice story because it showed that there was no stigma attached to being adopted and that the important thing was the brothers' relationship to each other and to their parents.

But in saying that I don't want to suggest that it would be necessarily undesirable for adopted people to be aware of this as a special category. My experience of adopted people in contemporary America and of adoptees in premodern Europe is that some do have such an identity and some don't. Some parents never tell their adopted children that they're adopted and so, of course, those children never have any such identity. Some who are told decide that they are well-rid of their biological parents or see little hope of ever being able to locate them. Others become obsessed with finding their biological parents and feel trapped between two worlds. That may well be comparable to being gay in many ways because unlike many other minorities, gay people are in most ways part of the straight world. They are socialized as straight people because they usually aren't known to be gay until they are adults. They come from straight families, unlike Jews who come from Jewish families or blacks who come from black families. Gay people are not even in the position that women are, in that a woman must at least have had another woman as an immediate ancestor. For a gay child, that's not so, and that's a lot like being adopted. You're anomalous in some important ways, but you're also socialized in a normal way. You're not brought up in a ghetto, but you're nevertheless different from most everyone else around you. So there is a sense of difference at the same time that there's a sense of being the same. In some ways, I think that's even more troubling than being simply different, as with someone brought up in a ghetto, but who at least has the support system of others who are also different.

On the other hand, I don't want to overstate this. I think the experience of a great many Jews in America, for instance, is very like the experience of gay people, because there are a lot of places in America where being a Jew doesn't really separate one from the majority, and one is only aware of being different at certain times — at Christmas, for example. The odd, empty feeling that an assimilated Jew might feel at Christmas is, I think, quite comparable to the way a gay person might feel at a straight wedding. There are many ways in which the experience of assimilated Jews and gays are the closest two minority experiences today in America.

MASS: At the conclusion of your review of Greenberg's book, you say that you "look forward to the next stage of conceptual development in the scholarship of homosexuality." Do you have any thoughts about what that stage will consist of?

BOSWELL: What I'd *prefer* is that we went back into a more empirical mode where methodologies didn't run ahead of findings. The main criticism I have of constructionism is that it assumes something and looks for it, rather than gathering lots of data and then cautiously sifting it for answers. I would prefer that nonempirical assumptions and ideologies about what sexuality is be dropped until, say, two decades from now, when there's enough of a body of data to have an empirical basis for pulling together a conceptual framework. But I don't think that will happen. What I do think will happen is that constructionism will gradually fragment into varieties of constructionism, some stricter and some looser and some adapted to different time periods, so that the movement will become more flexible and less monolithic and will therefore provide a less hostile focus for attacking everybody who doesn't subscribe to it. That is, once it becomes more diverse itself, I think that diversity will lower the tone of debate. That will be almost as good as what I would prefer, so I look forward to it.

On the Future of Lesbian and Gay Studies

A Dialogue with Will Roscoe

Will Roscoe is an independent historian and author. He has been coordinator for the History Project of Gay American Indians in San Francisco since 1984 and is editor of *Living The Spirit: A Gay American Indian Anthology* (St. Martin's Press, 1988). Other publications include *A Blessing from Wovoka* with Harry Hay (Vortex Media, 1988) and the "Bibliography of Berdache and Alternative Gender Roles Among North American Indians" (*Journal of Homosexuality*, volume 14, nos. 3/4, 1987). Mr. Roscoe is a member of the Editorial Board of the *Journal of Homosexuality* and the recipient of a Van Waveren Foundation Fellowship for his study of Zuni berdaches. In 1986, he received the Crompton-Noll Award of the Gay and Lesbian Caucus of the Modern Language Association. His essay, "Making History: The Challenge of Lesbian and Gay Studies" (*Journal of Homsexuality*, volume 15, nos. 3/4, 1988) was the subject of a colloquium of The Center for Lesbian and Gay Studies of the City University of New York in March of 1989. It is likewise the focus of this exchange, conducted by correspondence in the spring of 1989.

[Ed. note: Throughout our dialogue, there is reference to the concept of "sociosexual specialization," which Mr. Roscoe summarizes in his essay, "Making History," as follows:

A model of continuity-within-change and unity-within-variation encompassing both continuous and discontinuous elements of homosexual expression and identity. The conceptual and symbolic constructs of different societies can be compared in terms of similarities *and* differences and by *degrees* of relatedness. The unity that links "sodomite," "Uranian," and "homosexual" is a dense network of cross-references. When viewed historically, there is no constant meaning to any of these terms; they are all concepts-in-process. But if 'gay' and 'lesbian' are defined as a hypothetical construct of *elements* and *patterns* shared among diverse social forms, they can be legitimately employed on a cross-cultural and historical basis.]

MASS: Your article, "The Zuni Man-Woman," in *Out/Look* (Summer, 1988) was criticized by Ramon A. Gutierrez in a subsequent issue ("Must We Deracinate Indians to Find Gay Roots?" Winter, 1989). In his critique, Gutierrez asks "How do we reconcile the ridicule and low status the berdaches had in Zuni society with the high status and praise others lavish on them?" Is Gutierrez correct? Is your understanding of the Zuni Man-Woman "shrouded" in "romantic obfuscations?"

ROSCOE: Having reviewed hundreds of published sources, conducted research in several archival collections, and spoken with Zunis and other American Indians, I have never found data supporting the kind of assertions Gutierrez makes. Indeed, when Gutierrez claims that berdaches occupied a low social status, he contradicts not only my own findings but the consensus of every scholar who has published on this subject in recent years. Paula Gunn Allen, Evelyn Blackwood, Charles Callender and Lee Kochems, David Greenberg, Sue Ellen Jacobs, Maurice Kenney, Harriet Whitehead, and Walter Williams—to name a few—all agree that berdaches were accepted, often respected members of their tribes. And, of course, as I related in my original article in *Out/Look*, I have presented my material on the berdache We'wha at Zuni and been invited to return.

How then did Gutierrez reach such conclusions? I think one example will suffice, although I could cite others. Gutierrez writes,

> During one of the *sha'lko* [Sha'lako] dances Parsons saw at Zuni, the audience "grinned and even chuckled" at U'k; "a very infrequent display of amusement during these *sha'lko* dances," Parsons confided. After the dance ended, Parsons' Cherokee hostess asked her: "Did you notice them laughing at her [U'k]? . . . She is a great joke to the people."

This is his evidence of the "ridicule and low status the berdaches had in Zuni society." But here is the complete passage from Parsons's 1916 article:

> When U'k fell out of line the audience, an audience mostly of women with their children, girls, and a few old men, grinned and even chuckled, a very infrequent display of amusement during these *sha'lako* dances. "Did you notice them laughing at her?" my Cherokee hostess asked me on my return. "She is a great joke to the people—*not because she is a* lha'mana, *but because she is half-witted.*" (emphasis mine)

Poor U'k was developmentally disabled—a "simpleton," according to another informant—and a bad dancer to boot. The portion of the comment from Parsons's informant that Gutierrez failed to quote makes it clear that *lhamana* status is definitely *not* a basis for ridicule.

Beyond this, I would simply refer readers to my original article and to the evidence I present there. I think they will find a more sophisticated discussion of change and continuity between berdache and gay roles than Gutierrez's characterization of me allows.

I must add that I find it ironic to be accused of taking Zuni berdaches "out of context." In my forthcoming book, *The Zuni Man-Woman*, I devote separate chapters exploring historical, social, religious, and psychological aspects of the role. It is, to my knowledge, the first book-length study of berdaches in a single tribe. I think readers will find in it exactly what Gutierrez calls for: a thorough treatment of berdaches in the context of a specific social organization, world view, religion, and sex/gender system.

MASS: In your commentary on Arthur Evans's book, *The God of Ecstasy: Sex-roles and the Madness of Dionysos* and Mark Thompson's *Gay Spirit: Myth and Meaning* for the *San Francisco Jung Institute Library Journal* ("What Child Is This?" vol. 8, no. 2, 1988), you observe that these books "record (and are part of) an increasingly influential movement from within [the gay and lesbian] community to seek the cultural and historical roots of gay identity." You note that Evans and Thompson "believe that gay traits and social functions exist independent of prevailing social conditions."

Your studies of American Indian berdaches have led you to a more qualified but similar belief. As you put it in this review:

> The fact that contemporary gay American Indians now claim the berdache tradition as their own (as I report in my contribution to Thompson's anthology), that individuals who fulfill these roles in tribes that have maintained the tradition call themselves gay or are called such by their tribespeople, and that native words once used to refer to berdaches are now used to refer to homosexuals (the case at Zuni)—makes this evidence all the more enticing.

You're saying that contemporary gay American Indians are claiming connectedness with—a kind of direct descendency from— the berdaches of premodern history. Walter Williams concluded much the same thing in his study, *The Spirit and the Flesh*. And that's likewise very similar to what Thompson is claiming in seeking "the cultural and historical roots of gay identity." But the fact that a popular majority of us may all believe in this connectedness isn't the same thing as actually demonstrating it. I mean, isn't it possible that contemporary gay American Indians are simply looking at themselves and their history with the same mind-set—that being gay is a transhistorical, constitutional essential—that has shaped the consciousness of most contemporary gay- and lesbian-identified persons?

ROSCOE: I do not believe that gay and lesbian American Indians are using an essentialist model when they claim berdaches as their ancestors. They are using *Indian* models of identity and history that in many ways are more sophisticated than those of western sociology and psychology. As Jamake Highwater points out, "Indians find it incredible that a person must retain one identity, one name, one persona for his or her entire existence, no matter what immense changes may take place in that person's life. . . . Not only does a primal person have a variety of ways in which he or she may fit into the social structure, but people also have a very wide potentiality for changing themselves and their identities even after they have been defined by social circumstances and roles." Indians recognize, to put it simplistically, both "nature" and "nurture." Similarly, when contemporary gay Indians contemplate the traditional berdache, they perceive underlying continuities while recognizing outward changes.

It is important that we pay attention to the actual words that gay Indians are using. When Randy Burns, co-founder of Gay American Indians, says that berdaches were "our traditional gay ancestors," he means something specific. By using the word "our," he means "Indian" — that is, berdaches may not be the "gay ancestors" of non-Indians, and this challenges us to conceptualize the possibility of more than one historical tradition of homosexuality. "Traditional" distinguishes berdaches from their present day counterparts — and this modifier acknowledges differences between past and contemporary roles. And finally, in the case of the word "gay," we must not assume that our Indian brothers and sisters define this term as we do. I have found that Indian people often think of "gay" as a multidimensional social role, not merely a synonym for homosexual. Even nongay elders prefer the term "gay" over "homosexual" for this reason.

This implicit multidimensional perspective allows Indians to recognize the difference between traditional and contemporary roles on specific dimensions while perceiving continuity on others. The most important difference between berdaches and contemporary gay people, as Indians often point out, is not, as you and I might think, the fact that berdaches engaged in cross-dressing and we do not, but that today's gay social role lacks an acknowledged spiritual dimension. At the same time, however, berdaches were craft specialists — and arts and crafts remain important for many gay Indians. Berdaches were go-betweens and mediators — and leaders like Randy Burns and Erna Pahe often serve as mediators between the white gay community and the urban Indian community. And both male and female berdaches formed long-term and casual relationships with their own sex — there are obvious continuities on that level as well.

One of the questions this raises is not new to American Indians but has not so far been addressed in gay and lesbian studies — and that is the question of assimilation versus pluralism. In our increasingly multicultural, global community, Indians are not the only

group with a tradition of homosexuality distinct from that of western society. Latin Americans, Asians, Pacific Islanders, Africans —
all have their own customs, traditions, values, and roles surrounding homosexuality and gender. Does joining a contemporary gay
community and enjoying the benefits of gay liberation require the
abandonment of traditional roles like the berdache, the *mahu* (Pol-
ynesia), the *bayot* (Philippines), the *hijra* (India), the *bicha* (Bra-
zil), the *ricchione* (Southern Italy)? Must nonwhite, non-Anglo homosexuals become clones to join the gay movement?

Your question also points to a fundamental problem that I perceive in the theory of social constructionism, so popular in gay and
lesbian studies. Suggesting that the historical perceptions of gay
Indians — or any gay or lesbian person for that matter — are filtered
through an anachronistic mind-set is a euphemistic way of saying
that these perceptions are myths, and, by implication, that there is
some more "real" form of historical connection. But what other
source of connection might there be besides that of memory, that is,
historical knowledge, which is itself a construct — unless it were
something biological or natural? Social constructionism sets up
conditions for historical continuity that are impossible to meet. By
asserting that symbolic and discursive continuities are not "real" it
posits the presence of what it denies — that there are "real," "essential" forms of continuity between historical periods and cultures, albeit lacking in the case of gay men and lesbians.

That gay Indians perceive a connection with berdaches, represent
this connection in various ways, use this connection in dialogues
with family and tribal communities, and allow knowledge of this
connection to inform their actions makes it a historical fact. If this is
mythology it is nonetheless having a concrete impact on countless
lives, leading both Indian and non-Indian gay people to take actions
that have political as well as social ramifications.

To evolve a gay studies perspective relevant to our multicultural
world and its multiple historical traditions we have to take a step
back. We have to develop a more generalized perspective that can
encompass the varieties of ways in which different cultures value,
symbolize, socialize, and utilize sex and gender variance.

Describing berdaches as mediators, for example, is a generalization. In each tribe this took distinct forms. Here in California, berdaches were often responsible for burying the dead — they could mediate the realms of the living and the nonliving. Among Plains Indians, berdaches had visions and foretold the future — they mediated the social and supernatural worlds. Elsewhere they functioned as go-betweens in arranging romantic liaisons between men and women. At Zuni, a berdache kachina appeared in an important ceremony carrying symbols of farming and hunting, male and female — powerful cultural oppositions. These are all elaborations of the principle of mediation, and, for this reason, we are warranted in calling these berdache roles despite this variation. What I am proposing for gay and lesbian studies is the adoption of the same type of generalization — a family tree if you will — that allows us to recognize the variety and the continuity of gender mediation and homosexual social patterns.

On the other hand, if we don't broaden our definitions, gay and lesbian studies will continue to be plagued by anomalies. What are we to make, for example, of the fact that Crow berdaches, eighteenth century French sodomites, and contemporary gay men have all used the kinship term "sister" to refer to others who shared their social status? Social constructionism, with its overemphasis on social regulation, has no way of explaining this continuity between otherwise separate and unrelated cultural milieus. Are we to conclude that this correspondence is determined by genetics? I don't think so. This is simply a case where a common instrument, the human mind, being applied to a common problem comes up with similar answers. The problem here is how to represent a nonsexual relationship between two people of the same sex otherwise attracted to the same sex. The kinship category of "sister," serves this purpose equally well among Plains Indian berdaches, enlightenment sodomites, and modern homosexuals, since, in each of these societies, sex with one's sister is taboo.

At the same time, by making our focus of study not merely those configurations of homosexuality identical with contemporary western roles, but configurations of sex and gender variation in general — including such cultural forms as the use of "sister," cross-dressing, cross-gender occupational choice, female marriage resistance, and same-sex sexuality — we provide a meaningful constant between all the diverse projects currently being pursued under the rubric of lesbian and gay studies. We study this collection of practices and roles—gay cultural forms, gay social roles, and gay identities if by "gay" we mean "alternative configurations of sexuality and gender"—because it is through them that unique contributions have been made in the past and can be made today.

MASS: But there are "alternative configurations of sexuality and gender" that, at least ostensibly, have little or nothing to do with being gay or lesbian. For example, heterosexual transvestism. Are you saying that we should henceforth regard heterosexual transvestites as "gay?"

ROSCOE: Absolutely not. You must understand exactly how I am using these terms. I would definitely not say that heterosexual transvestites "are gay." I am suggesting, however, that the *practice of cross-dressing* is a form of sociosexual specialization, and, if we accept "sociosexual specialization" as the technical definition of "gay," then we can call this a "gay practice."

But how can we call cross-dressing a gay practice if some heterosexuals engage in it? Because I believe that cross-dressing has a strong empirical and historical association with homosexuality and the other dimensions of sociosexual specialization I have described. I offer my own work on homosexual, cross-dressing berdaches as evidence. The fact that there are exceptions to this pattern, that heterosexuals do sometimes engage in cross-dressing, does not negate its validity. Most people who call themselves lesbian or gay are homosexual, but few have never had heterosexual experiences, and a good percentage of heterosexuals have had homosexual experience. The occurrence of such exceptions, however, does limit our ability to make predictive statements—for example, calling a person "gay" based solely on the evidence of cross-dressing. This is why, whenever someone makes a statement like "gay men are artistic," someone else always mentions a gay man who is not artistic or a nongay man who is. The answer is that it takes more than being artistic to be gay and, by the same reasoning, nonartistic people can still be gay through other dimensions of sociosexual variation.

Again, I am arguing for multiple criteria in defining our subject and not just a single variable like sexuality or cross-dressing. The heterosexual transvestite as we understand him is variant only on the dimension of cross-dressing, and even this variance is largely a private activity. He is otherwise indistinguishable from the general population in terms of sexuality, social roles, etc. What I refer to as sociosexual specialization — and, informally, the gay pattern — entails variance on more than one dimension.

But you must understand the difference between calling the transvestite "gay" and referring to cross-dressing as a *gay practice*. The failure to distinguish between behavior and cultural forms, on the one hand, and identity on the other has been the cause of many fruitless (excuse the pun) debates over the use of labels. We must disabuse ourselves of the idea that we can ever apply the label "gay" to individuals of other cultures and historical periods in the same way we apply it to ourselves: referring to a conscious identity based on sexual orientation. Here I agree with the social constructionists. The identity is the historical product of modern western culture.

However, the *patterns of behavior* that we find associated with today's lesbians and gay men are *not* unique. These patterns are not the product of just one culture, but occur in many cultures. And while the meanings and values attributed to them and their configuration into social roles are highly variable, the elements of sociosexual specialization appear to be fundamental to the human condition. That is, homosexual behavior is a universal physiological potential of humans, while the dual division of labor based on sex, a nearly universal feature of human society, always poses the possibility of mediation. In short, the *practices* we engage in as lesbians and gay men — our forms of sexual and emotional expression, our patterns of communication, the semiotics of our dress and adornment, our sex-role nonconformity, our uses and interpretations of cross-dressing, our occupational choices, our relationship to religious expression, and even the forms and customs of our subculture — *do* have a history. Further, we can claim this as *our* history because we are the ones who today cherish and maintain these practices and carry forward the exploration of their social potentials.

In conclusion, I would again stress that the advantage of a multi-dimensional model is that it allows us to accommodate and account for the great diversity in gay and lesbian people in a way that a single-dimensional model cannot. Not all individuals who today identify as gay manifest all these practices or traits all the time. In this regard, the model describes an ideal or statistical type. Nor do I mean to say that, as gay men and lesbians, we should or should not manifest these patterns—only that we often do. Finally, I have not addressed myself to the individual causes of the behaviors involved in sociosexual specialization. As an historian, my concern is with the forms these behaviors take in society, their meaning and function, and their relationship to social and historical developments.

MASS: In your review of *The God of Ecstasy* and *Gay Spirit*, you note that the movement to seek the cultural and historical roots of gay identity

> has sought to combine "New Age" spirituality and human growth psychology (including, in no small part, ideas of Jung) and draws from self and group explorations as well as historical and religious inquiry. The goal of this movement for gay personal growth is, in the words of Thompson [in *Gay Spirit*], "to affirm our past and, in the process, make a history—to reimagine, reinvent and retell our lives; to reconnect at the deepest level of our dreams; to make our own myths."

Later, you identify yourself as both a participant and chronicler of this movement. Could you describe the nature of this movement as you see it and the particular impact it has on your work?

ROSCOE: You know, I would never want to deny the place of the gay personal growth movement and fairy gatherings in particular in my life. Yet, I feel I should provide a context before answering your question as I have found that this subject tends to trigger very strong reactions, sincerely felt, but often based on erroneous, preformed judgments. The piece in *Out/look* that you mentioned earlier was an entire article devoted to branding my work on berdaches as "romantic obfuscation." In other cases, I have seen works that have been important to me for their intuitive insights and willingness to speculate—by Judy Grahn, Mark Thompson, Arthur Evans, Harry Hay, and others—bitterly denounced, even ridiculed, for what appears to be the crime of seeking truth outside of scholarly discourse. It's as if we were the drag queens of gay scholarship—

showing up uninvited, sullying the image of our brothers and sisters in the eyes of the larger world.

But I see no reason why a mythico-poetic exploration of our experience, employing intuition, self-examination, and introspection, should be inimical to other, more academic methods. In fact, I believe that the desire to "make a history" — the existential dilemma that Harry Hay referred to forty years ago as "the homosexual in search of historical continuity," what a scholar of the Romantic movement has termed "redemption through historicizing" — impinges upon every gay and lesbian studies project, even the most academic and technical. It may not be apparent when you read the papers printed in the *Journal of Homosexuality*, but it is obvious when you go to the events where lesbian and gay scholars present their work. Whether in academic or community settings, it is not at all unusual these days to see talks on sexuality and gender draw standing-room only audiences. I don't see how gay studies scholars could fail to have these audiences in mind when writing their reports and papers or ignore their urgent questions. The fact is, the very existence of lesbian and gay studies would not be possible apart from this imperative to "affirm our past," for this is the same spirit that motivates the lesbian and gay political movement.

Does this mean that objective scholarship is not possible or that all research by lesbians and gay men is biased? No. As Nietzsche explains, objectivity cannot mean "disinterested contemplation," which we now recognize as a central myth of the western epistemological tradition, but for an ability to "have one's pros and cons within one's command and to use them or not, as one chooses." Rather than attempting to repress or circumvent the existential circumstances of our intellectual inquiries, we should learn to channel them, to balance or offset them when necessary, and to draw inspiration and insight from them when needed.

Having framed your question this way, I would say that my own experiences in gay men's spirituality have been the source of countless insights, a means of unblocking emotional and intellectual logjams, a testing ground for ideas, a creative inspiration — all treasures I have taken back from fairy gatherings to later re-examine, follow-up, substantiate, research, and test. I find the process of fairy circles, which are simply a type of leaderless rap group in which we can share experiences with each other, particularly valuable. Listening to the stories that gay men have to tell—and, we discovered, we all have remarkable stories to tell—it really became clear to me in the most definite way how much more is involved in being gay than simply having a homosexual orientation. Again and again we found shared experiences, preferences, and values in our childhood memories. Examining our lives as gay adults, we found more common ground in the special roles we often fulfill in interpersonal relationships, work, and families. The multidimensional model that I describe in "Making History" really grew out of these dialogues with gay men, which have been going on at fairy gatherings for over ten years now.

I might add that I believe the reason that this kind of sharing does not happen more often in our community is that so many of our early memories are associated with painful experiences. These were the years before coming out when we discovered that being "different" caused us to be rejected and persecuted by family and society; you might say every lesbian and gay man was a battered child. The wounds we received are now an obstacle to remembering our earliest self-awareness—especially our awareness of the specific behaviors that triggered the homophobic reactions of others. To reclaim our marginal memories of "differentness," we must confront this pain. In the safe space of the gatherings, held in secluded, natural settings, we more easily discover that, although we were alone when we first faced homophobia, we are not alone now. We all share this pain. From this follows the trust necessary for interpersonal exploration.

One of my disappointments with the fairy movement, on the other hand, has been its failure to build bridges by which to bring these insights and processes back to the larger gay men's community. The fairies have tended to remain insular and cliquish, which has limited their impact (see, for example, my critique in *RFD* #34). This may be changing, however. I recently attended a statewide gay conference in northern Maine. I hardly expected to encounter radical fairies in that corner of the world, so I was quite surprised the first morning when one of the local organizers announced that there would be a fairy circle immediately after breakfast. He had everyone, women and men, stand in a circle, hold hands, sing a couple of songs, and exchange hugs. It was definitely a generic version of a fairy circle, but I felt it made a real contribution to the spirit of unity at the conference, and I was proud to see this being offered by a gay man and a fairy.

MASS: In your essay, "Making History: The Challenge of Lesbian and Gay Studies," you critique both essentialist and constructionist schools of lesbian and gay history and propose a new, synthetic approach, one that has struck some readers as easier to conceptualize than to implement. You introduce this new definition of lesbian and gay studies, which you call *sociosexual specialization*, and for which you provide a general definition. The essay then continues with "a discussion of six possible dimensions of sociosexual specialization with relevance to gay and lesbian studies: sexuality, subjectivity and identity, gender, social roles, economic roles and spirituality." First, were there any other dimensions you considered but decided to reject?

Second, how did you come up with the term sociosexual specialization? Did you consider other terminology?

ROSCOE: "Making History" was originally written in 1984, rewritten many times, and finally published in late 1988. Although I made slight alterations in the wording along the way, I employed six "dimensions" from the earliest drafts. It took longer to settle on "sociosexual specialization," primarily for aesthetic reasons. I did consider calling it simply "social specialization," because I saw no reason to privilege the dimension of sexuality, but I was afraid that if I decentered sex to that extent my readers would find the formulation too disorienting. So I kept the reference to sex, with the qualification that it refers to both sexuality and sex roles.

MASS: In your discussion of one of these categories, gender status, you state the following.

> This knot of symbolic and behavioral relationships between sociosexual variance and gender crossing, reversing, blending, and triangulating awaits untangling. Such a project is especially needed in the study of historical and non-Western cultures, where a mish-mash of unqualified terms — from "hermaphroditism," to "transsexualism," "transvestism," "bisexualism," "androgyny," "effemination," and "sexual

inversion, congenital or acquired, partial or complete" — have obscured the subject through a century of cross-cultural and ethnological study.

You explain how the problem of gender dualism has obscured appreciation of the people who continue to be stereotyped as "the" American Indian berdache. "Instead of assuming that all social roles and behavior patterns fit into one or the other of two genders, gay and lesbian studies must begin to recognize patterns that are neither male nor female, but specific to sociosexual specialization."

What you're saying is very persuasive. But what's not clear is how we would use this new conceptual framework. First, what would the language, the terminology, of sociosexual specialization be? That is, would sociosexual specialization mean developing new, more specific and more flexible terms or categories to replace the mish-mash, as you so aptly put it, of older, unqualified, terms? ROSCOE: Well, let me say that I am not one to spend a great deal of time devising taxonomies and terminology. In my own work, I tend to develop new terms and categories on an as-needed basis, or borrow them if appropriate ones already exist.

But the question about language is a good one. For me the problem is not so much a matter of categories, but of wording, of writing in a more open, inclusive style. I have often been challenged on this by the audiences who attend my slide-lecture on We'wha, the famous Zuni Indian berdache. When I spoke in Denver in 1987, for example, my sponsors had thought to send an announcement to a local transsexual organization. Half-way through my lecture, during the intermission, I looked up to find five transsexuals standing before me politely but earnestly wanting to know why I was referring to berdache status as a "traditional gay role" when We'wha was so obviously a transsexual. My reaction was not to argue with them over the definitions of transsexual, gay and berdache, or which of these pigeon-holes Zuni berdaches belong in, but to re-examine my script to see if I could find wording that would leave room for both transsexual and gay audiences to relate to my material.

You can find examples of this wording in my comments here.

Expressions like "customs, traditions, values and roles surrounding homosexuality and gender," "variation in sexuality and gender," "gender mediation," "configurations of sexual variation and gender variation," "alternative sex and gender practices," and "gay cultural forms, gay social roles, and gay identities" are all attempts to use language that allows for the "homosexual traditions" of more than one historical period, more than one cultural context.

While more flexibility is needed at the level of terminology, greater specificity is needed at the level of description. Whatever terms a writer uses, we need to know exactly what is being referred to. Terms cannot be a substitute for description. And descriptions must be more rigorous and thorough. That's what I'm proposing with the six "dimensions" of sociosexual specialization. It seems to me that, whatever historical or cross-cultural configuration of homosexuality we describe, if we make reference to each of these dimensions we can be sure of a broad enough base of data to make empirical comparisons and valid pronouncements on the distance or proximity of a given configuration to our present day gay and lesbian identities.

You might look at this as a way of merely saying that we need an interdisciplinary view of our subject, one that synthesizes the previously discrete perspectives offered by psychology, sociology, anthropology, and history. And after all, if we are to claim that gay and lesbian studies is something distinct from these existing disciplines, then it must have some perspective, some way of looking at its subject different from what these disciplines offer. That perspective, I argue, should be a multidimensional view of sexual and gender diversity as a factor in human history and society.

MASS: The conclusion of your essay begins by asserting that "The multidimensional strategy can be deployed in many ways and adapted to the needs of different disciplines. Its value is threefold." You then list three categories of deployment: conceptual, methodological, and theoretical. Under the subheading of *Methodological* you say that:

A multidimensional approach can have *heuristic* value by providing an initial delimitation of the field and provisional criteria for gathering and handling evidence. It can have *strategic* value by guiding systematic description. Finally, it can have *formal* value when descriptions are standardized for controlled comparisons.

Again, you're saying that we need to develop new categories that allow for the overlapping borderlines of multiple "gay roles" in history and across cultures. I'm persuaded by the conceptual and theoretical aspects of your approach, but I still can't see how it is to be implemented. Are you saying we can develop a kind of ratings system, for example, like the Kinsey scale? That is, would we take the six dimensions of sociosexual specialization you've proposed and develop measures of say, 1 to 10 or 1 to 100 or 1000, and come up with some formula that would allow us to conclude that someone who's in a gray area — a heterosexual transvestite in Victorian England, for example — is more or less authentically connected to contemporary lesbian and gay experience based on her or his score in our new system of ratings? I know you're saying that persons would no longer be conceptualized in terms of rigid dichotomies. What you really want and expect the new framework of sociosexual specialization to do is, first, to make clear to what extent this Victorian heterosexual transvestite's experience *is*, more or less, authentically connected to contemporary lesbian and gay experience. Ideally, the new framework should also be able to tell us *how* it's connected. The only border of lesbian and gay studies, you're saying, is the condition of zero sociosexual specialization. Everything else would be of some interest, pertinence and connectedness to lesbian and gay studies.

But isn't that too broad? Won't we quickly find ourselves returning to the problem of needing to more grossly delimit the borders of lesbian and gay studies? Or are you saying something more profound — that as our understanding broadens, lesbian and gay studies, like what we currently understand to be our lesbian and gay identities, will be subsumed within much broader areas of understanding; that lesbian and gay identities will be perceived in relation to broader phenomena of sociosexual specialization in much the same way that identities of color and ethnicity will ultimately be perceived in relation to such broader phenomena of physical "specialization" or variance, if you will, as eye, hair and skin color, right versus left-handedness, etc., or to such broader phenomena of social specialization or variance as capitalism and socialism?

ROSCOE: The heuristic value of a multidimensional model arises at the onset of research. Rather than simply "shopping" through history for evidence of practices comparable to modern homosexuality (to use Mary McIntosh's phrase), data on sociosexual specialization is sought on all six dimensions and this inventory is used to create an empirical description. This avoids the pitfall of only looking for evidence consistent with the homosexual model of a particular period, namely the present.

By the strategic value of a multidimensional model I mean simply that the six dimensions provide a checklist for collecting data that can help the researcher avoid overlooking evidence in less obvious areas. In this regard it is similar to the set of categories an anthropologist uses in the field when preparing a classic enthnography.

In suggesting that the model has formal value, I was, in fact, thinking of the use of scales and other statistical methods based on the six continuums or dimensions. In my own work, I have used an approach like this to assign gender ratings to the costume elements used on Zuni kachinas (masked representations of supernatural beings) and then analyze the patterns by which gender was represented on male, female, and the berdache kachina. Perhaps there are other applications.

An example of how I see the multidimensional model being used might be helpful. The Dutch historian Theo van der Meer was recently in San Francisco speaking on his research into eighteenth century Dutch sodomites. He has been using official court records of the time that reveal a good deal about their day to day existence. I would say that van der Meer employed a multidimensional approach because he described not only the sodomites' sexual practices, but their social roles, their place within families, their class and occupational background, their gender status, and their sense of identity. In his talk he related all this beautifully, but because he had not (at that time) made this multidimensional model explicit he slipped into an old error — that is, he structured his account in a way that privileged the dimension of sexuality.

Of course, this is what we, as modern homosexuals, would first notice about the sodomites — that they engaged in sexual practices similar to those employed in today's gay subcultures. But the material van der Meer presented regarding the self-perceptions of these sodomites made it clear that they considered themselves gender variant first, sexually variant second. They were operating under a different gender ideology than our present notion of two natural, biological sexes, and in their ideology intermediate positions were possible. In other words, homosexuality was conceptualized in terms of gender, not sexuality. This is an important difference between contemporary and sodomite social roles. On a continuum of gender it places them somewhere between berdaches and contemporary homosexuals. These distinctions become clear when a multidimensional model is used — and the pitfall of giving precedence to any one dimension before considering the others is avoided.

At the same time, I would argue with anyone who would deny us the sense of connectedness we feel as gay men today with the sexual customs and desires of these sodomites — or the connections that lesbians feel with the romantic friendships between women of the same period that Lillian Faderman has documented. This is, after all, our history, and we have fought hard for the right to uncover it and speak about it. If we do not live exactly like the sodomites of two hundred years ago, neither do we live exactly like our grandparents, but we are still connected to both. We must treasure every detail that scholars like van der Meer manage to resurrect.

Is sociosexual specialization too broad, as you suggest? Wherever we draw the boundary of gay and lesbian studies we should always be careful that we don't exclude too much. We should study the heterosexual Victorian transvestite, for example, because he or she outwardly appears to engage in a practice with a long history in homosexual subcultures — namely, cross-dressing. Yet we also feel somehow that the transvestite's practice is not the same as the practice of gay drag. The process of exploring and specifying this difference, however, is indispensable to the project of deciphering the meaning and history of those cultural forms we do want to call gay. Eventually, we may be able to "prune" our family tree of alternative sex and gender roles, deciding certain traditions — perhaps Melanesian initiation rites or prison homosexuality — are indeed more related to other fields than what we call lesbian and gay studies.

As for the final part of your question, whether we won't eventually come to see our modern lesbian and gay identities against a larger background of sociosexual specialization, yes, I do believe this will happen.

In and of itself, sociosexual variance is a largely neutral phenomenon, like skin color or even sex (although comparison to other forms of social and economic specialization, as opposed to biological traits, is probably more apt). Identities and valuations based on variance, however, are always cultural constructs. There is no universal black identity, for example, but only specific black identities in specific historical contexts, so that, ultimately, "being an Afro-American" does not mean having black skin color but "socialized to Afro-American cultural forms." This is even more apparent among American Indians, for whom being socialized within a tribal tradition is more important than the purity of one's blood line.

In this regard, our current gay and lesbian identities reflect only one of the possible configurations of sociosexual specialization. Gay identity—that is, the sense of belonging to a group because of one's sexual orientation—is certainly an interesting and perhaps unique development, but it is not the *sine qua non* of being gay. That is, one need not have a gay identity to be gay, or, more technically speaking, to engage in behaviors typical of sociosexual specialization. If you doubt this you might think of your own experiences before and after coming out. Obviously you were gay before you discovered a label for your feelings and behaviors and willingly adopted it. While the label made it possible to reflect on your feelings and, therefore, more effectively act on them, it did not create those feelings. Social constructionism has no way of accounting for the very real manifestations of sociosexual specialization that can exist independent of sexual labels.

We must remember that we are creating a discourse where discourse has been diverted or suppressed. I have no doubt that the more we discuss these things the clearer our perceptions will become of the multiple traditions of sociosexual specialization, the relative historical and social contributions of each form and each tradition, and their value to ourselves and society.

Index